The
Catholic Parent
Book of
Feasts

The
Catholic Parent
Book of
Feasts

Celebrating
the Church Year
with Your Family

Michaelann Martin

Carol Puccio

Zoë Romanowsky

Our Sunday Visitor Publishing Division
Our Sunday Visitor, Inc.
Huntington, Indiana 46750

Table of Contents

Introduction 7

Part One — Customs Tailored to Your Hearth 9

Advent 12

Christmas 22

Carnival 25

Lent and Easter 31

Ordinary Time 63

Part Two — Celebrating the Liturgical Year 93

Feasts of the Saints 93

Prayers and Devotions 161

Glossary 177

Bibliography 181

Appendix 185

Index 187

Introduction

"It should be our noble right and duty to bring up our children in such a way that they become conscious of high tide and low tide, that they learn that there is 'a time to weep, and a time to laugh, a time to mourn, and a time to dance.' "

— Maria von Trapp, *Around the Year with the Trapp Family*

. . . People are instructed in the truths of faith and brought to appreciate the inner joys of religion far more effectively by the annual celebration of our sacred mysteries than by any official pronouncement of the teaching of the Church. Such pronouncements usually reach only a few and the more learned among the faithful; feasts reach them all. The Church's teaching affects the mind primarily; her feasts affect both mind and heart and have a salutary effect upon man's whole nature.

— Pope Pius XI

Following Christ is no easy task in today's world. How can we bring our faith into daily life and pass it on to those we love? Thankfully, the Church has already sanctified time and space by patterning her year on the life of Jesus Christ and His Church throughout history.

By participating in the seasons of our Faith, we live out the natural rhythm that God has created for us. Modern society has given us another rhythm, a very fast-paced one that leaves little time to slow down and feel the world turn. Many families live under the constraints of heavy work-schedules, two careers, extracurricular activities, and the competition with the media world. Many parents don't have the knowledge they feel is necessary to pass on their faith to their children. The natural rhythm of the year is a gift from God, through which He means to reveal more about Himself. By learning to live in this rhythm, we can take advantage of the wonderful celebrations, devotions, and teaching moments inherent in God's plan of time.

All that we need to know about our God and His family can be found in living the liturgical year, the Church year. Holy Mother Church, in her wisdom, teaches us every day about God — Father, Son, and Holy Spirit. We find Him in the Mass, the Scriptures, the sacraments, the prayers of the Divine Office, the Liturgy of the Hours, the feasts, and the celebrations throughout the liturgical year. But the life of faith, and its seasons, are meant to be incorporated into our daily lives in practical and relevant ways. Just as a child learns to walk and run, to talk and eat, to love and hurt, under the care of their parents at home, we learn the essentials of our Faith by living every day in the arms of our mother, the Church, guided by Our Father in Heaven.

Most of us can recall traditions that were woven into the fabric of our family celebrations and holidays — a special dish served only at Easter, gingerbread men made as a family on Christmas Eve, a bouquet of fresh flowers placed by Mary's image every May first — and the list goes on. Perhaps you don't even remember why certain traditions were kept, but their meaning remains, never to be forgotten.

This book is designed to help even the busiest family inject some of the Church year into their daily lives . . . to take their faith from the church to the home. It is designed for parents who may feel less than adequate in their own faith to effectively pass it on to their children. This book is written for your average, everyday Catholic, just trying to live a good life!

The Catholic Parent Book of Feasts is meant to be an easy-to-use activity guide. We do not think, even for a moment, that anyone will use every activity in this book all year-round. Hopefully, there are enough choices for you to find the activities and devotions that best suit your family and can go on to become lifelong family traditions. As a rule, it is best to begin with one or two activities and add others in the coming years. Your family can also develop their own customs. This can be done by adapting some traditional customs to your unique family situation. If there is anything we want to emphasize, it's *consistency*. It is better to choose a few activities and be consistent, than to do many that won't become traditions.

Our prayer is that this book may help your family to live and love Christ and His Church more and more through the coming years!

Michaelann
Carol
Zoë

PART ONE

Customs Tailored to Your Hearth

Each family is unique. Your home has its own style and the people who live in it have their own personalities. *The Catholic Parent Book of Feasts* will work for you only if you custom-tailor the traditions to your particular family. This can begin with simple decorations in the home and through the celebrations that are unique to the members of your family.

The Home

St. John Chrysostom said the home should be a "little church," a miniature kingdom of God in which the father strives to represent the qualities of Christ and the mother seeks to make herself like the Blessed Mother.

The home should be seen by the family and their guests as the dwelling place of God. We live in a world of deep mystery, in which even the most mundane of locations or chores holds in it an importance beyond our immediate vision. Thomas Howard says:

> *It is hard to see ourselves . . . as carrying on the commonplace routines*
> *of our ordinary life in the presence of mighty mysteries that would ravish*
> *and terrify us if this veil of ordinariness were suddenly stripped away.*
> — Thomas Howard, *Hallowed Be This House*

How do we impart this idea to our children? We start by reminding *ourselves*! In decorating your home it is always good to display a crucifix or religious object in each room. Also, a small shrine can be set up in a corner with a statue or crucifix, a votive candle, and the Bible. Sometimes an old free-standing kneeler can be found in the basement of a church. Many families have small holy-water fonts at the entrance of their homes. A fun spring project could be to construct a grotto in the yard with a statue of our Lord, the Blessed Mother, or the family's patron saint. For those very creative souls, a fountain or pool can be added. This can provide another quiet place for prayer and contemplation.

The proper environment in a Catholic home should foster a sense of the sacred, a love of the liturgy, and a desire to love God more completely each day.

Name-Days

The *Catechism of the Catholic Church* (2156) states, "The patron saint provides a model of charity; we are assured of his intercession." It is important that we share this wealth of information with our children. It may take a little research to learn about a patron saint, or to help a child choose which saint to adopt as his patron. There are so many great saint-books available that this is not too big a job. If anything, it is interesting and challenging to read about the great lives of the saints in the process. We recommend that the family celebrate yearly the feast day of each member's patron saint. Try to discuss the saint's virtues and life struggles. It is a great idea to begin the family tradition of praying each night to everyone's patron saint. All it takes is a little planning. Mark the name-days and all other family feast days on your new calendar in January, then follow along and feast it up.

Unfortunately, the custom of giving children saints' names is not as common these days. No worry, you can still celebrate name-days! If any family member's first or middle name is not that of a saint's, a patron should be chosen. If the family member took a confirmation name, this is a natural choice for a patron. If not, do a little research and choose an appropriate patron. Each year the name-days should be celebrated as a family.

What is a feast? The dictionary says it is a "religious festival or celebration." But it is more. According to Catholic author Romano Gaurdini, it means "to wait for our Lord, to invite Him, to go to receive and honor and praise Him, to be with Him, drawn in to the intimacy of communion with Him (and through Him into communion with the name-day saint) that is the Christian feast," and the true meaning of a name-day.

How should we celebrate? There are many ways, and each family can develop its own, but here are a few ideas to start you off. On the feast day of the saint (or beginning on the vigil, the night before):

- attend Mass;
- pray the "collect" from the Liturgy of the Hours for the day;
- bake a cake decorated with symbols representing the saint (see below);
- invite friends over for dessert;
- give a dramatic presentation of the life of the saint;
- have Dad recite the following prayer over the family member:

> Let us pray. *(Everyone extend hands or lay hands on person.)* Dear heavenly patron whose name N. is proud to bear, always pray to God for him/her. Confirm him/her in the faith. Strengthen him/her in virtue. Defend him/her in the fight that he/she may deserve to conquer the malignant foe and obtain glory.
>
> All: Amen. Christ conquers, Christ reigns! (loudly)

According to *Catholic Household Blessings and Prayers* (United States Catholic Conference, Washington, D.C., 1-800-235-8722, publication #292-6), parents have the ability to bless their children on their name-day by making the sign of the cross on the child's forehead or heart and reciting this prayer:

"God of glory, Whom we name in many ways, when we brought this child to your Church we were asked, 'What name do you give this Child?' We answered, '(Child's name here),' and so our child was claimed for Christ by that name. May St. (Name) ever pray for him/her, may he/she guard him/her so that (Name of child) might overcome all evil and come at last to that place where his/her name is written in the book of life. We ask this through Christ our Lord. Amen."

Crown Cake

A mark of victory or distinction for all those who have attained heaven.

Bake or buy a round, two-layer cake, unfrosted.

You'll need two thin cardboard strips, 20 inches long and 7/8-inch wide, colored yellow or gold.

Cut slots in the cake at four opposite spots about 1½ inches up from the bottom. Bend each cardboard strip downward in the middle. Stick one end in a slot and bend it up and over (the bend in the middle will touch the center of the top of the cake). Place the other end in the opposite slot. Do the same with the second piece so that it fits at a right angle to the first and its middle bend rests on top of the first piece. If necessary, tie the centers together with thread.

Cut a circle to set on the top center. Frost and decorate cake and crown with appropriate colors (white on cake, yellow on crown), and use bright-colored candies to resemble jewels around the bottom and along the top of the crown. Put a symbol of the saint in the center.

Advent

Quick Activities

Christ Candle

Decorate the candle to be your family "Christ Candle." Use Jesse tree symbols, alpha, omega, Pax Christi — whatever your family chooses. See the "Appendix" for the symbols.

Christmas Eve

Put up the family Christmas tree and decorate for Christ. Make this family time and talk about the ornaments and their significance.

Many families bless their Christmas trees before lighting them. (See the "Prayers and Devotions" chapter for "Blessing of the Christmas Tree.") The Christmas tree provides our children with a concrete reminder of a tree's role in both the fall of man and the victory of Christ.

The Christmas tree itself traces its origin to the paradise plays that were popular in medieval Germany during Advent. In the plays, the garden of Eden was represented by a fir tree hung with a apples, representing both the "tree of life" and the "tree of discernment of good and evil." After the plays were suppressed in the German churches, the paradise tree found its way into the homes of the faithful as a symbol of the coming Savior.

In the fifteenth century the faithful began adding small white wafers, representing the Holy Eucharist, to the apples. Thus the tree that had borne the fruit of Adam's sin now bore the saving fruit of the sacrament of Christ's sacrifice. Only in later usage were the white wafers gradually replaced by angels, bells, and other religious ornaments.

Light the Night

You'll need electric candles or a string of white lights.

Put lights in the front windows. A candle in a window was

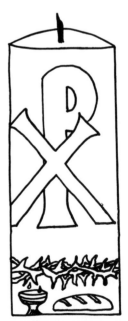

A Christ candle with Jesse tree symbols.

a symbol of Christianity, an outward sign of welcome to passersby that Christ resides in the house, as well as a welcome for the coming of Christ at Christmas.

Service

Pray for the foreign missions. Try to attend Mass as a family and continue to do good works and pray for your "*Christkindl*" (Christ Child).

SUPPLIES

construction paper
markers and/or
  crayons
glue
glitter
old Christmas
  cards
paper clips
scissors

Tree Decorations

Using old Christmas cards, allow the children to cut, stencil, or draw symbols of Christmas. These can all be made fairly sturdy with paper and glue. They can even be used to help tell the story of Christmas to the younger children.

Jesus' Ancestors

Dress tiny dolls to represent Christ's ancestors to hang on the tree. Include Jesse, David, Our Lady, St. Anne, St. Joachim, St. Joseph, Adam and Eve, etc.

With clay and paint add a tiny apple and a serpent to give Eve significance and make more real the reason for Christ's redemption. You can add symbols to the other characters, too.

SUPPLIES

paper or
  cardboard cut-
  out dolls
scissors
construction paper
paper clips
clay
paint
glue

Family Trip for Christmas Tree

Make an outing of selecting and purchasing your family Christmas tree. If you can, try to find a cut-it-yourself tree farm. Bring your special tree home, trim branches if necessary, and shake it out well before bringing it inside to decorate.

If you can't decorate the tree right away, cut a one-inch slice off the trunk and put it in a bucket filled with water. Keep the tree in a cool place, such as in the garage, until you can bring it inside. Select the area in your home where the tree will be placed, and prepare it before bringing the tree inside. Have a sturdy stand ready that can be filled with water after the tree is placed in it.

The tree is a symbol of life. Green stands for giving life and hope.

Family Trip to a Barn

Travel to a barn or cave together. Talk about the weather, the animals, comfort, discomfort, smells, etc. Explain how Mary and Joseph were very tired, yet settled in a similar place, where Mary delivered the Son of God. Jesus was laid in a manger, the food trough for the animals. There is much to learn when you experience the discomforts first-hand, such as detachment and simplicity.

Try to prepare a feast for dinner since it is Sunday, the day to remember the resurrection of Christ.

Family Service Outing

Take the family to a nearby nursing home. It would be nice to take a gift such as cookies, decorations (bows for the doors, for example), or flowers. Practice songs to sing. It's even fun to plan this activity with a couple of other families and sing the carols that await Christ's coming, such as "O Come, O Come, Emmanuel."

Honor the Blessed Mother

Try to go to Mass as a family, taking a special moment after Mass to invoke Our Lady's prayers to prepare our hearts to better receive Christ this Christmas.

If the weather permits, prepare an outdoor meal in remembrance of the journey of Mary and Joseph. Plan a barbecue of hamburgers, a salad, and soft drinks. Dinner conversation could focus on eating outside, grilling outside, or what traveling might have been like for Mary and Joseph.

SUPPLIES

a family photo, or
photos of each
member

white paper,
8"x10"

tape or glue

pens, crayons, or
markers

Write a Family Christmas Letter

Have each family member write or dictate an individual message on the letter. Tell something special about the past year or hopes for the next. Tape or glue pictures to the paper. Have children add artistic touches and signatures. Finish the family letter by photocopying the number you want to send out. (If your family has a computer and printer, some of this could be done using word processing and other programs.) Address the envelopes and stamps. This is a great family gift to send and fun for all ages.

Christkindl Brief

"*Christkindl Brief*" is German for "letter to the Christ Child." You'll need white paper (letter size) and pens, crayons, or markers.

Write a letter to the Christ Child explaining your love and anticipation for His arrival. Explain how you are trying to prepare your hearts (and the soft manger!) for Him. Add artwork if you want, and place on the family altar. This activity is especially fun and meaningful for young children.

More Advent Activities

Make a Jesse Tree

The decorations can depict messianic prophecies.

The Jesse tree shows the ancestry of Jesus through symbols and relates the scriptural story of our redemption and the purpose of Christ's coming, from creation to the birth of the promised messiah. The tree can be cut from any large sheet of paper, posterboard, or cardboard. Make sure it is large enough to accommodate all the symbols. Even a leafless branch from a tree in your yard will do. Write these verses at the base of the tree:

"There shall come forth a shoot from the stump of Jesse, / and a branch shall grow out of his roots. / And the Spirit of the LORD shall rest upon him, / the spirit of wisdom and understanding, / the spirit of counsel and might, / the spirit of knowledge and the fear of the LORD" (Isaiah 11:1-2).

The symbols depict the ancestors of Jesus or Old Testament events leading to Christ. Explain each and read related scriptural passages. The symbols can be drawn, made of clay, cardboard, etc., then hung on the tree each day. See the "Appendix" for patterns for the symbols.

The symbols include:

Adam and Eve: apple with two bites gone
Abraham and Isaac: a ram
Solomon: a temple
Moses: two tablets of the law
David: a star
Isaiah: hand or burning coal
Rebecca: silver pitcher
Ruth: wheat
John the Baptist: shells
Jacob: ladder
Creation: sun or moon
Noah: ark
Joseph: coat with many colors
Samuel: scrolls
Jesse: flowering rod
Joseph: carpenter's tools
Zachary and Elizabeth: a slate board
Christ: chi-rho, rose
Mary: lily, crown of twelve stars
Nativity: donkey, star, angel
Anne and Joachim: golden gates of Jerusalem, doves

It is a good idea to put Mary's crown at the top with Christ's rose above her, because he is "stemmed" from the root of Jesse.

Christmas Baking

The week before Christmas is the traditional time to spend a few afternoons baking for Christmas day.

Christstollen is a German bread whose crisscross shape reminds us of the Child in swaddling clothes. It is especially fun for children to take part in the kneading and baking of Christmas foods. Prepare yourself for a little more mess and lots of fruitful discussion and questions. Ingredients appear at right.

Dissolve yeast and one teaspoon sugar in warm water. Cover and allow to rise. Cream shortening and 1¼ cup sugar. Add eggs and scalded milk (cooled to lukewarm). Sift flour with salt and nutmeg. Add yeast mixture. Knead until smooth. Add fruits and flavoring. Cover and let dough rise to double its bulk. Knead dough again. Shape dough into ropes about 1½ inches in diam-

SUPPLIES

Materials around the house that might be used: toothpicks, felt, foil, buttons, calendars, magazines, cards, crayons, markers, glue, tape, paper clips

CHRISTSTOLLEN INGREDIENTS

1 cake yeast
1 c. shortening
1¼ c. plus 1 tsp. sugar
¼ c. lukewarm water
2 eggs
6 c. flour
1 c. raisins
½ tsp. nutmeg
1 tsp. salt
1 c. currants
2 c. scalded milk
½ c. blanched almonds
½ c. chopped citron
1½ tsp. lemon extract

**CHRISTMAS
LADY COOKIE
INGREDIENTS**

2 eggs,
  separated
1 tsp. vanilla
½ c.
  confectioner's
  sugar
½ c. cake flour
¼ tsp. salt
wax paper

eter. For each large *stollen*, make one rope three inches long and two that are 2½ inches long. Braid the dough. Bring the braid to a point at either end. Place the braid on a greased cookie sheet. Bake in a hot oven (400°) for 25 minutes or until brown. This recipe will make two large *stollen*. (**Note:** All temperatures given in recipes are in degrees Fahrenheit.)

Christmas Lady Cookies

Beat egg whites until stiff; add ¼ cup sugar, beating all the while. Beat the yolks until thick and lemon-colored, then beat in remaining ¼ cup sugar. Fold the white mixture into the yolks, then fold in vanilla, flour, and salt. Drop on ungreased wax-paper-lined cookie sheets and bake for 15 minutes in a slow oven (300°). When cool, remove from paper and sprinkle with confectioner's sugar.

Cranberry Muffins

For Christmas morning

Wash and clean the cranberries, cut in halves, cover with sugar, and let stand overnight. Combine the other ingredients gently — don't worry about lumps. Add the cranberries and fill well-greased muffin pans two-thirds full. Bake in a 400° oven for 20 to 25 minutes. Makes 12 two-inch muffins.

**CRANBERRY
MUFFIN
INGREDIENTS**

1 c. fresh berries
2 tbs. melted
  butter
½ c. sugar
2 eggs, beaten
2 c. prepared
  biscuit mix
¾ c. milk

**PFEFFERNUESSE
INGREDIENTS**

2 c. corn syrup
1 tsp. soda
2 c. dark
  molasses
2 tsp. cinnamon
1 c. shortening
¼ lb. cintron, cut
  fine
½ lb. brown sugar
¼ lb. almonds,
  chopped fine
10 c. flour
1 lemon (rind and
  juice)

Pfeffernuesse

A favorite!

Warm syrup, add shortening and lemon juice, then the remaining ingredients in the order given (soda mixed with flour). Roll into little balls and brush with egg white. Place on greased pan spaced far apart, and bake in a 350° oven until brown. Roll the cookies in confectioner's sugar.

This recipe is from the Trapp family.

Rum Balls

Grind wafers very fine. Add nuts, cocoa, syrup, and rum. Stir until well-blended. Dust hands with confectioner's sugar and roll mixture into balls the size of a walnut. Let stand for about an hour, until partially dry. Then roll in confectioner's sugar.

**RUM BALL
INGREDIENTS**

½ lb. vanilla
  wafers
½ c. light corn-
  syrup
2 tsp. cocoa
¼ c. rum or
  brandy
1 c. pecans, finely
  chopped
confectioner's
  sugar

NUT BUSSERLN INGREDIENTS

1 egg, beaten
1 c. chopped walnuts
1 c. sugar
5 tbs. flour

EGGNOG INGREDIENTS

6 eggs
1 pt. brandy
1-1/8 c. sugar
½ pt. rum
1½ pt. cream
1 qt. milk
½ c. confectioner's sugar

Nut Busserln

Beat egg and sugar until very light; stir in chopped nuts, then add flour. Drop by teaspoonful on greased cookie sheet and bake in a moderate oven, 375°, for 10 minutes.

Christmas Punch for Children

Boil sugar, water, lemon rind, and spices until flavored. Mix with the rest of the ingredients, boil five minutes, and serve hot in punch glasses.

Eggnog

Beat egg yolks with sugar; add brandy and rum slowly, so eggs will not coagulate. Beat in milk and pint of cream. Fold in three stiffly beaten egg-whites. Beat remaining egg whites very stiff; add confectioner's sugar and ½ pint cream. Float this egg mixture on the eggnog. Chill overnight before serving.

PUNCH INGREDIENTS

1 qt. grape juice
1 stick cinnamon
2 qt. water
juice of 2 lemons
juice of 2 oranges
2 c. sugar
½ tsp. whole cloves
rind of above oranges and lemons

Nativity Preparation

Find your Nativity set and unpack, always including the children in the preparation as much as possible.

Unpack the angel and shepherds last, building momentum for the journey to Bethlehem.

Begin to set up the Nativity with animals and shepherds. Have Mary and Joseph traveling far away — across the mantle or table. Spend one a day a week focusing on how to make the Nativity more comfortable and clean for the Holy Family's arrival. A beautiful custom from France is adding straw to the bed of the Savior. Decide what each child can do to make Jesus' manger more comfortable. This can be done with your family manger, or you can make a larger version of the manger for smaller children.

Make a Manger

Explain that every time anyone in the family does a loving act or act of service in preparation for the coming Christ Child, he/she will put a piece of hay, straw, or cotton in the manger to make a nice, soft bed for the baby on Christmas morning. Having a list may aid in giving ideas for good works and practices. Every time a good deed is completed or an extra prayer said, the children may place a piece of straw or a cotton ball in the manger. By their good deeds they are making the Christ Child more comfortable and welcome in their home. This is especially good for younger children. This can be done throughout Advent in preparation for Christ.

SUPPLIES

a box to act as a manger
straw, hay, or cotton balls
a small infant doll to be Jesus
many acts of love and service

Review the Messianic Prophecies

There are five significant stories in the Old Testament where the coming of the messiah is foretold. You might meditate each day on one. Read the passages as a family and talk about the significance of Christ's coming. After dinner might be a good time. There are also short activities that might help the children more clearly understand the meaning of the passage.

1. Born of the House of David

2 Samuel 7:12-16; Psalms 89:2-52, 132:11

Fulfilled in Matthew 1:1-25

2. Virgin Birth

Isaiah 7:14

Fulfilled in Matthew 1:20-25

3. Bethlehem

Take a long walk and talk to the children about the journey that Mary and Joseph took. Talk about the discomfort of riding on a donkey and walking on foot, the long distance traveled, the weather conditions experienced, and not having any family around to help. Pack a meager snack to eat while out on your venture. Trail-mix consisting of nuts, granola, and dried fruits is always a healthy reminder of nature, and probably not far from the real foods that Mary and Joseph ate while traveling.

For the prophecy, see Micah 5:1-3

Fulfilled in Matthew 2:5-6

4. Wise Men and Their Gifts

Isaiah 49:23, 60:5 and Psalm 72:10-15

Fulfilled in Matthew 2:9-12

Explain what the gifts were.

Frankincense: Offered as incense in Old Testament

Gold: Used in the making of the Old Testament tabernacle

Myrrh: Used in preparation of holy ointment

5. Holy Innocents

Jeremiah 31:15

Fulfilled in Matthew 2:16-18

Make an Advent House

The Advent house has seven sealed windows concealing symbols of Christ derived from the Old Testament. Beginning December seventeenth, the little house is hung against a light or window, and the beautiful "O Antiphons" of the Liturgy become a morning prayer. I'm sure your little ones will hardly be able to wait to break the seal on each window.

Make a house-shape out of cardboard and cut seven "hinged" windows. Behind each window, glue an "O Antiphon" symbol, which can be copied from the following pages. This is especially good for older children who have outgrown ready-made Advent calendars. Do this after dinner as a family activity.

Review the canticles of Mary from the *Liturgy of the Hours*.

December 17: O Sapientia

Wisdom, O holy Word of God, you govern all creation with your strong yet tender care. Come and show your people to salvation.

December 18: O Adonai

O sacred Lord of ancient Israel, who showed yourself to Moses in the burning bush, who gave him the holy law on Sinai mountain: come, stretch out your mighty hand to set us free.

December 19: O Radix Jesse

O Flower of Jesse's stem, you have been raised up as a sign for all peoples; kings stand silent in your presence; the nations bow down in worship before you. Come, let nothing keep you from coming to our aid.

December 20: O Clavis David

O Key of David, O royal power of Israel controlling at your will the gate of heaven: come, break down the prison walls of death for those who dwell in darkness and the shadow of death; and lead your captive people into freedom.

December 21: O Oriens

O Radiant Dawn, splendor of eternal light, sun of justice: come, shine on those who dwell in darkness and the shadow of death.

December 22: O Rex Gentium

O King of all the nations, the only joy of every human heart; O Keystone of the mighty arch of man, come and save the creature you fashioned from the dust.

December 23: Door Of House Opened

Picture of Jesus on Mary's knee.

Illustrations of O Antiphon symbols.

Trapp Family Custom — Herbergsucher (seeking shelter)

Most kids like to draw, so today have each draw a picture of Mary and Joseph. Perhaps show Mary on a donkey (looking tired) and Joseph knocking at the innkeeper's door. For the nine evenings before Christmas you can sing or recite this little Austrian song called *"Wer Kopfet an"* (any tune will do) and display the pictures:

Who's knocking at my door?
Two people poor and low.
What are you asking for?
That you may mercy show.
We are, o sir, in sorry plight,
O grant us shelter here tonight.
You ask in vain.
We beg a place to rest.
It's "no" again!
You will be greatly blessed.
I told you no! You cannot stay.
Get out of here and go away.

Sing this song for nine nights in a row (which makes a novena), then on Christmas Eve a place is lovingly prepared for the Christ Child called *Herbergsucherlied*.

Octave Of Christmas
Begins on December 17

Begin the "O Antiphons" on December seventeenth, by opening the first window of the Advent House that you made last week. Write out "O Antiphons" on three-by-five-inch cards and read at dinner. Then open the windows of the house after dinner. Remind everyone to do something for their *Christkindl*.

Season-Long Activities

Make an Advent Wreath

The four candles represent the four weeks of Advent. The purple represents a time of penance, although a different sort of penance than that of Lent. This is more of a longing, a realization of the need for Christ in our lives. The pink candle is for the third Sunday, *Gaudette* Sunday, when the priests wear rose-colored vestments and when we shout for joy at the promise of the Savior being fulfilled soon. Green is the color of hope and a symbol of eternal life in Christ. The ring is a symbol of the eternal nature of God.

Place the candles in the ring, and decorate with the greenery. White ribbons could be added as a symbol of divine innocence.

Start an evening Advent ceremony before or after the evening meal when the family is together. If you have children, they can altarnate the lighting and blowing out of the candle, and the

> **SUPPLIES**
>
> 3 purple candles
> 1 pink candle
> greenery
>   (evergreens or
>   anything in your
>   yard will do)
> ring of wood,
>   wire stand, or
>   Styrofoam)

nightly reading of Scripture. When all are involved , there is more understanding and attention given. Light the first purple candle and read 1 Samuel 16:1-13.

Study the Saints

Have each member of the family choose a patron saint to read about and pray for intercession in the coming year. If children are younger, parents may need to read aloud to them about "their" special saint for the year. Try the following great resources:

Butler's Lives of the Saints

Any biographies written by Mary Fabian Windette

The Saints and Our Children, Mary Reed Newland (TAN)

Saints and Feast Days, Loyola University Press

Christkindl

You'll need small pieces of paper with a different family member's written on each, and a hat or bowl in which to place them. Fold name-papers and place in the hat or bowl. Pass around and each person should each choose a paper.

The name on the paper is your *Christkindl* (German for Christ Child). This is the time to commit to praying for and doing little things for that person as a gift to them, and through this to the Christ Child. This is a fun tradition for all ages and it doesn't cost any money, either. The best gifts are acts of love and service to one another, in imitation of Christ Himself.

St. Nicholas Story and Traditional Shoe Goodies

Read the story of St. Nicholas in preparation for his feast day, December 6. Explain the practice of putting out the shoes and then don't forget on December fifth to do it!

**An example of an
Advent wreath.**

Christmas

Quick Activities

Significant Days — Feast of Christ's Birth

Either after midnight or morning Mass, celebrate Christ's arrival by putting a doll or a Christ figure in the crèche, singing hymns, and revealing *Christkindls* with a small gift of love from each. Then feast it up! You have been baking all week, now bring on the treats and rejoice! Also light your Christ candle (made at the beginning of Advent) and remember to light it every Sunday throughout the year to remember that Christ is the Light of the World. Light your Advent Wreath one last time and read John 1:1-18.

Feast of the Holy Family
First Sunday after Christmas

This is a great day to celebrate the family in your own home. Read Paul's Letter to the Colossians 3:12-17, noting the phrase about the "cloak of kindness." Discuss how the "cloak of kindness" is or is not seen in your family. Practice "wearing" it by words and actions. (You might even use an actual cloak, perhaps using a towel or sheet, with each family member taking a turn wearing it and acting out how kindness acts in a holy family.)

Feast of the Epiphany
January 6, or the Sunday following the Feast of the Holy Family

Act out the Christmas story. In *The Year and Our Children*, Mary Reed Newland tells of her family enacting the story. The children would be the kings, father would be Herod, and mother his scribe. The kings began their journey in the farthest room from the main living area. They would look out the window for the star (if one could not be seen they would pretend) then journey to Herod (in the dining room) to ask where they would find the new-born King of the Jews.

Herod (father) calls his scribe (mother), who reads Micah 5:1-3 from Scripture. When they discover He is to be born in Bethlehem, the kings promise Herod (who gives them an appropriately sinister smile) that they will return and tell him where the baby is.

The kings head to the Nativity by the longest route possible. When they arrive, they lay their gifts and pay tribute to the Christ Child. Soon one king points to an invisible being in the corner. This, of course, is the angel warning them to return to Herod using another route. Which they do, avoiding the dining room where Herod (still in character) is pacing and mumbling about irresponsible foreign kings. All at once there is a great giggling and the episode is over.

When the family is all together again, "Herod" (now Dad again) is welcomed to eat crown-cake and open Epiphany gifts (usually a few Christmas gifts saved for the occasion).

Feast of the Baptism of Our Lord
Sunday following Epiphany

"And when Jesus was baptized, he went up immediately from the water, and behold, the heavens were opened and he saw the Spirit of God descending **like a** dove, and alighting on him; and a voice from heaven saying 'This is my beloved Son, with whom I am well pleased" (Matthew 3:16-17).

As St. Augustine said: "The Lord desired to be baptized so that he might freely proclaim through his humility what for us was to be a necessity." The sacrament of baptism is to us a necessity *and* a great moment of grace, and we celebrate the anniversary of our baptism. It seems only fitting that we celebrate the anniversary of Christ's baptism also. If you have started this tradition in your home for family members, you can plan a celebration similar to it with Christ as the guest of honor.

If you have not started the tradition, now is the time to do it. First, you must find and write down the dates of every family member's baptism. Parents, this also means you. Don't make the mistake of one teacher we know and love, who, after two years of celebrating every student's baptismal day in her second grade classroom, did not know her own! Imagine her embarrassment when someone finally asked! So, begin today and develop a tradition that fits your family. See the the "Prayers and Devotions" chapter on sacramental days for ideas.

Christmastide ends with the Feast of the Baptism of Our Lord. This feast replaces the first Sunday in Ordinary Time and is followed by Ordinary Time, sometimes called Carnival.

The "Twelve Days of Christmas"

The origin of this carol is found in an old Hebrew hymn which begins, "In those twelve days." The hymn was originally arranged as a dialogue between a leader and singers. Each of the verses was repeated in the style and tune of "This is the house that Jack built." Later in the Middle Ages, the Church rewrote the hymn in Latin.

From the Latin hymn developed the English hymn in 1645 called "In Those Twelve Days." In the eighteenth century, that song evolved into a Christmas carol, "The Twelve Days of Christmas" (from *The English Carol* by Erik Routley, Greenwood, 1973).

Each number is a symbol for a truth of the Faith. It was used often as a teaching tool. The numerical symbolism goes like this:

Partridge in a pear tree = the one true God
Two turtle doves = two testaments, old and new
Three French hens = three Persons of the Trinity
Four colley birds (colley means black; some versions say "calling" birds) = four evangelists
Five golden rings = the five books of the Pentateuch

Six geese a-laying = six jars of water at Cana (the first miracle)
Seven swans a-swimming = seven sacraments
Eight maids a-milking = eight beatitudes
Nine drummers drumming = nine choirs of angels
Ten pipers piping = Ten Commandments
Eleven ladies dancing = eleven faithful disciples (or eleven stars seen in Old Testament)
Twelve lords a-leaping = twelve tribes of Israel (or twelve apostles).

Carnival

Carnival is the time between Christmastide (Advent) and Lent. It is a time of celebration after Christmas and in anticipation for the season of Lent. Lent and Advent are the two periods of the liturgical year that are considered closed times. They are both times of fasting, sacrifice, and prayerful preparation. In Austria Carnival is called *Fasching*, and in Latin countries, *Carnevale*, which is translated as "meat-farewell." (*Carne-vale!* One feature of fasting is abstaining from meat.)

This celebration has come to be almost wholly associated with Mardi Gras in New Orleans on the day before Ash Wednesday. However, Carnival is a season extending over several weeks, *culminating* in the Mardi Gras (or "Fat Tuesday") celebration. The whole season is important and the final celebration on the evening before Ash Wednesday brings it to a close and moves us into our time of sacrifice and preparation in Lent.

You may want to plan a series of seven parties building up to the celebration on the night before Ash Wednesday. The season should be one of merriment and fun. It is good for our children to truly experience the highs and lows of the liturgical tide. The parties should be as little work as possible and certainly can be adapted to your needs and interests. They should be for adults *and* children and should be planned, attended, and participated in equally by both.

Here's a format for planning and preparation for the week preceding each party:

Monday: Plan — discuss theme; assign tasks; write out guest-list. Coordinators needed are listed. This job can be done alone or delegated. Try to portion the jobs out evenly between kids and adults.

Tuesday: Invite — invitation coordinator makes and delivers invitations or phones the guests.

Wednesday: Choose entertainment — the coordinator of entertainment gathers materials needed for skits, songs, games, or dances appropriate to the party.

Thursday: Practice entertainment (skits, etc.) and/or choose music to play during the party.

Friday: Clean house.

Saturday: Cook and finish cleaning.

Saturday night or Sunday: Party!

Seven Party Ideas

Family Get-together: For immediate family and possibly grandparents. This is a night to get together to share family history, stories, and look at pictures or home movies. It should be joyful, fun, and relaxing. The menu should be light and easy and preparation minimal.

Poetry Night: This party can be a wonderful opportunity to learn poetry as well as practice memorization and public speaking skills. This could be the opportunity for the budding writer of the family to display his or her talent. The evening is meant to be fun for all, so in order to keep stress levels down, memorizing should be an option, along with reading aloud and writing original poetry. A theme may be chosen, such as love, nature, or nonsense. Inviting another family from the neighborhood might be fun. Desserts can be used as refreshments.

Bible Hero Party: This is a costume party in which each guest chooses his/her favorite biblical hero and dresses as that person for the evening. Skits and small plays can be planned to act out heroic stories containing the persons portrayed at the get-together. The meal can be a biblical dinner made with recipes from *The Continual Feast* by Evelyn Vitz. The guest list can include grandparents, aunts, uncles, cousins, as well as neighborhood and parish families.

Biblical Dinner: This meal as offered as a "culinary pilgrimage to the Holy Land at the time of Christ" by Evelyn Vitz in her book *A Continual Feast*. The menu follows. Please see her book for a wonderful commentary on the various recipes.

Menu
Broiled fish, biblical-style
Lentils with cumin and coriander
Cucumbers with cumin and yogurt
Wheat and barley loaves, flavored with mint and olive oil
Biblical "fruitcakes"

Broiled Fish, Biblical Style

Clean, rinse, and salt the fish. Rub with garlic and brush with oil.

Preheat broiler. Place the fish in an oiled pan. Broil small fish about three inches from heat, larger fish about five inches away. Broil split fish skin-side down. During the cooking, baste generously with olive oil and a little vinegar or lemon juice.

Serve the fish on a bed of lettuce, surrounded by Greek olives. Sprinkle with mint leaves, if you wish. Yield: four to six servings

Cucumbers with Cumin and Yogurt

See next page for ingredients. Combine all ingredients and chill for one hour or more. Yield: six to eight servings.

Lentils with Cumin and Coriander

See next page for ingredients.

Rinse the lentils and carefully look over to remove any pebbles.

BROILED FISH INGREDIENTS

2 lbs. of fresh or frozen fish (defrosted) (any small fish, fish fillets, fish steaks, or larger fish, split)
salt
4 cloves garlic, chopped
olive oil
red wine vinegar or lemon juice
lettuce
Greek olives or other strongly flavored olives
optional: ½ c. chopped fresh mint leaves

CUCUMBER INGREDIENTS

2 cucumbers,
  peeled and
  grated
1 medium onion,
  finely chopped
1 tsp. cumin
  seed, heated
  briefly in a dry
  skillet, or 1 tsp.
  ground cumin
3 c. plain yogurt,
  lightly whipped
Salt to taste
Freshly ground
  pepper to taste

Bring five cups of water to a boil in a large saucepan. Add lentils, and boil for two minutes, then remove them from the heat and set aside for one hour.

In the meantime, sauté onions and garlic in olive oil. After the lentils have soaked for one hour, add the onions, garlic, cumin, and coriander to the pan with the lentils. Cook, partly covered, for one hour or more, stirring occasionally, until the lentils are quite soft and the water is mostly absorbed. Add more water if necessary to keep the dish from drying out too much, but the mixture should be very thick.

Add salt and freshly ground pepper; taste for seasoning. Yield: four to six servings.

LENTIL INGREDIENTS

1 c. dried lentils
5 c. water
2 medium onions,
  chopped
2 cloves garlic
¼ c. olive oil
1 tsp. ground
  cumin
1 tsp. ground
  coriander
½ tsp. salt
freshly ground
  pepper

Wheat and Barley Loaves

Mix the honey with the water in a large bowl. Sprinkle in the yeast and let rest until foamy.

Stir in the barley flour and the salt. Gradually add the all-purpose flour, mixing well between additions. Add the olive oil and the mint. Mix thoroughly.

Place the dough on slightly floured work-surface. Knead it for about 15 minutes, or until it is shiny and elastic. Add more flour while you are kneading if the dough is too sticky.

Form the dough into a ball, and place it in a greased bowl. Cover with oiled wax-paper and a towel, and let the dough rise until approximately doubled in volume, 1½ to 2 hours. When a finger inserted into the dough leaves a hole that remains, the dough is ready.

Punch the dough down with your fist. Put the dough on your work surface and cut it in half with a knife.

Knead each half into a ball. Cover the balls and allow them to rise for 15 minutes.

Form each ball in to a large, flat loaf and place on an oiled pan. Make several slashes — or a cross — with a very sharp knife on the top of each loaf.

Bake for 45 minutes at 350°. The loaves are done if they sound hollow when tapped on the bottom (these loaves won't brown as much as regular bread). Yield: two eight-inch flat loaves.

WHEAT AND BARLEY LOAF INGREDIENTS

1 tsp. honey
2 c. warm water
  (100°-110°)
1 envelope dry
  yeast
1 c. barley flour
2 tsp. salt
5 c. all-purpose
  flour
¼ c. olive oil
2-3 tsp. crushed
  dried mint leaves

Biblical "Fruitcakes"

Mix the fruits, honey, and cinnamon. Form the fruit mixture into small cakes (about two inches across) or into little balls.

Roll the balls or press the cakes onto the chopped nuts, coating them well. Yield: about 12 cakes or 20 balls.

> **FRUITCAKE INGREDIENTS**
>
> 1 c. coarsely chopped dried figs
> 1 c. coarsely chopped pitted dates
> ¼ c. honey
> ½ tsp. cinnamon
> 2 c. chopped walnuts (or almonds)

International Evening: This can be the time to practice some of your grandmother's favorite recipes, or one of your own. The recipe need not be from your heritage but it should be something different. Children can help with cooking (and eating!) and especially with decorations. This would be a good time to reinforce geography and learn about the flags of different countries. The guest list can be small, perhaps one neighbor family. Try to invite a family whose cultural background is different from your own. You might want to invite guests to share about their cultural background. Costumes can be optional. This party can be as elaborate or as simple as you would like it to be. It can be an evening dinner party, a dessert party, or a Sunday brunch. It's up to you. This would be a good time to learn an international song or dance (such as the famous Mexican Hat Dance!) to share with guests at the party.

Family Tree Night: This party might be a good follow-up to International Evening and the Family Get-together. The guests should be the immediate family and grandparents. Extended family such as aunts, uncles, and cousins can also be included. This is the time to look into your family's past and discover its heritage. What country did grandparents or great-grandparents come from? What does your name mean? You might want to interview grandparents and older relatives on family history (on film, videotape, or audiotape if possible!). Think about what you might want future generations to know. If you are taping, feel free to ask questions to which you already know the answer, since future generations may not know it. Focus especially on the faith of your ancestors. These are the roots of your own faith. Gather old pictures, letters, and other memorabilia to arrange on tables. Make a family tree on a large piece of butcher-paper and fill in the names. For food, consider asking guests to bring their favorite dish along with the recipe for it. This could be a good time to begin putting a family cookbook together.

Mardi Gras Preparation Week: The Mardi Gras party is the culmination of the Carnival season. It marks the end of "the time to dance" and the beginning of "the time to mourn." It should be a true celebration for all family members. Unfortunately, the celebrations usually found around the country on this feast are less than Christian. That does not mean that we should stop celebrating, though. In the past six weeks you and your family have played and danced and sung. This evening should be a combination of all of these. Remember, though that good parties have good planning behind them. Plan well, celebrate heartily, and move into Lent with a spirit of mourning and sacrifice.

Plan

Your guest list should include all of the guests of the past weeks and more if you like. You might consider using a parish hall. The Mardi Gras party traditionally ends at midnight, the official beginning of Lent. At this time the dancing, singing, and playing stops and all kneel down for a prayer led by the father of the host family or a priest, if one is present. Then all will go home in relative silence to mark the true character of the season that is beginning. Guests should be forewarned of this tradition so that they can prepare themselves and their children. They might want to make sure they can stay until midnight also. The entertainment should be planned and scheduled as much as possible. All that you have learned about feasting and hospitality will be put to use in this one evening. You might want to enlist the help of another family to share the burden of the chores.

The time and place should be decided early. Write out a guest list and a general food list. This party should be pot-luck! (Remember those international dishes!)

Invite

Invitations should be festive and handmade if possible. Include the time of the party with a brief explanation of the nature of the evening. Also include the date and time of practice (to practice dances and songs), as well as the food that you wish invitees to bring. Include an RSVP for the party. Be sure to ask what recipe each guest family will bring.

Entertainment

We have a vast history of dances in this country that touch on many different cultures. Many have been lost by disuse and replaced with other forms of entertainment. Wouldn't it be nice if families could regain the ability to play musical instruments, sing songs, and do folk dances for fun, instead of watching TV? Carnival is the perfect season to try this. After all, "All things have their season. . . . There is a time to weep and a time to laugh, a time to mourn and a time to dance" (Ecclesiastes 3:1-4).

The purpose is to learn and enjoy folk dances and songs from this country and others. Ideally, you would spend some weeks learning these dances in a class or on videotape. If this is not possible, this is the week to learn from friends or family members. The dance and song "experts" should be involved in today's activities. Don't forget to ask around for friends and family with dance experience or knowledge of a particular cultural dance or song. They could be a great resource.

One song should be chosen to end the season and be sung at midnight. A suggested song would be "The Glory of These Forty Days" sung to the tune of "Praise God from Whom All Blessings Flow." Both of these hymns can be found in *The Liturgy of the Hours*. Another Lenten song may also be chosen.

Search libraries and used-record stores for folk-dancing music and books. A record, CD, or videotape would be best; however, a book could suffice. Choose the easiest and most enjoyable dances and songs. Remember to keep it simple. It is better to learn two or three very well than five or six not so well.

Menu Planning

Make a list of what is being brought from the RSVPs. This will give you an idea of what gaps need to be filled. Also, remember to purchase paper products and decorations.

Clean

This is the final party of Carnival season, so really make the house shine! The children have been learning to respect their home and have pride in its appearance. This is the opportunity to put that into practice. Each family member should have a cleaning task in the general living area, as well as the task of cleaning his or her bedroom. Make this an entire day's event. Listen to music as you work, and take a lunch break together.

Decoration and Set-up

Spend time arranging tables for food set-up and decorating the general living area. Be sure to arrange an area suitable for dancing as well as one for spectating.

Final Countdown

It is best to have things ready as far ahead of time as possible to allow for some rest and quiet time before guests arrive. This way the hosts can be fresh and relaxed. Remind the children that although this party is meant to be fun for all, as the host family, you have a special responsibility to make sure your guests achieve this goal, even before yourselves. There are great rewards for this kind of generosity and it is never too early to teach this to our children.

Have a wonderful Mardi Gras and remember to have someone (Dad?) watch the clock for midnight. Here is a prayer from the Liturgy of the Hours for Ash Wednesday that can be used to move you into the next season of the Church year: Lent.

> God our Father brings us to the beginning of Lent. We pray that in this time of salvation he will fill us with the Holy Spirit, purify our hearts, and strengthen us in love. May we be filled and satisfied, by the word which you give us. Teach us to be loving not only in great and exceptional moments, but above all in the ordinary events of daily life. May we abstain from what we do not really need, and help our brothers and sisters in distress. May we bear the wounds of your Son in our bodies, for through his body he gave us life.
>
> Lord, protect us in our struggle against evil. As we begin the discipline of Lent, make this day holy by our self-denial. Grant this through our Lord Jesus Christ, your Son, who lives and reigns with you and the Holy Spirit, one God, for ever and ever.

End with the Lenten song that was chosen and quietly say good-bye to your guests. A small speech thanking the guests for sharing the Carnival season with your family and wishing them a blessed Lenten season may facilitate this process.

Lent and Easter

Quick Activities

Pre-Lenten Lessons And Activities

Teach the difference between mortal and venial sin. Begin to prepare hearts for confession by reviewing the ten commandments at dinner.

Sin: Every sin is a rebellion, a choice of one's own will instead of God's, a repetition of Adam's fault in the garden. These choices between one's own way and God's way are forming habits in us.

Mortal sin is a choice against God, which results in death to one's soul.

Venial sin is a surrender of some of the soul's vitality, an impairment of its splendor, for the soul, like the body, has the faculty of forming habits.

Confession: It is very important to be truly sorry for all sin, and do penance sincerely. Lent is the perfect time to ponder these things, from the very beginning in sin to the renewal in baptism.

Mortification: What is it? It means to offer something up for love of Jesus or for the poor souls in purgatory. Why? To remind us to pray, to help us live in the presence of God, and remember our need to be positive. It will help us develop real love for Jesus so that we will miss him on Good Friday and Holy Saturday. Mortification introduces our children to the three ancient good works — prayer, fasting, and giving alms — with which we can atone for our sins and prepare ourselves to walk with Christ.

How? As an example of individual mortification, have each child pick something to offer up. Examples: Make your bed in the a.m. and say a morning offering. Don't buy candy, but instead put the saved money into a collection for the poor, and explain the call for almsgiving. Whatever is decided, put it in writing on a small piece of paper and place the deeds before God on your family altar or before a prominent picture of our Lord.

As a family, decide on a Lenten offering or sacrifice. Examples include: no desserts after dinner, family Rosary each night, attend daily Mass, attend Friday night Stations of the Cross.

When? Keep in mind that the first four weeks of Lent are to focus on our own mortification. Passion Sunday focuses on our Lord's suffering and public life. Then the last week focuses on the Passion of Christ.

Significant Days

The first day of Lent is Ash Wednesday.

Good-Deed Counter Jar

Dye lima beans purple to be used as counters in a jar.

Dye the lima beans as directed. Draw a large cross on the poster-board. Explain that purple is a color for royalty, for Christ is our risen King. Every time a child does an act of charity, penance, or alms, he/she will receive a bean to place in his/her jar. Every Friday during Lent, glue all the week's beans onto the poster, filling in the cross. This shows that we are all helping Jesus to carry His cross. Each bean helps Jesus carry the cross and helps us prepare for Good Friday and Christ's Passion.

Note: Save purple dye in a plastic container for next week's activities.

> **SUPPLIES**
>
> 1-lb. bag of lima beans
> 1 package of purple dye
> 1 large poster-board
> 1 jar per child to display on altar

Middle Cross Day

This day literally marks the half-way point of Lent. It would be a good time to review how your Lenten penances are going. Renew your commitment as a family to do your Lenten readings, mortifications, and giving of alms. You could take the money collected thus far and decide on a charity to give it to, either through your parish mission program or other needs you may be aware of.

We help Jesus carry His cross.

Laetare (Rejoice) Sunday

Also called "Rose Sunday."

This day celebrates the middle of Lent. As if to give us a break, the Church interrupts our mourning with the wearing of rose-colored vestments and a call to rejoice. There are even flowers on the altar. This Sunday was known in ancient times as "Mothering Sunday," when people visited the main cathedral, or mother church, as inspired by the Fourth Sunday of Lent Epistle: "That Jerusalem which is above, is free, which is our Mother."

In England, children who did not live at home visited their mothers on this day and gave them a gift. This is the precursor of our modern celebration of Mother's Day. In expectation of the children, the mothers are said to have baked a special cake for them, with equal or similar amounts of sugar and flour, like the *Simmel* cake. Prepare the family for the rose-colored vestments at Mass. Explain that this signifies the middle of Lent and a sign of hope amidst the mourning.

> **SIMMEL CAKE INGREDIENTS**
>
> ³/₄ c. butter
> ¹/₃ c. shredded lemon and orange peel
> 2 c. sugar
> 2 c. flour
> 1 c. currants, dates, or raisins
> 4 eggs
> almond paste (marzipan)
> ½ tsp. salt

Simmel Cake

Cream the butter and sugar until smooth. Add the eggs one at a time, beating after each addition. Sift flour and salt and add to the first mixture. Dust the peel and currants with a little flour and add to the batter. Line cake tin with waxed paper and pour in half the dough. Add a layer of almond paste and remaining dough. Bake at 300° for one hour. Ice with a thin white icing, flavored with a few drops of almond extract.

Lenten Activities

Shrouding Sacred Statues and Pictures

Take out purple dye and reheat. Count your statues and holy pictures, then cut strips of cloth to dye and use as shrouds for the artwork on Passion Sunday, just as the shrouds are used in church. This reminds us that with the arrival of Passion Sunday, the last most solemn and sorrowful weeks of Lent have begun.

> **SUPPLIES**
>
> purple dye (from bean activity)
> white cloth (old or new)
> (or buy new purple cloth)

Practice Silence

Make a point to all family members not to bicker with each other over small matters, but offer up the silence to our Lord. If the children come to a parent to tell them of their heroics, "Mom, I want you to know that I offered up not bickering today," it would be appropriate to put a bean in their jar. If we explain this well, we might cultivate some truly good habits throughout the coming year.

Jesus said, "Whatsoever you do to the least of my brethren, you do it to me" (Matthew 25:40). So explain to your children that when they tease each other, they tease Christ. This is a special time of year to work on being good, especially for love of Christ.

Make a Family Altar

Clean off your fireplace mantle and transform it into a family altar. You could include the candelabra used for the stations, a bowl with Lenten offerings, the jars with purple beans, and a crucifix on which to meditate.

Use today to clean out the toy-box or game-room. Include the children and decide what things are in excess of their needs, even toys they like but don't play with much. This is a great opportunity to instill a generous heart in our children. We can also teach the virtue of detachment, by always emphasizing that all of our belongings are gifts from God and we are to use and share them to ultimately give Him glory. Make up a box for a needy family or homeless shelter in your area.

Collect Toys for the Needy

As a family, try to deliver the toys collected when cleaning on Thursday. You might try the hospital, a needy family, church play-room, or homeless shelter. If you have time it might be fun to visit your adopted grandparent, too.

Jonah Story

Read Matthew 12:22-50 (paraphrase for younger children), then in order to see exactly what happened to Jonah, find the book of Jonah in the Old Testament and read it aloud.

In discussion you may ask how we are like Jonah. We also like to have things just so, and often demand answers from God. He is very merciful, but often we are not. Lent is a magnificent example of God's mercy. We adored him at Bethlehem, and soon after, we betrayed Him with our sins, big and small. We ought to pay with our very lives, for even they are a gift from Him. But Christ in His Church offers us forty days to fast and pray; and at the end, He promises, His love will triumph over sin and death. At the end He will show us the sign of Jonah. Jonah is a sign of resurrection since he came out of the whale in three days.

A Jonah Project

The patterns for the ship, fish, and Jonah are shown in the illustration. The fish, measuring 8"x5½", is cut from the folded piece of paper with the top of the head and tail on the fold. Paste the tails together and spread apart the base so that it will stand. The ship is 6" high and 6 ½" wide, with the top of the sail on the fold. Cut this from one piece of folded paper. Cut another sail from another color and glue over the first; spread apart to stand. Jonah is 3" high with his hands on the fold. Paste his heads together and spread his legs apart. Use different colors for each piece and decorate them to suit your desire. On the sail of the ship paint a single eye, a symbol of the watchfulness of God the Father, who saw Jonah run away and sent the storm at sea.

SUPPLIES
colored construction-paper
scissors
paste or glue
crayons
markers
glitter or paint

This is how they are used: Pour sand or corn meal on a tray and the figures will stand up in it. At the beginning of Holy Week, Jonah is in the ship. He is standing with his arms up, ready to be thrown overboard. On Good Friday he is put into the fish. On Easter Sunday, the first child awake runs to take Jonah out of the fish and put him on the shore, where he stands with his arms up in a joyful "Alleluia!"

Until then, display in central location.

Almsgiving

Almsgiving during Lent is as much an obligation as fasting and penance, although somehow in modern times the impression is that it is optional. St. Basil tells us:

> Is God unjust that he distributes goods unequally to us? Why do you wax rich, while he begs, except that you may gain the merits of a good distribution, and he may be crowned with the laurels of patience? It is the bread of the famished that you retain; the cloak of the naked that you keep in your cupboard; the shoes of the barefoot that rot in your keeping; the money of

An example of the "Jonah Project."

the needy that you keep hidden away. As much as yet remains in your power to give, by so much do you harm others.

Now is the time to do more cleaning out and more giving away. Go through your closets today and pack those extra clothing items that are not being used. Every member of the family can have a bag to donate.

You might deliver the clothing collected to a homeless shelter, nursing home, or needy family. Don't forget about your adopted grandparent, or if you are within traveling distance, visit your biological grandparents, or family members.

Make a Paschal Candle

An Easter candle is fairly easy to make and helps mark the resurrection with a visible sign of light. It is lit on Easter morning after the first child up has taken Jonah out of the fish. The second child claims the privilege of lighting the Paschal candle after the others have gathered. The same type of candle is used for the Christ candle in Advent.

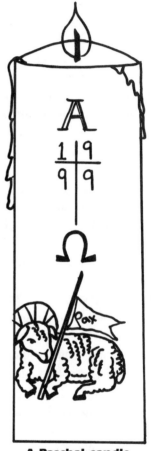

The instructions for cutting the cross, the alpha (A), omega (like an upside-down U), and the numerals of the year on the Paschal candle are given with the text of the restored Easter Vigil, available in booklet form and also in missals printed since the Vigil was restored.

To make these cuts visible, they may be stained or painted with red oil-paint. You can add other symbols of redemption like the lamb, pelican, grapes and wheat, or phoenix, according to your taste. Insert cloves at the ends of the cross and the center to symbolize the nails. As with the Christ candle, you must plan time together in the evenings in order to prepare the candle and discuss the doctrine relating to these symbols.

The Stations of the Cross

The tradition of the Stations of the Cross probably originated around the years 1095-1270. When visiting as pilgrims to the Holy Land, people would prayerfully travel the road to Calvary. The Latin word *statio* means "halting place," and is the root for the word "stations." After the Crusades, the Muslims captured the Holy Land and forbade the walking to Cal-

A Paschal candle.

vary, so many people kept the practice of walking in Jesus' footsteps by making special markers in their own towns. This walking of the stations became very popular in Europe during the Middle Ages.

In the eighteenth century, Pope Clement XII decided that the number of stations would be fixed at fourteen, based on the Gospel accounts of Jesus' crucifixion and death. As a result, churches were allowed to feature the fourteen stations inside. Some markers are very elaborate and others are simple crosses.

SUPPLIES
holy cards
pictures of the passion
paper
crayons, markers
glue or tape
scissors
yarn

Make Stations of the Cross Booklets

Either gather holy cards, order pictures, or draw and color each child's book. The Mother of Our Savior Company, Inc., catalog has great supplies (call 1-800-451-3993). Each family member can then use the booklet when doing the Stations of the Cross together. This helps younger children to pay attention.

The Apostles and Prayer

Read Matthew 4:18-23 and 9:9-13, where Christ chooses the twelve. Talk about them being His closest friends. How much time did they daily spend with our Lord? Did they miss Him after His death? Now relate this to your own relationship with Christ. He has called each one of us to have a close relationship with Him. How are we to imitate that close friendship with our Lord? Prayer! We are all called to pray, to spend time talking with Jesus and listening to Him. Spend some quiet time today instructing your children on prayer. Make a family commitment to pray every day, and try to develop that closeness with Jesus. Recite a few prayers and then allow for quiet prayer, a time to listen to Jesus.

There are five types of prayer listed in the *Catechism of the Catholic Church* (2626-2643). They are: blessing and adoration, petition, intercession, thanksgiving, and praise.

Honor St. Joseph

In honor of St. Joseph, the foster-father of Jesus and spouse of Mary, encourage everyone in the family to do a chore for another person who is not expecting it. This should be a surprise and could be anything from taking out the trash to cleaning the house. Remember to do it with love and offer it up to St. Joseph so he may offer it to our Lord as a gift of love.

Prepare a St. Joseph Table

This is a tradition in Sicily, where everyone prepares breads and feasts. Then a priest comes and blesses the food. Invite the guests who St. Joseph would invite: the poor and the unfortunate. You could even make this a group effort with neighbor families. One special item is St. Joseph Sfinge (see page 41).

Holy Eucharist Discussion

Discuss the Last Supper, which happened on Holy Thursday. Catholics believe in the Real Presence of Christ in the Holy Eucharist. Transubstantiation, when the bread and wine are transformed into the body and blood of Christ, occurs in the Holy Sacrifice of the Mass when the priest, in the "person of Christ" (*in persona Christi*), says the words of the consecration. Depending on the ages of your children, your discussion might include reading the Eucharistic Prayers, Scripture, and the *Catechism of the Catholic Church* (1322-1419).

Holy Angels

Make a special effort to say a family prayer to the angels asking for their help and guidance in preparing our hearts to sorrow in Christ's brutal passion and death and to long for His resurrection.

Learn the Prayer to the Guardian Angels

"Angel of God, my guardian dear, to whom God's love commits one here, ever this day be at my side, to light and guard, to rule and guide. Amen."

Here is a special angel poem that Michaelann's children love to recite.

"Four corners to my bed, four angels around my head, one to watch, two to pray, and one to keep all fear away" (author unknown).

Learn to Make a Spiritual Communion

It might be a good idea to make a visit to your home parish and say "hello" to our Lord. He is always present in the Blessed Sacrament and He waits there, longing for us to come and visit Him. Word your own Spiritual Communion. Here's an example:

Spiritual Communion Prayer

"O my Jesus, I believe that You are here, that You see me and hear me. I wish to receive You with the same humility and reverence with which Your most holy mother Mary received You. Amen."

Vigil of Passion Sunday

Now is the time to take out the purple shrouds and drape your crucifixes, statues, and religious pictures. You could make this a family ceremony in the evening, where all help in shrouding the art, as will be done in our churches. This is to call our minds to remember that Christ's Passion is soon approaching and we should be sorrowing in our hearts.

Passion Sunday

This day has been known as Silent Sunday and Quiet Sunday. This is the week to meditate on Christ's public life. If you are not yet reading the Bible together, this would be a great time to start reading the Gospels. Begin with Matthew and work your way through the New Testament. It is a good idea to set a certain period of time aside (for example, for thirty minutes beginning at eight p.m.) for Gospel reading. At that time, gather as a family and read aloud. The older children can even take turns reading.

This week's readings at Mass might sound familiar and promote great family discussions.

Don't forget to continue with your other Lenten reading program.

Review the Spiritual Works of Mercy

The spiritual and corporal works of mercy are charitable actions where we aid our neighbor in his need, both spiritual and physical.

The spiritual works of mercy are: instructing, advising, consoling, comforting, forgiving, and bearing wrongs patiently (CCC 2447). Discuss in your family how you can increase your spiritual works of mercy and make a resolution to do one together this week.

Review the Corporal Works of Mercy

"The Corporal Works of Mercy consist especially in feeding the hungry, sheltering the homeless, clothing the naked, visiting the sick and imprisoned, and burying the dead. Among all these, giving alms to the poor is one of the chief witnesses to fraternal charity: it is also a work of justice pleasing to God" (CCC 2447). What can you do in the remaining weeks of Lent to better live out these corporal works of mercy? Make a resolution as a family to commit to doing one or more together.

SUPPLIES

construction
paper
wire hangers
string
glue or tape
crayons or
markers

Make a Works of Mercy Mobile

Have your family review all of the works of mercy. Then either draw or cut out pictures from magazines to fit the description of each work. Attach to hanger with tape and string and hang in your dining room to remind you to do these good works during the remainder of Lent.

Review on Fridays the Seven Sorrows of Mary

All are found in the New Testament.
1. Prophecy of Simeon
2. Flight into Egypt
3. Jesus lost in the temple
4. Jesus meets His afflicted mother
5. Jesus is crucified
6. Jesus is taken down from the cross
7. Jesus is laid in the tomb

There is also a beautiful Litany of Our Lady of the Seven *Dolors* (Sorrows) that is found in *A Prayerbook of Favorite Litanies* by Father Albert J. Hebert, S.M. (TAN Publishing).

This is a day traditionally devoted to meditating on the seven sorrows of Mary. It could be further emphasized by making the Seven-Herb Soup (the recipe appears in the section "Great Recipes for Lent").

Review Acts of Charity

This might be a good time to plan and collect some food items for the poor. You could take the time to plan an Easter meal for a needy family, with all of your family favorites and not just canned goods that nobody cares for. This will show your family that their personal sacrifices are going to bring great joy to those less fortunate. It might even encourage each member to do more in this last week of penance.

If you have older children, you might want to encourage them to consider doing some type of volunteer work this Lent. There are nursing homes, church functions, food pantries, etc. that could probably use their energy and spirit.

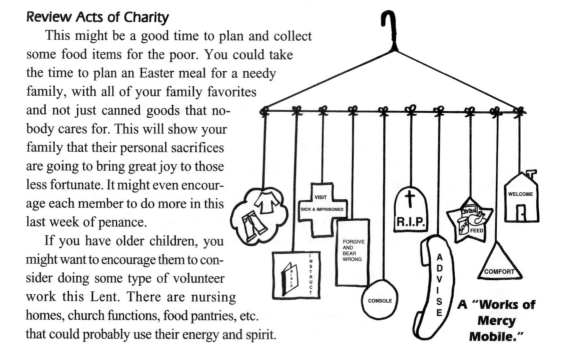

A "Works of Mercy Mobile."

Great Recipes for Lent

The Pretzel Story

During Lent, the early Roman Christians (fourth century) observed a strict fast — no milk, no butter, no cheese, no eggs, no cream, and no meat. They created a bread which they called *bracallae* ("little arms") which was shaped into the form of a person's arms crossed in prayer to remind them that Lent was a time of prayer and penance. They sprinkled the top of this pastry with salt.

Later, when the monks introduced these breads to the northern countries, the Germanic people coined the word *bretzel* from the Roman *bracellea*, from which comes our word "pretzel."

Pretzel Making Is Fun!

Dissolve the cake yeast or package of dry yeast into 1½ cups warm water. Add one teaspoon salt, and one tablespoon sugar. Blend in four cups of flour (two cups whole wheat, two cups enriched).

Knead dough until smooth. Cut into small pieces. Roll into ropes, and twist into desired shape. Place on lightly greased cookie sheets. Brush pretzel with one beaten egg. Sprinkle with coarse salt. Bake immediately at 425° oven for 12-15 minutes.

(For hard pretzels, use only 1¼ cups water, and ¼ cup melted butter. Make pretzels smaller and bake until brown. These keep well over a period of days.)

Serve a pretzel to each family member at dinner.

> ### PRETZEL INGREDIENTS
>
> 1 cake yeast (or 1 package of dry yeast)
> 1½ c. warm water
> 1 tsp. salt
> 1 tbs. sugar
> 4 c. flour — 2 c. whole wheat, 2 c. enriched
> 1 egg
> optional: melted butter

Bread

Fridays are bread days! Begin in the morning so that the bread has time to rise.

> ### WHOLE WHEAT BREAD INGREDIENTS
>
> 1½ qt. milk
> 14 c. whole-wheat flour
> 4 tsp. salt
> 2 cakes of yeast
> 3 tbs. molasses
> 1 c. lukewarm water
> 3 tsp. fat
> sesame seeds

Whole Wheat Bread

Scald and cool milk. Add salt, molasses, and fat. Stir in eight cups of flour until smooth. (If you have an electric mixer, let it beat the dough until it is stiff.) Dissolve yeast in water for 10 minutes. Add yeast and remaining flour to the first dough.

Knead and let rise until doubled in bulk. Knead again, shape into six loaves, and place into 5"x9" inch bread-pans. Let rise until doubled in bulk. Bake at 350° for 15 minutes. Then turn the oven up to 400° and bake for five minutes or until brown.

Have extra sesame seeds to make designs of fish and crosses on your loaves. The seeds remind us that we must die to ourselves so that Christ may give us new life.

HOT CROSS BUN INGREDIENTS

¼ c. shortening
2 c. scalded milk
¾ c. sugar
1 cake yeast
2 eggs
½ c. lukewarm
  water
4-6 c. whole
  wheat flour
1 c. currants or
  raisins

Our Daily Bread — Hot Cross Buns

Scald and cool milk. Add shortening, sugar, and eggs. When lukewarm, add yeast that has been dissolved in ½-cup lukewarm water. Stir in four cups flour, and beat hard. Add enough flour to make a soft dough. Stir in raisins. Keep in refrigerator until ready to use. Shape into buns and cut with cross; let rise 60 minutes. Bake in hot oven (425°) for 15 minutes. Brush with melted butter and mark with icing cross.

Dark Rye Bread

Dissolve yeast in one cup warm water until it starts to rise and make bubbles. Pour this on the flour. Add three more cups of warm water to the flour and stir until fluid is all soaked up. Then knead (with your own hands) until it is a firm, fairly stiff dough. Put in a warm place to rise, covering it with a cloth.

After two hours or more (depending on the temperature of the room), the dough should rise to twice the size. Punch it down and knead for about 10 minutes again. Cover it up and let it rise again until not quite doubled in size. It will rise in a short while (½ hour). Heat oven to 350°. Then put dough upside-down on a flour-sprinkled cookie sheet. Make holes in the dough with a knitting needle (or something similar) while in the hot stove. Leave there for an hour, then "wash" the bread: take it half-way out and brush it freely with water. Push back into the oven for another quarter of an hour, turning heat down to 300°. Then take it out. Makes one loaf.

DARK RYE BREAD INGREDIENTS

4 c. medium rye
  flour
½ tsp. caraway
  seed
2 c. regular white
  flour
1 cake of yeast or
  1 package of
  dry yeast
1 tbs. salt
4 c. warm water

RED BEANS AND RICE INGREDIENTS

1 lb. red kidney
  beans (soak in a
  pot of water
  overnight)
1 chopped onion
1 chopped green
  pepper
1 chopped clove of
  garlic (or more to
  taste)
2 tbs. oil
salt and pepper to
  taste
¼ tsp. ground
  cumin
⅛ tsp. cayenne
  pepper
½ tsp. ground
  thyme
½ tsp. basil
left-over ham-bone
  or cut-up ham, or
  2 lbs. of kielbasa
  sausage

Louisiana Red Beans and Rice

If using sausage, slice into rounds, cook ahead of time, and put aside until later. If using ham bone and left over ham, place it in the pot in the beginning of cooking process.

After the beans have soaked all night, pour out the old water and put in fresh water to cover the beans. Place the oil in a frying pan and brown the onion, green pepper, and garlic until all are soft. Add browned vegetables to the beans in a large pot and recover with water. Add in the ham, holding the sausage until later.

Let the mixture cook all day in a crock-pot or over a low flame. Taste and add seasoning to taste. Before serving, add the sausage and serve over cooked rice.

— Recipe from Carole Martin, my mother-in-law extraordinaire.

ST. JOSEPH SFINGE INGREDIENTS

1 c. water
1 tbs. sugar
¼ lb. butter
1 tbs. grated
 lemon peel
¼ tsp. salt
1 tsp. grated
 orange peel
1 c. sifted flour
4 eggs

St. Joseph Sfinge

Boil water and butter. Add flour and salt. Keep stirring until mixture leaves side of pan or forms a ball in the center. Cool. Beat in eggs, one at a time. Add sugar and grated peel. Drop tablespoonfuls of dough every three inches on a greased cookie sheet, or fill muffin tins half-full. Bake in a hot oven (400°) for 10 minutes. Reduce heat to 350°, and continue baking until light brown. Remove from oven. Open puff in the center of top to let steam escape. Cool.

FILLING INGREDIENTS

1 lb. cottage
 cheese
2 tsp. almond
 extract
2 tbs. grated
 chocolate
3 tbs. milk
1 tbs. grated
 orange-rind
18 maraschino
 cherries
½ c. glazed
 orange peel

Filling: See ingredients at right. Mix cottage cheese with chocolate and orange rind. Add flavoring, milk, and sugar to taste. Beat until smooth and custard-like. Fill puffs. Chill until ready to use. Before serving, top with cherry and orange peel. Yields about 18 cream puffs.

PRETZEL INGREDIENTS

1 tbs. honey
1½ c. warm water
1 package active
 dry yeast
1 tsp. salt
4 c. flour
coarse salt
1 egg, beaten

Pretzels

Add the honey to the water; sprinkle in the yeast and stir until dissolved. Add one teaspoon salt. Blend in the flour and knead the dough until smooth. Cut the dough into pieces. Roll it into ropes and twist into pretzel shapes. You can make small pretzels with thin ropes, or large ones with fat ropes, but to cook at the same rate, your pretzel batch needs to all be the same size.

Place the pretzels on lightly greased cookie sheets. Brush them with the beaten egg. Sprinkle with coarse salt. Bake in a 425° oven for 12 to 15 minutes, until the pretzels are golden brown.

TOMATO-LENTIL SOUP INGREDIENTS

⅔ c. dried lentils
4–5 c. water
½ head of garlic
 (8–10 cloves)
2 stalks celery,
 sliced
3 carrots, sliced
1 tsp. tamari
1 tbs. fresh
 parsley, chopped
½ tsp. marjoram

Tomato-Lentil Soup

Place lentils and four cups of water in a saucepan or large skillet. Bring to a boil, reduce heat and simmer. Peel and mince garlic, add celery and carrots to lentils. Simmer until vegetable and lentils are tender. Stir in tamari, tomato paste, herbs, and enough additional water to make desired consistency. Leftovers can be frozen for later use. Another variation is Chili-Lentil Soup. Just add one tablespoon of chili powder and ½-teaspoon of cumin powder.

— *From the kitchen of Diane Aquila*

Soup de Sante (Soup of Health)

Brown vegetables in butter. Add enough water to cover. Let boil until tender. Add flour and stir until smooth. Add fish broth, wine, seasonings, and parsley. Place French rolls in soup toureen and cover with hot soup. When the bread is soaked, garnish with bits of carrot.

— *From* Cooking for Christ

SOUP OF HEALTH INGREDIENTS

1 c. shredded
 celery
½ tbs. flour
1 c. endive
4 c. fish broth
1 c. sorrel
⅓ c. white wine
½ c. chervil
1 tsp. salt
1 c. cabbage
¼ tsp. pepper
2 onions
1 tsp. parsley
2 tbs. butter
French rolls
2 c. water
carrot sticks

CALZONE DOUGH INGREDIENTS

2–3 c. of flour
1 c. warm water
1 package of
 yeast
1 tbs. honey

Calzones

Dissolve the yeast in water and add it to the flour. Stir in the honey and knead for five to 10 minutes. Let rest for two hours or more to rise.

Wash spinach and steam until wilted. Remove from water and cut into pieces. Sauté onion, garlic, and butter until translucent and soft. Combine cheeses and pour sautéed onion mixture into cheese and add spinach.

Divide dough and roll into ¼-inch thick pieces. Fill and place filling on one-half of the circle, leaving ½-inches to pinch closed. Fold the empty side over and crimp the edge with your favorite fork dunked into water. Prick it here and there. Bake on oiled tray at 450° for 15 to 20 minutes or until lightly brown. Brush with melted butter and serve.

— *From the kitchen of Diane Aquila*

CALZONE FILLING INGREDIENTS

1 lb. fresh spinach
2 cloves garlic,
 crushed
2 c. mozzarella
½ c. minced onion
½ c. Romano or
 Parmesan
 cheese
dash of nutmeg

Herbed Lentils and Rice

See the ingredient list on the next page.

Combine broth, lentils, onion, uncooked rice, wine, basil, salt, oregano, thyme, garlic, pepper, and shredded cheese. Turn

HERBED LENTILS AND RICE INGREDIENTS

2¾ c. chicken or vegetable broth
¾ c. dry lentils
¾ c. chopped onions
½ c. brown rice
¼ c. dry white wine
½ tsp. dried basil, crushed
¼ tsp. salt
¼ tsp. dried oregano, crushed
¼ tsp. dried thyme, crushed
⅛ tsp. garlic powder
⅛ tsp. pepper
½ c. shredded Swiss cheese (2 ounces)
8 thin strips Swiss cheese (2 ounces)

mixture into an ungreased 1½-quart casserole dish with a tight lid.

Bake, covered, at 350° for 90 minutes to two hours. Serves four to six adults.

— From the kitchen of Marilyn Grodi

Clam Sauce

Make this to serve over linguine or spaghetti.

In a pan, sauté garlic in oil. Pour in the clam juice and white wine and simmer.

At the same time you put your linguine or spaghetti in boiling water, put the clams in the sauce mixture. Cook pasta according to package directions, then drain. Pour the clam sauce over the pasta.

Top with Romano cheese. You can add parsley, broccoli, mushrooms, and/or lemon.

— From the kitchen of Diane Aquila

CLAM SAUCE INGREDIENTS

1 tbs. olive oil
4 cloves of garlic
½ c. white wine
3 cans minced or chopped clams
basil or oregano to taste
1 lb. linguine or spaghetti
parsley
Romano cheese

Food to Share

Next is a great recipe that is easy to make and perfect to share. Plan on having a family over to share your meal or plan on taking dinner to a needy family. Maybe your pastor knows of needy families in your parish.

This would be a great time to practice the corporal works of mercy and charity, which were so important to our Lord. Read: Luke 3:11, Luke 11:41, James 2: 15-16, and 1 John 3:17.

Vegetable Soup

Cook vegetable broth and herbs. Add diced vegetables and spices. When the soup is well-cooked, add the egg yolk. Serve hot.

Seven-Herb Soup (Siebenkraeutersuppe)

See the ingredient list on page 44.

The mixture of the first five herbs should total seven

VEGETABLE SOUP INGREDIENTS

1 qt. vegetable broth
3 carrots, diced
½ c. borage
2 onions, diced
½ c. endive
2 c. cabbage, diced
¼ c. marigold
pinch of cloves
½ c. sorrel
pinch mace
2 c. whole spinach
pinch of nutmeg
1 turnip, diced
1 egg yolk

SEVEN-HERB SOUP INGREDIENTS
dandelions
chervil
cress
sorrel
leafnettle
parsley
onions
butter
flour
2 egg yolks
¼ c. milk or sour cream

ounces. Whether bought at the market or picked from your herb garden, they should be washed well. Steam in butter with finely chopped onions and parsley. Press through a sieve into a flour-soup and let boil. You may put in one or two egg yolks, one to two tablespoons of cream, or ¼ cup milk. You also may use sour cream.

Recreate a Last Supper Meal

Traditional items needed are bitter herbs: parsley, chives, and celery greens. Unleavened bread is served with the herbs.

Then the feast day meal of yearling lamb is roasted, and eaten with bitter herbs and the traditional brown sauce. Each time you dip into the herb sauce, remember our Lord answering sadly the question of the apostles as to who was the traitor: "He who has dipped his hand in the dish with me, will betray me" (Matthew 26:23).

Afterwards the table is cleared and in front of the father is put a tray of unleavened bread and red wine. He blesses them and hands some to each individual, each drinking and eating, remembering our Lord, Who must have celebrated such "love feasts" many times with his apostles. This was signifying our Lord's great farewell.

Unleavened Bread

Mix salt, flour, and egg. Add water, mix dough quickly with a knife, then knead on a board, stretching it up and down to make it elastic until it leaves the board clean. Toss on a small, well-floured board. Cover with a hot bowl and keep warm one-half hour or longer. Then cut up into squares of desired size and bake in 350° oven until done.

UNLEAVENED BREAD INGREDIENTS
1½ c. flour
1 egg, slightly beaten
¼ tsp. salt
½ c. butter
⅓ c. warm water

ROASTED LAMB INGREDIENTS
leg of lamb
20 cloves of garlic
dry white wine
rosemary

Roasted Lamb

Place leg of lamb fat-side-up and make many slits in the fat. Stuff the sliced garlic in these slits.

Place the lamb in a roasting pan. Pour white wine over it so that there is liquid in the bottom of your pan. Sprinkle rosemary on top.

Cook at 350°, calculating the length of time at 20 minutes per pound.

Other Lenten Activities

Adopt-a-Grandparent

As a family, visit a nursing home and adopt a grandparent for Lent. Try to visit him or her often during this season and possibly throughout the year.

SUPPLIES

12 white candles
2 shoe-boxes, or 2
tissue-boxes, or
a 2"x4" board
with 12 holes
plaster of Paris
black paint

Candelabrum

Use with the Stations of the Cross.

Twelve candles in one candelabrum, or two shorter candelabra holding six candles apiece, or twelve separate candleholders are needed. The candelabra may be made a number of ways. If you have a length of 2"x4" board, bore 12 holes for the candles. If you have two shoe-boxes, cut six holes in each for the candles. To use plaster of Paris, make two candelabra. One at a time, pour the plaster into two empty tissue-boxes. Hold the candles in place (six in each) for a few moments until the plaster hardens. These may be moved after 24 hours and painted black.

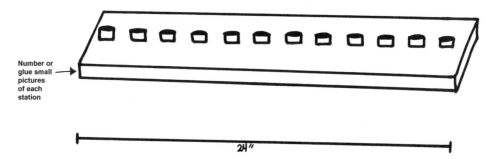

Number or glue small pictures of each station

24"

It is not difficult for children to give meaning to the Stations of the Cross. This activity involves so many senses that it appeals to all ages. All twelve candles are lit at the beginning; one is blown out after each station. This involves and interests most children. They become actively involved in the prayer and understand the meaning of Christ's suffering. When you have finished the twelfth station (Jesus Dies on the Cross), the last candle is snuffed, and the room is in complete darkness. Why? Because Jesus was the light of the world, and when he died, the light was gone out of the world. This is a great discussion starter. Do this every evening or on Fridays.

Holy Week

Palm Sunday

This is the beginning of Holy Week, in which we accompany our Lord day-by-day through the last week of His life, as it is told in the Gospels. So too we are here at His triumphant entry into Jerusalem on Palm Sunday.

The solemn blessing of the palms was added to the liturgy in the ninth century. It is a great idea to prayerfully read and meditate on these beautifully rich texts some time today. If you need to take a missal home from your church, then do so. There are many booklets available with the texts in them. (See the book list at the end of this book.)

Ask the family what was different about the liturgy today. Answers: No "Gloria," purple shrouds on the statues, and the prayers at the foot of the altar are much shorter, all because these are holy days of mourning.

Place blessed palms in prominent spots, behind the crucifix or another statue, as placemats for your thorn centerpiece, and in every room. This could be done in a family procession around the house and grounds, while praying for God's continued blessings.

Burn Last Year's Palms

According to ancient tradition, the three days after Palm Sunday are devoted in many places to a thorough cleaning of the house, the most vigorous of the whole year. Design a family job-list and divide it over the three days. This traditional spring-cleaning, of course, is to make the home as neat as possible for the greatest feast of the year.

Since the ashes at Mass on Ash Wednesday are from the year past, at home you could burn old palms and use them to bless your labors, such as in a family garden. This is an old custom in the Alps, except that the Austrian people distributed the ashes not over the garden, but the fields. If you have a garden, try it.

SUPPLIES TO COLLECT

- moss (you will find it growing around the roots of trees)
- attractive stones and pebbles
- shells if near an ocean or Great Lake
- some nice damp-earth flowers, daisies, and celandines
- small twigs for cross and fence
- some carrot-tops
- small mirror (cosmetic)
- large plate, tray, or box

Make an Easter Garden

Continue to complete cleaning jobs on the family job-list and encourage the children to offer up these sacrifices in preparation for the great feast of Easter.

First, go for a walk to collect the necessary bits and pieces for the Easter garden. Everyone should carry a suitable box or bag to collect the various things.

You make the garden by putting a layer of soil on the tray, then planting the moss on it. Create a little "lake" by putting the mirror in a suitable corner and carefully planting moss and placing pebbles around it. Carrot-tops, if placed on wet moss and watered every day, will start to sprout and look like mini-ferns. In the corner, create a hill or mound using earth and pebbles. This will be your Calvary. Cover it with moss and stand three crosses on top, the one in the middle being larger. Make crosses by wrapping the purple thread around two perpendicular sticks, in a criss-cross style. Almost anything can make the garden look pretty. One idea is to leave the garden free of flowers until the evening of Holy Saturday and then it can be transformed into a bower of Eas-ter, with white and gold ribbons and flowers everywhere.

Holy Thursday

It would be a good custom to go from church to church (try to visit seven in honor of the seven sorrows of Mary) on Holy Thursday. On this day, the churches are decorated with a profusion of flowers, as a sign of love and gratitude for the Holy Eucharist. The contrast with the bare churches on Good Friday (tomor-

A plan for an Easter garden.

row) is all the more striking and gives a tremendous feeling of desolation that Christ is gone. Point out that the candle being lighted on Holy Thursday and not on Good Friday depicts Christ, the light of the world, Who is present when the candle is lit and not present when it is not lit.

Good Friday

Remember that today is a day of fast and abstinence. That means that we don't eat meat and the food we do eat is less than normal. The guidelines are to eat two small meals and one larger meal. It is important to keep in mind that the two small meals, if combined, should not equal the size and quantity of the larger meal. The main idea is that all the meals are smaller than usual and penitential in substance.

It is a great idea to spend some time in church between 12:00 and 3:00 p.m., the time when Christ was crucified and died. Most churches have services of some kind and, depending on the ages of your children, you can choose which activities will best suit your families' abilities. If you are unable to attend services, then keep as silent as possible throughout the day and really make the afternoon a solemn prayer-time. You may want to say the Stations of the Cross, the Rosary (sorrowful mysteries), or prayerfully talk to your little ones about the great sorrow of this day.

Note: Isn't it interesting that our Lord died at the sixth hour, on the sixth day, of the sixth week of Lent?

Divine Mercy Novena and Chaplet

In a revelation to Blessed Sister Faustina, Christ asked that a Novena of Divine Mercy precede the Feast of Divine Mercy, the Sunday after Easter. The novena begins on Good Friday; one must say the Chaplet of Divine Mercy for nine days. (See the "Prayers and Devotions.")

On different days, remember different groups of souls as follows:

Day 1: All mankind, especially sinners

Day 2: Souls of priests and religious

Day 3: Devout and faithful souls

Day 4: Souls of those who do not believe in Jesus or do not know Him

Day 5: Souls of heretics and schismatics

Day 6: The meek and humble souls of children

Day 7: "Souls who venerate and glorify My mercy"

Day 8: Souls in purgatory

Day 9: Souls of those who have become lukewarm. This group "wounds My heart most painfully," Christ said.

In the evening, the older members of the family can put the Easter garden or gardens on the table, and turn out the lights and have candles on either side of it and pray together.

Holy Saturday and Easter Vigil Activities

Color Eggs

This is a great activity for all family members. You can use muriatic acid to etch patterns onto eggs. Easter songs, staves, notes, and words are very good ideas. Paint can also be used to create a lamb, or a risen Christ, the Blessed Mother, or patron saints of the family. You can fasten dried ferns, flowers, or herbs to the eggs before you dye them, then that area will be a white silhouette. All of these eggs can appear in baskets on Easter Sunday morning at the foot of the altar for the solemn blessing of the food.

Call your parish priest and ask if he will be blessing the Easter food and baskets at Mass. Afterwards, they can be distributed at the Easter breakfast. The egg symbolizes the tomb and its opening on Easter morning, symbolizing Christ's resurrection.

Recite the Divine Mercy Novena and Chaplet

If your children are older, you may want to attend Midnight Mass together. This is the most holy liturgy of the entire year and a true blessing to attend.

Bring home holy water to fill your family fonts.

Season-long Activities

Family Time and Lenten Reading Program

When counting the forty days of Lent, Sundays are not counted. The Church teaches that the feast of Christ's resurrection supersedes the fast. Explain to your family how Sunday is a weekly feast, a mini-resurrection. It would be good to have a special dessert at dinner to emphasize the celebratory aspect of the day Christ rose from the dead.

Abstain from television and entertainment, so that you can spend time reading silently. There will be time for reading aloud as well. Find something for the mind, the heart, and the soul. Examples include:

For the mind, something intellectual

A Lenten Yule log.

— a history of the Church, history or information about the sacraments, or selections from papal encyclicals.

SUPPLIES

2 pieces of the trunk of your Christmas tree, 12" and 7" long
nails
hammer
6 candleholders
6 candles
purple ribbon

For the soul, spiritual reading — *The Ascent of Mount Carmel*, by St. John of the Cross; *The Introduction to a Devout Life*, by St. Francis de Sales; *The Story of a Soul*, by St. Thérèse of Lisieux; *The Spiritual Castle*, by St. Teresa of Ávila; or *The Soul of the Apostolate*, by Abbot Chautard.

For the heart — biographies of the saints. St. Augustine said, "If he could do it, and she, why not I?"

And most importantly, the Holy Bible.

Have family members share what they are reading. One great benefit will be the exchange of the spiritual goods obtained from everyone's reading. Continue every Sunday to have family reading time. You may want to decide on a family book to read aloud.

Make a Lenten Yule Log

Gather the supplies listed in the box on page 48.

Nail the logs together, then tie ribbon around the center. Make sure that the cross lies flat and then attach the candle holders, either with screws or with glue. Place the candles in the holders and light one candle a week, like with the Advent wreath. This can be a wonderful centerpiece for your dining room table or used during family reading time.

Easter and Beyond

Easter Sunday is the feast of feasts! The Feast of the Resurrection is celebrated as the greatest and most important feast day of the whole year. Paschaltide then lasts from Easter night until after Pentecost. But in fact, every Sunday is a "little Easter," consecrated to the memory of the risen Christ.

Following ancient customs going back to the tenth century, all kinds of foods that were forbidden during Lent are placed in baskets and blessed by the priest at Mass on Easter morning.

Continue with your Easter celebrations by feasting together and rejoicing in Christ's resurrection. A ham dinner symbolizes that although the Jews were forbidden to eat pork, we are made new through Christ. This is a celebratory meal. Set the feast table using a white tablecloth and use your Paschal candle as the centerpiece.

Shower your home with fresh flowers and have the children design place-cards in the shape of a lamb. Say the blessing standing up to show special reverence to the great Easter feast.

Significant Days

Trinity Sunday is last day in the octave of Pentecost. "Easter-time" officially ends today.

It might be a good idea to review the seven gifts and the twelve fruits of the Holy Spirit at dinner tonight. Think of short quiz-questions to measure how well everyone understands these great and helpful gifts from God. Then, as a closing prayer, ask our Lord to truly send His Holy Spirit to shower each member of the family with His gifts and fruits. If one member needs a particular gift, encourage each person to make his petitions known to God.

12 Fruits Salad

See the ingredient list at right. Wash all the fruits gently and pat dry with a paper towel. Slice and prepare the fruits, adding the lemon and drop of honey when finished. Serve plain or over pound cake, waffles, or ice cream.

---

12 FRUITS SALAD INGREDIENTS

apples (symbol of salvation and the New Eve)
pears (symbol of Mary)
oranges (symbol of purity and generosity)
peaches (symbol of the heart)
strawberries (symbol of righteousness)
blueberries (blue for Our Lady's mantle)
cherries (symbol of good works)
grapes (symbol of the Eucharist)
lemon (symbol of fidelity)
figs (symbol of fruitfulness)
a drop of honey (symbol of the sweet ministry of Christ)
slivered almonds (symbol of divine approval)

Mercy Sunday

What a perfect time to concentrate on and ask for Christ's mercy for you and your family. It would be nice to have a special dinner with white linens. The children could help prepare a special meal, and afterwards everyone could share how Christ has been merciful to them. It would be nice to have a centerpiece of white and red flowers as well. (White for mercy, red for our sins.)

The Feast of St. Mark and the Three Days Before the Ascension

Formerly known as rogation days.

Rogation days were a time to see God in visible things, like new leaves on the trees and new green grass, and the promise of what is invisible, like the seed buried in the earth. They are a great time for family celebration. Long ago, there were outdoor processions and requests for God's blessings on one's crops. Rogation days were a time of prayer and penance to appease God's wrath and ask for protection and blessings.

Today have the family take a nature walk and discuss the beauty of new life, and how that relates to our life in the risen Christ as well.

Great Easter Recipes

Strawberry Cake

Mix the yeast in warm milk with ¼-cup flour. Cover and let rise until light. Cream shortening and sugar. Add lemon rind and salt. Beat in eggs, one at a time. Add yeast mixture and the rest of the flour. Beat for 15 minutes.

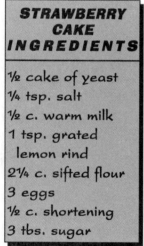

STRAWBERRY CAKE INGREDIENTS

½ cake of yeast
¼ tsp. salt
½ c. warm milk
1 tsp. grated lemon rind
2¼ c. sifted flour
3 eggs
½ c. shortening
3 tbs. sugar

GLAZE INGREDIENTS

1 c. strawberries (mashed)
whole strawberries
½ c. sugar

RUM SAUCE INGREDIENTS

½ c. sugar
3 tbs. rum
¾ c. boiling water

Pour the bubbling dough into a greased tube-pan. Allow the dough to rise until doubled in bulk. Bake in a 350° oven for 45 minutes.

When the cake is done, remove from the oven. Turn pan upside down and let the cake slide out. Stab the bottom of the cake with a long-tinged fork. Place the cake in a dish containing:

Rum Sauce

Boil the water with the sugar for 10 minutes. Take the syrup from the stove and add the rum. Allow the cake to absorb the sweet rum flavor. Then spread the top with:

Strawberry Glaze

Cook mashed berries with sugar before spreading them on the cake. Use the whole berries to decorate the cake.

Eternity Cake

See the ingredients on the next page.

The resurrection was our passport from death to new life, so on each succeeding Easter we begin our immortality with the renewal of our baptism. Our Christian life is our heaven here on earth. It is the beginning of our eternity, our never-ending circle, just as these cakes are.

Cream shortening and sugar. Stir in whiskey. Add egg yolks and flour. Roll dough into a long strip. Cut the strip in five equal parts. Roll each strip between palms of your hands until it is as thick as your little finger.

Arrange in circles on greased cookie sheets. Brush with egg white and sprinkle with sugar. Bake at 350° for 15 minutes.

ETERNITY CAKE INGREDIENTS

2 c. shortening
2 c. flour
2 c. sugar
2 tbs. whiskey
4 raw egg yolks
1 beaten egg
4 cooked and
  diced egg yolks
sugar

Angel Food Cake

Bring the egg whites to room temperature. Sift powdered sugar and flour together three times. In a large bowl, beat the egg whites, cream of tartar, and vanilla with an electric mixer on medium speed until soft peaks form (tips curl). Gradually add sugar, about two tablespoons at a time, beating until stiff peaks form (tips stand straight).

Sift about one-quarter of the flour mixture over beaten egg whites; fold in gently. (If the bowl is too full, transfer to a larger bowl.) Repeat, folding in remaining flour mixture by fourths.

Pour into an ungreased 10-inch tube pan. Bake on the lowest rack in a 350° oven for 40 to 45 minutes, or until the top springs back when lightly touched.

Immediately invert cake (leave in pan); cool thoroughly. Loosen sides of cake from pan; remove cake. Makes 12 servings.

ANGEL FOOD CAKE INGREDIENTS

1½ c. egg whites (10–12 large eggs)
1½ c. sifted powdered sugar
1 c. sifted cake flour or sifted all-purpose flour
1½ tsp. cream of tartar
1 tsp. vanilla
1 c. sugar

Easter Activities

Emmaus Walk

In honor of this day's Gospel, which tells of the two disciples who went to Emmaus and met our Lord on the way, Easter Monday can become a visiting day. Visit the old, the sick, the shut-ins, and the dying.

Learn the Litany of All Saints

This would be a good time to say the Litany of All Saints in preparation for an Ascension Thursday procession. See page 171 for an example of the Litany of All Saints.

Jesus appeared to the eleven in Jerusalem. They were afraid, but Jesus assured them not to be. He ate broiled fish and honeycomb with them. Then he instituted the Sacrament of Penance. Read John 20:19-29.

Picnic Breakfast

Try to go to Mass on a Saturday morning, then have a family picnic breakfast, as Jesus did with the seven disciples in today's readings. This could be done on your porch, in your yard, or at a park. It might allow for fruitful discussion about the readings. This is where the primacy of the pope is explained, and Peter appointed as the first. Read John 21:1-25.

Note: The *Catholic Commentary on Holy Scripture* states, "Before memory and the spoken word were replaced by documents and signatures, a recognized way of making a good juridical disposition was to solemnly repeat three times in the presence of witnesses." Thus, before witnesses, Peter was made head of the Church and the faithful were in his care, as they would be in the care of all the "Peters" who would follow him. Jesus called Peter "a rock" and said, "On this rock I will build my Church." Here our Lord defines the papacy. We must teach this to our children.

Study the Holy Eucharist

Make a special effort today to visit either your parish church or another local Catholic church to visit our Lord in the Blessed Sacrament.

What a great testament to your faith and belief in the Real Presence this will be for your children.

Meditate on the Passion

On any Friday: Even though we are now in the Easter celebration, we are still called by the Church to remember that Friday is the day to remember Christ's passion and death. We need to remind the family to do some form of penance or offering for our Lord in remembrance and thanksgiving for the great price He paid for our eternal life.

You might to do the Stations of the Cross, or go to confession on Fridays.

Our Lady

This is a great time of year to buy fresh flowers. It would be a great gesture of love and devotion to Our Blessed Mother to take fresh flowers to a shrine in her honor. This could be at your local parish or at another Catholic church in your area. You might even want to encourage the family to say the Rosary while on this little pilgrimage.

Honor the Holy Angels

In honor of the angels make an angel food cake (see page 51) for dessert tonight. If you have children that like to help out in the kitchen, by all means make this an occasion of celebration and fun. You might mention that the snowy white cake represents the purity of the angels.

Try and honor your angels by reciting the Prayer to the Guardian Angels together after dinner. Then take time to thank your angels for taking such great care of you.

During your family reading time, encourage all of the members to keep reading about their patron saint for the year.

Here is another addition about angels by Mary Dixon Thayer, from her book *A Child On His Knees*:

> *Dear God, I'm sure the Angels keep their arms around me while I sleep!*
> *For sometimes, when I wake at night — Yes, when my eyes are still shut tight —*
> *I hear all sorts of little things, that sound just like an Angel's wings!*
> *It wouldn't be a great surprise If when I did open my eyes,*
> *I saw an Angel by the bed and touched the halo 'round his head!*

Ways to Gain Better Formation

In your family reading time, begin the Letter of St. Paul to the Romans. You might want to purchase the *Navarre Study Bible* for Romans and use it as a commentary to better explain the Scriptures. It is imperative that we foster a love for Sacred Scripture in our homes, and what better time than together in the evening. To set the mood you might light three candles, one for the Father, one for the Son, and one for the Holy Spirit.

Set an allotted time and stick to it. Allow for questions, too.

Work As an Offering

It might be a great help to a neighbor for your family to offer to help with some task. Babysitting, mowing the lawn, taking out the trash, watering the lawn, whatever they might need. This should be done with the spirit of St. Joseph's giving heart. Remember how he lovingly took care of Mary and Jesus. He provided food, shelter, and protection for them faithfully and without complaint. We could do some small task and ask for his intercession for a generous heart.

Honor the Holy Eucharist with Poetry

As a creative family project, write poetry together in honor of our Lord in the Eucharist. A *cinquain* poem is written in the following form:

Cinquain

Line 1 — Consists of a noun with two syllables

Line 2 — Uses adjectives totaling four syllables

Line 3 — Words ending in "ing" totaling six syllables

Line 4 — Sentence or phrase using eight syllables

Line 5 — Synonym of line one, also with two syllables

Example:

Jesus

Truly present

Loving, dying, rising

Let us honor and worship

Savior

Another type of poetry that is easy to write is *haiku*. Follow the format given, then share your poems with each other. Do this in your family time before or after you read aloud.

Haiku

Line 1 — Five syllables

Line 2 — Seven syllables

Line 3 — Five syllables

Example:

Jesus in the host

You gave your life for all men

Let us adore you!

Now let your family try to write some of their own.

It would be a great gift to make a visit to our Lord in the Blessed Sacrament today. It

Honor Mary with a garden.

doesn't have to be a long visit, just enough time to tell Him you love Him and make a spiritual communion.

Honor the Blessed Virgin Mary

Honor the Blessed Virgin Mary today by making an effort to go on a fresh-flower hunt in your yard or neighborhood. Then have the children bring the flowers to Our Lady and put them in water at the foot of a statue or image of her in your home. This can help foster a true devotion to our Blessed Mother.

Honor her with a special dessert, like fresh blueberries over vanilla ice cream. The blue symbolizes her mantle and the white symbolizes her purity.

These are just little ways to introduce our children to the richness of our Catholic Faith.

Celebrate This Feast Day

Try to make Sunday a true day of rest, as we are instructed in the second commandment. Spend leisure time with the family and plan to go somewhere together. If you live by a cathedral or older church, you might want to make a little visit and explain their architecture and history.

Sunday Activities

Today is a day to celebrate the risen Lord. A time for the family to grow in love and unity. Try to plan something so you can enjoy your leisure together. Explore some great work in music: *Gregorian Chants for All Seasons*, Choir of the Vienna Hofburgkapelle, Josep Schabasser, Director, by Vox Box, is available at your local library, for example.

An idea for spending family time together today might be to go on a hike or bike ride. Maybe you live near a state park or have trails close by your home. Whatever the case, these outdoor activities always build family unity and are fun in the spring.

In order to review the seven sacraments, look for flowers with seven petals on a nature walk and recite one sacrament for each petal. If you would rather draw or cut out seven-petaled flowers at home, that would work as well.

Remember to celebrate at dinner with your Paschal candle and a white tablecloth, too. This drives home the fact that we are still celebrating the risen Lord's feast.

Honor the Apostles

Read one of the parables with Jesus and His apostles, allowing the children to request a favorite, then encourage the children to draw the story. These could be shown and explained after the evening meal or during the family reading-time.

Honor St. Joseph

If the weather permits, you could organize a trip to a nearby nature center or Audubon area. This might foster the opportunity to talk about nature and how the Holy Family lived in a rather rustic style, using creation as God designed, for food and shelter. St. Joseph always protected and provided for their safety and well-being.

After the evening meal's blessing have the father say, "St. Joseph," and the family responds, "Pray for us."

Lamb-and-Flag Drawing

At the time of Jesus, lambs were sacrificed in the Jerusalem temple as part of an act of worship. Jesus was described by John the Baptist as "the Lamb of God," the lamb that would be sacrificed to take away the sins of the world. Only this lamb was victorious, rising to a new life. The standing lamb then represents Jesus, and the flag is the sign of his triumph.

Either have the children design a lamb-and-flag picture for a centerpiece, or use a stuffed lamb and flag and put them in the center of the table during dinner. Then explain the richness of the symbolism of the lamb and Christ.

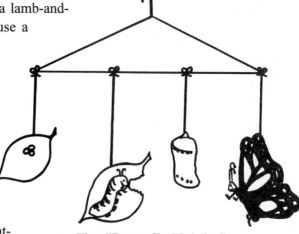

The "Butterfly Mobile."

The Butterfly Project

Plan a trip to your local library and check out some books on butterflies. Or, if your local zoo has one, visit a butterfly garden. Children find it fascinating to learn how the caterpillar goes into a cocoon (a type of tomb) where it seems to die, then emerges to a new life as a beautiful butterfly. It is a terrific symbol of Christ's death and resurrection.

Rather than skip over this symbol, create a project based on different butterflies and their life cycles. Don't forget to point out the symbolism; it is a most valuable way of tying in God's creation with His work of re-creation. Today, have your children draw the four stages of growth: egg, caterpillar, cocoon, butterfly.

SUPPLIES

1 hanger per child
construction paper
pictures of
 butterflies
books for ideas
glue
string
paper clips

The Butterfly Mobile

Today your family can design a butterfly mobile.

Explain that you will make a mobile of the life of a butterfly, then add other butterflies. Draw, cut, glue, etc. Allow the children to be creative and help the little ones.

Attach the egg, caterpillar, cocoon, and butterfly pictures to the hanger with string and hang in prominent places.

Remember to explain the symbolism to Christ and His resurrection.

Caterpillar Hunt

This time of year there are sure to be many caterpillars scooting around your yard, so make an adventure out of hunting for one. Capture and place in a ventilated jar. Feed it leaves and branches, then watch it make a cocoon and transform into a butterfly or moth. This will take a few weeks, but it is fascinating for the young and old.

If you have time to get to your local library, you could check out some science books on butterflies and make this a real time of learning science and the Faith together. Allow the children time to share their knowledge with dad during the family time in the evening.

(There is a butterfly kit available through *Insect Lore*, P.O. Box 1535, Shafter, CA, 93263, 1-800-LIVE BUG.)

What Are Sacramentals?

The *Catechism of the Catholic Church* describes sacramentals as follows: "These are sacred signs which bear a resemblance to the sacraments. They signify effects, particularly of a spiritual nature, which are obtained through the intercession of the Church. By them men are disposed to receive the chief effect of the sacraments, and various occasions in life are rendered holy [*SC* 60; cf. CIC, can. 1166; CCEO, can. 867]" (CCC 1667). Various forms are: holy water, blessings, scapulars, medals, etc. "Sacramentals do not confer the grace of the Holy Spirit in the way that the sacraments do, but by the Church's prayer, they prepare us to receive grace and dispose us to cooperate with it" (CCC 1670).

After reviewing that description, see how many sacramentals you and your children can name in your home. You could even travel together from room to room to count.

Family Leisure Time

It's time again to plan a family activity. What about going to a local zoo, or, for a little culture, an outdoor symphony or concert in the park. Be looking for outdoor activities such as these for you and your family.

Plan a family garden. Pick the spot, until the soil, and plant seeds or seedlings. It's a great opportunity to experience the wonder of spring, God's bounty and glory in this world, as well as elevate our minds and discussions to the holy. Whenever we do something outdoors, our children are inspired to ask both profound and sometimes silly questions, but such conversations usually cause us to realize how blessed we are. Try it and see if you have the same results.

It's still a good idea to celebrate the Sunday feast with your Paschal candle and white tablecloth. Soon it will be Ordinary time and our celebrations will not be as plentiful.

Bless Your Seedlings
Blessing of the Sprouting Seed
 V. Our help is in the name of the Lord.
 R. Who made Heaven and Earth.
 V. The Lord be with you.
 R. And with your spirit.

Let us pray: To Thee, O Lord, we cry and pray: Bless this sprouting seed, strengthen it in the gentle movement of soft winds, refresh it with the dew of heaven, and let it grow to full maturity for the good of the body and soul. (Sprinkle with Holy Water.)

(From *With the Blessing of the Church*, National Catholic Rural Life Conference, Des Moines.)

Bless Your Young Crops and Garden

V. Our help is in the name of the Lord.

R. Who made Heaven and Earth.

V. The Lord be with you.

R. And with your spirit.

Let us pray: We appeal to thy graciousness, O Almighty God, that thou wouldst shower thy blessing upon these first fruits of creation, which thou hast nurtured with favorable weather, and mayst bring them to a fine harvest. Grant also to thy people a sense of constant gratitude for thy gifts, so that the hungry may find rich nourishment in the fruits of the earth, and the needy and the poor may praise thy wondrous name. Through Christ our Lord. Amen. (Sprinkle with holy water.)

(From *With the Blessing of the Church*, National Rural Life Conference, Des Moines).

Other Activities

Ascension Thursday
The Ascension of Our Lord into Heaven — Holy Day of Obligation

Today we begin the nine days of waiting and preparing, together with the apostles and Mary, of the coming of the Holy Spirit. This is a great time for families to discuss the "gifts of the Holy Spirit" and the "fruits of the Holy Spirit" every evening. It might be helpful to keep a list of the gifts and fruits of the Holy Spirit near the dinner table for easy reference in these following weeks.

The daily reflections and ideas on the gifts of the Holy Spirit are taken from Maria von Trapp's *Around the Year with the Trapp Family*, Pantheon, 1955.

The *Catechism* states: "The seven *gifts* of the Holy Spirit . . . belong in their fullness to Christ, son of David [Cf. Isa 11:1-2]. They complete and perfect the virtues of those who receive them" (1831).

Study the Seven Gifts of the Holy Spirit
Gift of Knowledge

The gift of knowledge is offered to help us in our dealings with things and people. It teaches us to make use of them wisely, and to refrain from what is dangerous. Consider a typical day: We use this gift almost every moment. Younger ones might discover that the gift of knowledge helps them to remember that they have to make use of created things, such as the toothbrush and the shower.

In fact, at all times of the day we make decisions about using something or dealing with somebody, and we need the immediate help of the Holy Spirit to carry us safely through the day.

Reminder: Pray for the gift of knowledge.

Gift of Understanding

The gift of understanding is extended to us to help us to comprehend, with both mind and heart, of revealed truth as we find it in Holy Scripture and the liturgy. This gift is needed for our hours of prayer and meditation. It fulfills the Lord's promise: "The Holy Spirit whom the Father will send in my name, He will teach you all things" (John 14:26).

Reminder: Pray for the gift of understanding.

Gift of Counsel

The gift of counsel helps us to distinguish, in every moment of our life, what is the will of God. We need this gift when someone turns to us for advice. It is most necessary for parents, teachers, priests, and all persons in authority. But above all, it should help us to make the right choices in everyday life, even in such matters as: Should I do this work now or later? Or: Should we watch this movie or not?

Reminder: Pray for the gift of counsel.

Gift of Fortitude

The gift of fortitude helps us overcome our own will. This may start with getting out of bed when the alarm goes off; with giving up smoking; cutting back on sweets; with keeping silence when we might have an answer ready; with doing little things for others at the cost of our own comfort; and it may lead to the ultimate test of aiding in the heroic decisions of thousands of contemporary martyrs who are called to lay down their lives for God. This is a gift that is needed every day!

Reminder: Pray for the gift of fortitude.

Gift of Piety

The gift of piety infuses our hearts with a special love, directed toward everything belonging and related to God: all persons consecrated to His service, the Holy Father, bishops, priests, missionaries, nuns, and lay brothers and sisters. Also for all things set aside for God only — church, altar, chalice, monstrance, vestments, the sacramentals at home like rosaries, holy water, and medals. This precious gift makes us eager to devote time to the service of God. It helps overcome morning laziness when it is time for Mass. It makes us want to visit our hidden God once in a while in the tabernacle. It instills the interest for the supernatural in our souls.

Reminder: Pray for the gift of piety.

Gift of Fear of the Lord

The gift of fear should lead us to a state of mind which makes us afraid to sin because it would hurt our Lord. If a person loves another very much, you may often hear him say: "I'm afraid to wake her up, she needs her sleep"; or, "I'm afraid to disturb him." In other words, love is afraid to hurt the beloved one; so it is with this gift of fear of the Lord.

Reminder: Pray for the gift of fear of the Lord.

Gift of Wisdom

The gift of wisdom seems to sum up all the gifts of the Holy Spirit, just as charity sums up all His fruits. If we ask throughout out all of the days for the other gifts of the Holy Spirit and cooperate with them, if we examine our conscience every night about the use we made of them, then we will naturally grow in wisdom.

The gift of wisdom has nothing to do with ordinary human intelligence, or with book knowledge. One doesn't even have to be able to read and write in order to become wise. Once in a while we meet elderly people, who may not be learned in the eyes of the world, but may deeply impress us with a true wisdom expressed in all simplicity

Reminder: Pray for the gift of wisdom.

Pentecost Sunday
Begin Day Nine of the Novena to the Holy Spirit

Use your white tablecloth and continue to use your Paschal candle at dinner. If your children like to draw and cut, you could have them make place mats and or placecards in the shape of doves or tongues of fire, to symbolize the arrival of the Holy Spirit.

Fruits of the Holy Spirit

The *Catechism of the Catholic Church*: "The *fruits* of the Spirit are perfections that the Holy Spirit forms in us as the first fruits of eternal glory. The tradition of the Church lists twelve of them: 'charity, joy, peace, patience, kindness, goodness, generosity, gentleness, faithfulness, modesty, self-control, chastity [Gal 5: 22-23 (Vulg.)]" (1832).

Study the First Three: Love, Peace, and Joy

Love or charity is the constant love of God and neighbor.

Peace is calm and quiet, living at rest with God and neighbor.

Joy means spiritual joy; cheerfulness in spite of trials and sufferings.

Sing "Come, Holy Ghost" at dinner. Then review the first three fruits of the Holy Spirit and the seven gifts.

Since we normally give honor to the Blessed Virgin on Saturday, this would be a great time to discuss how Mary received and lived out these gifts.

Patience

Patience means not being easily upset when things go wrong, but bearing sorrows and troubles for the love of God.

Have each member of the family say or write down one way to live patience. Then try to do it.

Kindness

Kindness means thoughtfulness of others.

Share one way that each family member can be kind and thoughtful and make a resolution to do a kind act for another today.

Goodness

Goodness means to stand for what is right, even though others fall for what is wrong.

Discuss what we as Catholics can do to grow in goodness and live this out. (At home, at school, in public places.)

Long-Suffering

Long-suffering means not to complain when things are hard or when disappointments come.

This is a great one to talk about in a family. So many times it seems easy to complain and sulk, and we need to ask the Holy Spirit to bear the fruit in our hearts. What about your family?

Mildness

Mildness is gentleness, even toward those who do us wrong.

Self-control

Self-control is the ability to harness our natural appetites, whether it be in eating or drinking, temper, or whatever one may do.

Mildness and self-control are necessities in family life. Try to discuss ways to grow and behave with these fruits. Children especially need reminders when dealing with things as "fair or unfair."

Modesty and Chastity

Modesty means being pure in speech, dress, and behavior.

Chastity is purity in thought, word, and action, according to one's state in life.

These fruits are under attack in our society. We need to show our children that modesty and chastity are difficult not just because they are counter-cultural, but because they are the way to eternal life. This is just as applicable to adults as it is to young people. I'm sure you will experience a fruitful discussion tonight.

Review of Sacraments

In your family reading time today or tonight, try to review the seven sacraments. As noted in the *Catechism of the Catholic Church* (1210 and 1212), Christ instituted the sacraments of the new law. There are seven: baptism, confirmation, penance, Holy Eucharist, anointing of the sick, holy orders, and matrimony. The seven sacraments touch all the stages and important moments of Christian life: they give birth to new Christians, increase holiness of the family's life in God, give healing, and give a sense of mission to the Christian's life of faith. The sacraments of Christian initiation are: baptism, confirmation, and the Holy Eucharist, because they lay the foundation of every Christian life. In the following week you can highlight each of the seven sacraments in your family time.

First Sacrament: Baptism

Explain: In baptism we are born anew. "Repent and be baptized, every one of you, in the name of Jesus Christ for the forgiveness of your sins; and you will receive the gift of the Holy Spirit" (Acts 2:38 NAB). We are told in Galatians 3:27 that we are to "put on Christ" (RSV), and that is what baptism does. Hence, baptism is a bath of water in which the "imperishable seed" of the Word of God produces its life-giving effect. St. Augustine says of baptism: "The word is brought to the material element, and it becomes a sacrament."

The *Catechism of the Catholic Church* covers this so beautifully. If you have time for further reading, read sections 1213-1284.

Act: Review your family baptismal days and mark each on the calendar, if you haven't yet done so. Then make a family celebration out of each baptismal feast day.

Sacrament of Penance

Explain: Sections 1422-1498 of the *Catechism of the Catholic Church* are specifically about the Sacrament of Penance and Reconciliation. This sacrament is one of conversion, penance, confession, forgiveness, and reconciliation. In order to make a good confession, one must examine his or her conscience, have true sorrow for sins, confess to a priest, and make reparation through penance and actions. "Sin is before all else an offense against God, a rupture of communion with Him" (CCC1440).

Act: The Catechism is waiting to be opened and read in your home, and is full of information. (See the "Prayers and Devotions" chapter for examinations of conscience.)

Sacrament of the Eucharist

Explain: Sections 1322-1419 in the *Catechism of the Catholic Church* are about the Holy Eucharist. At the Last Supper, on the night he was betrayed, our Savior instituted the Eucharistic sacrifice of his Body and Blood. "He did this in order to perpetuate the sacrifice of the Cross throughout the centuries until He should come again, and so to entrust to His beloved spouse, the Church, a memorial of His death and resurrection: a sacrament of love, a sign of unity, a bond of charity, a paschal banquet in which Christ is eaten, the mind is filled with grace, and a pledge of future glory is given to us (*Sacrosanctum concilium*, 47).

Act: Please take the time to read this beautiful section on the Blessed Sacrament. Talk about the celebrations and dates to remember, and look at photos from members of your family who have made their First Communion.

Sacrament of Confirmation

Explain: Sections 1285-1321 in the *Catechism of the Catholic Church* are about the Sacrament of Confirmation. It is one of the three sacraments of initiation, along with baptism and the Holy Eucharist. "It must be explained to the faithful that the reception of the sacrament of Confirmation is necessary for the completion of baptismal grace [Cf. *Roman Ritual*, Rite of Confirmation (*OC*), Introduction 1]" (CCC 1285). "It is evident from its celebration that the effect of the sacrament of Confirmation is the special outpouring of the Holy Spirit as once granted to the apostles on the day of Pentecost" (CCC 1302).

Act: You and your family are encouraged to read the information in the *Catechism* together. There is a great amount of Church history and tradition listed and it will broaden your understanding of the Faith.

Parents, display your confirmation pictures and talk about your personal experiences with your children.

Sacrament of Holy Orders and Anointing of the Sick

Explain: Sections 1499-1532 in the *Catechism of the Catholic Church* are about the Sacrament of the Anointing of the Sick. Sections 1533-1600 are devoted to the Sacrament of Holy Orders.

"By the sacred anointing of the sick and the prayer of her priests the whole Church commends the sick to the suffering and glorified Lord, asking that He may lighten their suffering and save them; she exhorts them, moreover, to contribute to the welfare of the whole people of God by associating themselves freely with the passion and death of Christ" (*Lumen Gentium*, 11). This is a sacrament to give grace to strengthen those who are being tried by illness. This sacrament was instituted by Christ in Mark 6:13 and James 5:14-15.

"Holy Orders is the sacrament through which the mission entrusted by Christ to his apostles continues to be exercised in the Church until the end of time: thus it is the sacrament of apostolic ministry. It includes three degrees: episcopate, presbyterate, and diaconate" (CCC 1536).

Act: Invite a priest to dinner and ask him to share about his life as a boy and hearing God's call to be a priest.

Sacrament of Matrimony

Explain: Sections 1602-1690 in the *Catechism of the Catholic Church* describe the Sacrament of Matrimony. Section 1601 of *Catechism* quotes the Code of Canon Law (canon 1055 § 1; cf. *GS* 48 § 1): "The matrimonial covenant, by which a man and a woman establish between themselves a partnership of the whole of life, is by its nature ordered toward the good of the spouses and the procreation and education of offspring; this covenant between baptized persons has been raised by Christ the Lord to the dignity of a sacrament." Wow! May you and your family discover the richness of the *Catechism*, together!

Act: Something fun to do would be to tell your courtship and wedding story to your children. Bring out the photo album for more conversation.

All-Season Activities

Forming Our Hearts and Minds in Christ

In order to give your children the great knowledge of the Faith, you need to spend time together. We all have to help each other in our daily struggle to follow Christ. So, you might think about spending at least one hour every evening together, for examination of conscience, prayers, reading aloud, and conversation. The most important job of parents is to form their children in Christ and this takes time and effort. We need to make sure our priorities are set with this being high on the list. During this time, place your Paschal candle in your midst to remind you that Christ has risen, and read and listen to His teaching. Your family will experience such fruit from this time that you will never regret making the sacrifices to spend the time together.

Making Beautiful Music Together

Another great way to spend time together is to explore great works in music. There are many accessible CDs and cassettes of Gregorian chant, works by Mozart, Tchaikovsky, Stravinsky, Mahler, Ravel, Handel, and Beethoven to name a few. There is a Music Masters Series, put out by Vox, that gives a great mix of historical narrative and a variety of works on individual tapes or CDs. (See Lifetime Books and Gifts in the bibliography for catalog information.) The beauty of good music touches the soul in a very powerful way. It is beauty of this sort that helps the young heart to yearn for the supreme beauty which is God.

Ordinary Time

Quick Activities

Significant Days — Feast Days in Ordinary Time

Trinity Sunday

This feast falls on the Sunday following Pentecost. It is a day to remind the family of the triune nature of God. The two common prayers which remind us of this are the Glory Be and, of course, the Sign of the Cross. Review these prayers with the younger ones or teach them to those who don't know them. They might also do an art project using the symbols of the Trinity: a triangle; three interwoven circles; a triangle in a circle. Older children can discuss the mystery of the Trinity as taught in the *Catechism* (232-237). The family itself is a symbol, or sign, of the Trinity: "The Christian family is a communion of persons, a sign and image of the communion of the Father and the Son in the Holy Spirit" (CCC 2205).

The art project can be used as a centerpiece for dinner. A white tablecloth can be used, since this is a feast. The meal should be special and a dessert would be appropriate. You might want to try the recipe for polenta, a favorite of Pope John XXIII, who was the pope responsible for approving the feast for all Catholics (until then it was only celebrated in certain areas).

Polenta

Heat three cups water to boiling. Combine corn meal, remaining cup of cold water, and salt; pour into boiling water, stirring constantly. Cook until thickened, stirring frequently. Cover; cook over low heat 10 minutes longer. Remove from heat.

Stir in cheese, butter, and pepper; stir until cheese and butter are melted. Serve hot. Makes six servings. If any is left over, it can be chilled, sliced, dusted with flour, and fried for another meal.

This would be a good prayer for today's meal (taken from the Liturgy of the Hours):

Father, you sent your Word to bring us truth
and your Spirit to make us holy.
Through them we come to know them mystery of your life.
Help us to worship you, one God in three Persons,
by proclaiming and living our faith in you.

> **POLENTA INGREDIENTS**
>
> 4 c. water, divided
> 1 c. yellow corn meal
> 1 tsp. salt
> ¼ lb. grated parmesan cheese
> 3 tbs. butter
> ⅛ tsp. pepper

We ask you this, Father, Son, and Holy Spirit,
*   one God, true and living, for ever and ever.*

Corpus Christi
Thursday after Holy Trinity; sometimes celebrated on the Sunday following

This is the feast of the Body and Blood of our Lord. The anniversary of the Eucharist is, of course, on Holy Thursday at the Last Supper. However, since this falls in the most solemn of weeks — Holy Week — it cannot very well be celebrated as a feast. Therefore, the Church in her wisdom has assigned another day to celebrate this special feast. According to Maria von Trapp, in the "old country," the day was celebrated with a joyous procession in which the whole community participated. It was a true parade, led by an altar boy with a crucifix, followed by school children in their Sunday best, various church organizations carrying banners, religious in their respective habits, and priests in their feast day vestments. These were followed by the pastor carrying the monstrance containing the Blessed Sacrament. He is carried most reverently, as a king should be, with small girls throwing flowers at His feet and altar boys ringing bells and soldiers marching along either side. The band and choir followed the King playing songs for the people to sing. At various points along the way, which was decorated with flowers, trees, and various finery, the pastor would have benediction. Altars had been prepared ahead of time for this and the raising of the monstrance would be marked by the salute of the soldiers' guns and the canons thundering from the outskirts.

Our equivalent, in this day and age, is Super Bowl Sunday! Let us begin to bring back the celebration of the truths worthy of such festivities. Let us help our children realize that festivity based on shallow grounds (i.e., football) can be an empty, unfulfilling celebration.

To celebrate the Most Blessed Sacrament in your home today, you can announce the feast day in the morning and plan some fun activities. Go to a park for a hike and pick wildflowers as a decoration for the family altar and the dinner table. Plan a special meal. Have a special dinner and serve dessert. Use your white tablecloth and decorate the table with fresh-cut flowers. Attend Mass as a family and, if your parish doesn't have a procession, look for one that may still do a procession for this feast.

Sacred Heart
Friday following the Second Sunday after Pentecost

This feast celebrates the most famous of the many revelations concerning the love burning in the heart of Christ for His beloved children. Jesus appeared to St. Margaret Mary Alacoque, a French nun of the seventeenth century, and made twelve promises for those who would venerate this symbol of divine love with devotion:

1. I will give them all the graces necessary for their state of life.
2. I will establish peace in their houses.
3. I will comfort them in all their afflictions.
4. I will be their secure refuge during life, and above all in death.
5. I will bestow large blessings upon all their undertakings.
6. Sinners shall find in My Heart the source and the infinite ocean of mercy.

7. Tepid souls shall grow fervent.

8. Fervent souls shall quickly mount to high perfection.

9. I will bless every place where a picture of My Heart shall be set up and honored.

10. I will give to priests the gift of touching the most hardened hearts.

11. Those who propagate this devotion shall have their name written in my heart, never to be blotted out.

12. I promise them in the excessive mercy of My Heart that My all-powerful love will grant to all those who receive communion on the first Friday in nine consecutive months the grace of final penitence; they shall not die in My disgrace nor without receiving the sacraments; My Divine Heart shall be their safe refuge in this last moment.

Today would be a good day to begin a devotion in your family to the Sacred Heart. Find a picture portraying the Sacred Heart of Jesus (there are various versions and styles) and display it in your home. Explain to the children the story of St. Margaret Mary and the deep love that Jesus has for them. There is a family consecration to the Sacred Heart on page 164. Also celebrate this day as a feast, with a special dinner and dessert, using a white tablecloth and centerpiece (maybe use the new picture or statue of the Sacred Heart).

Christ the King
Last Sunday in Ordinary Time

In the Old Testament, when God's chosen people were living under the rule of judges and God spoke to His people through prophets, the people decide that they wanted a king like the other nations. God warned them, through their prophet Samuel, that a king would subject them and take their men to war and force their women to work for him. He warned them that they would be unhappy, but the people pleaded and He gave in. They were ruled by kings for many years (starting with David) and all that God warned came to pass. But He brought them a good king eventually, one that would not enslave them, one that would love them as His own and lead them to His kingdom where all were happy, forever. This King was His only Son, Jesus Christ, and on this day we celebrate His kingship and His eternal kingdom.

Just as this King rules differently from the other kings of this world, the subjects of His kingdom are to live differently. He told us how we may inherit His kingdom, the Kingdom of Heaven, in the sermon on the mount. There he gave us the eight beatitudes so that we may "be" His subjects.

"The Beatitudes take up and fulfill God's promises from Abraham on by ordering them to the Kingdom of heaven. They respond to the desire for happiness that God has placed in the human heart" (CCC 1725).

Today seems a fitting day to review these "be-attitudes" and begin to live them more clearly everyday. These Scripture verses (Matthew 5:3-11) are good ones to memorize. After dinner tonight, reflect on these passages. Discuss the questions and how they relate to your lives.

Finish off this feast with a crown cake, as we described on page 11. A crown cake is your favorite flavor of cake, frosted, then decorated with a crown made of gumdrops. You might want to throw a gumdrop in the batter before baking and the family member who gets that piece can be "king" and be excused from chores for a day.

Blessed are the poor in spirit, for theirs is the kingdom of heaven.

Are our hearts attached to earthly goods?

Do we remember that the Lord is the rightful owner of all our earthly goods?

Could we be happy and at peace if our dearest possessions were taken from us?

How can we be more "poor in spirit"?

Blessed are those who mourn, for they shall be comforted.

Do we realize what a tragedy mortal sin is?

Do we reflect on the sins of the world we live in and our own responsibility for them?

Do we mourn not only for our sins but those of our brothers and sisters (all mankind)?

How can we do penance and repent more deeply for the sins of the world, including our own?

Blessed are the meek, for they shall inherit the earth.

Do we control our resentment at other's character or behavior?

Are we impatient or angry with other's weaknesses?

Do we understand that "meek" is not "weak"?

How can we practice this virtue?

Blessed are those who hunger and thirst for righteousness, for they shall be satisfied.

Do we thirst for justice and righteousness?

Do we remember that peace is the fruit of justice?

How can we charitably work for righteousness?

Blessed are the merciful, for they shall obtain mercy.

Can we see the gap between the mercy we show and the mercy we receive from God?

Do we truly see others as our brothers and sisters in Christ?

How can we be more merciful in our day-to-day living?

Blessed are the pure in heart, for they shall see God.

Do we walk in "holy simplicity," shunning sin and loving God?

Do we keep our hearts pure for God to rest in them?

Can we simplify our lives and sharpen our focus on God?

What can we do today as a family to be pure in heart?

Blessed are the peacemakers, for they shall be called sons of God.

Do we look deep into our souls where God indwells, and find peace?

Do we make peace with God daily?

How can we share that deep inner peace, the love of God, with others?

Blessed are those who are persecuted for righteousness' sake, for their is the Kingdom of Heaven.

Do we recall that suffering was the measure of God's love for us?

Do we make suffering the measure of our love for God?

Do we willing accept the crosses He sends us and shoulder them with humility, not pride?

How can we help each other to shoulder the crosses of family life?

Weekly Activities

Early Church history and tradition teaches that each day of the week has a theme which can help us to celebrate ordinary time.

Sunday: The Weekly Easter
Monday: Honor the Holy Angels
Tuesday: Honor the Apostles
Wednesday: Honor St. Joseph
Thursday: Reverence the Holy Eucharist
Friday: Meditate on Christ's Passion and Death
Saturday: Honor Our Blessed Mother

Sunday

This day of rest is seen by the Church as an echo of Easter. A day to celebrate Christ's resurrection and to renew our own baptismal vows for the coming week, Sunday is a feast day. We should celebrate with festive meals in honor of Christ and His resurrection. It should be day the family spends together, enriching the body, mind, and soul of each family member.

Preparation: Spend Saturday evening cleaning, laying out Sunday clothes, preparing food, planning.

On Sunday: 1. Go to Mass as a family.

2. Designate certain music to listen to or sing that praises God.

3. Designate special toys to play with only on Sunday.

4. Brainstorm activities that are family favorites: biking, cooking, movies, games, etc. Choose one each week.

6. Cook a special dessert or recipe — set aside budget restrictions or nutrition for that day — FEAST!

Family meeting: Schedule one day a month to meet as a family to discuss issues and share thoughts on your relationships as family. This is a good way to get children to talk about difficulties at an early age. Airing differences can be done in a controlled environment with adult guidance. Make sure that good things are discussed at family meetings also, such as vacations, major purchases, great achievements, etc.

Ideas for Sunday Activities — Family Activity Box

The Lord's day should be celebrated as a family. Make a family activity box, using small pieces of paper in Easter shapes, an empty can or jar, and leftover Easter decorations.

Each member contributes a few reasonable activities for the family. They are written on separate pieces of paper cut in Easter shapes (a lamb, a lily or an egg [as a reminder of the resurrection]) with the word "alleluia" written across the top. These symbols can also be used to decorate the box. (Old Easter cards and decorations would work, also.) Each family member takes turns choosing an activity out of the box (eyes closed, of course!). Enjoy your day celebrating with the family!

Flower Walk

You'll need various vases; a field, park, or generous neighbors with flower gardens (make sure you ask before you pick); and a scrapbook of family memories.

Flowers are signs of new life and gifts from God. Take a walk with the family today and find as many different flowers as possible. Use them to decorate the house and dinner table for this day. Choose a few favorites at the end of the day to dry and flatten in a scrapbook. Make sure to write the date and any relevant comments about this mini-Easter from family members on scrapbook page. Mark family favorites.

Read and Discuss

Read Exodus 20:8-11 and *Catechism* sections 1166-1167. Discuss how your family can rest on Sunday. What activities should you avoid? What activities might you add to your day of rest? To allow Mom to rest, the family might go out to eat, have meals of pre-made casseroles, or construct sandwiches buffet-style. Spend the afternoon sitting on the porch or in lawn chairs and chat about life and/or listen to classical music. Remember your family reading time (explained on the first Sunday in Lent).

SUPPLIES

(For each child, you'll need:)
1 empty eggshell (carefully break ¼ off the top)
1 egg c. (or small napkin ring)
1 damp cotton-ball
⅛ tsp. alfalfa seeds
set of colored fine-tipped felt markers

Grow Sprouts in an Eggshell

Eggs are signs of new life that help remind us of the resurrection of our Lord and our share in his new life (CCC 654). While doing this activity, discuss the various ways we experience new life through the sacraments (CCC 1130).

Set the empty eggshell in the egg cup or napkin ring and gently draw a face. Children can do self-portraits or draw the face of a saint or angel. Place a damp cotton-ball inside the eggshell and sprinkle seeds over cotton. Keep the cotton damp and in two or three days, seeds will begin to sprout. Put in a sunny spot and watch it grow. It may eventually need a haircut and the clippings can be added to a salad or sandwich.

Have a Bubble Party

Sunday is a day of prayer and worship. It is often hard for children (and adults!) to imagine that their prayers are being heard, *but they are*! To illustrate this fact, have a bubble party and explain to the children that the bubbles are like all of our prayers going up to heaven and when they pop (as they all will eventually) it is like God taking hold of that prayer and drawing it to His heart. Let them try to draw a bubble against their heart and see how it pops. Show them how some take a lot longer to pop than others.

SUPPLIES

¼ c. liquid dish-washing soap
1 gallon water
large bucket
various unbreakable "bubble-makers"

Some dishwashing soaps work better than others; try what you have on hand. We recommend Dawn if you have to purchase some. To make the bubbles, you might use: the plastic holders from six-packs of soda pop; plastic coat hangers; straws; paper cups, etc. Try anything that a little soap and water can't hurt; after all, our prayers and needs are as various as the "bubble makers."

Grow sprouts in eggshells.

"Sonday" Singalong

Today we celebrate the day the Son of God rose from the dead to conquer sin. What better way to celebrate than with song! You'll need books and/or tapes with familiar religious music; a few musically inclined friends and family, with their instruments; joy.

Using all three ingredients in any combination that works, sing old favorites and learn at least one new favorite. What a way to celebrate the Son of God!

Walk and Picnic

Maria von Trapp in her book *Around the Year with the Trapp Family* describes the joys of Sundays in the Austrian countryside. One particular memory is that of "a long, peaceful walk home from Sunday Mass." After Mass, take a long walk as a family. If your neighborhood does not hold any great interest, find another neighborhood or a park or wilderness area within driving distance, and then walk! Take a picnic. Here's a picnic recipe suggestion:

Potato Salad

Wash the potatoes. Place in a pot of salted water (use just enough water to cover the potatoes) and boil until just tender when pierced with a fork: about 15 to 20 minutes. Drain thoroughly. Combine potatoes with onions and peppers on serving platter.

Prepare the vinaigrette: Mix the olive oil thoroughly with the lemon juice. Add the mustard, garlic, salt, and pepper to taste, and the basil or dill.

Pour over the potatoes and vegetables. Let marinate for several hours, stirring occasionally. A few minutes before serving, stir in the parsley. Adjust seasoning. Garnish with basil leaves or dill sprigs, if you wish. Yields: 10 to 12 servings

Family Activity Box Activity

Choose an activity from the "Family Activity Box." Then, for energy and good taste, make:

Sandy's Healthy Cranberry Bread

Stir dry ingredients together, then cut in butter until mixture resembles coarse cornmeal. Combine honey, egg, and orange rind and pour into dry ingredients. Stir just to moisten, then carefully fold in nuts and berries. Pour into 9"x5" well-greased and floured loaf pan. Bake at 350° for one hour.

POTATO SALAD INGREDIENTS

- 10 small red potatoes
- 3 purple onions
- 3 bell peppers (red, green, yellow), cut into thin strips
- 1 c. olive oil
- ⅓ c. lemon juice or wine vinegar
- 1-2 tsp. Dijon mustard
- 3 cloves garlic
- 1½ tsp. salt
- freshly ground black pepper
- 2 tsp. dried or 4 tsp. fresh, chopped basil or dill
- 2 c. fresh, chopped parsley, preferably Italian
- optional: fresh basil leaves or sprigs of fresh dill weed

CRANBERRY BREAD INGREDIENTS

- 1½ c. unbleached flour
- 1 c. fresh cranberries, coarsely chopped
- ½ c. whole-wheat flour
- ¼ c. butter
- 1 c. honey
- 1 tbs. grated orange rind
- 1½ tsp. baking powder
- 1 egg
- ½ tsp. salt
- 1 c. chopped nuts

SCRIPTURE CAKE INGREDIENTS

1½ c. (3 sticks) Psalm 55:21

1 tsp., ½ tsp. 2 Chronicles 9:9 (cinnamon, nutmeg)

2 c. Jeremiah 6:20

2 c. 1 Samuel 30:12

6 Jeremiah 17:11

2 c. Numbers 13:23, chopped

½ c. Judges 4:19

1 c. Numbers 17:8, chopped or grated

2 tbs. 1 Samuel 14:25

4½ c. Leviticus 2:13

2 tbs. Amos 4:5

Attend Mass

Go to Mass as a family, then spend the day in restful celebration of this feast. Watch home movies and look at old pictures, and reintroduce the children to relatives who have gone before them.

Remember your family reading time.

Scripture Cake

Today, make Scripture Cake. Have the children look up the Scripture verses. This famous old New England favorite is not only yummy but helps us learn the Bible.

Preheat oven to 350°. Butter and flour loaf pans or a bundt or tube pan. Cream the butter. Beat in sugar until light and fluffy. Add eggs one at a time, beating well. Stir in milk and honey. Sift in flour with the salt, baking powder, and dry spices. Add the dry ingredients gradually to the wet mix only until blended. Stir in the raisins, figs, and almonds. Put into pans. Bake about 50 minutes. Yields: one large or several small cakes.

Remember family reading and the saint for the day.

Monday

Monday has been traditionally dedicated to honoring the Holy Angels. This would include guardian angels and archangels. Making mention of this at morning prayer and evening dinner would allow for fruitful spiritual discussion.

Recite Angel Prayers

St. Michael the Archangel,
defend us in battle;
be our defense against the wickedness
and snares of the devil.
May God rebuke him, we humbly pray.
And do you, O prince of heavenly host,
by the power of God
thrust into hell Satan and all the evil spirits
who prowl about the world
for the ruin of souls. Amen.

Angel of God, my guardian dear, to whom God's love commits me here, ever this day (or night) be at my side, to light and guard, to rule and guide. Amen.

Learn the Guardian Angel Prayer

Remind children (and adults!) that their guardian angel is always at their side helping them to pray, to fight back when they are tempted, to warn them to steer clear of situations which will turn them away from God. Give your guardian angel a special gift by taking him to a church for some quiet time in front of the Blessed Sacrament.

Raphael the Archangel Place Mat

You'll need light-colored construction paper; markers and/or crayons; and clear contact-paper (optional).

Read the book of Tobit (especially chapters 4 to 12). You can use a children's Bible version, or have an adult or older child read and paraphrase the story. Try to read the words of Raphael in chapter 12. Discuss the role of the Angel Raphael. How did he help Tobias? What was his message to Tobias and his father? The symbols for Raphael are a pilgrim's staff, a wallet, or a fish. Children can decorate a piece of paper with the symbols and/or what they think he looked like to Tobias to make a place mat. They can also add favorite verses from the story. When finished, the place mat can be covered with clear contact-paper and used at dinner.

C&H Box (Charity and Humility)

SUPPLIES

Catholic
  dictionary
paper
crayons, markers,
  pencils
empty shoe-box
  with lid
foil or wrapping
  paper to cover
  box

Criticism is an activity that seems to come naturally to adults and children alike and creeps up most often among close friends and family. Fortunately for us, God sent our guardian angels to help us with just such problems. Charity and humility are the virtues that help combat criticism. Today would be a good day to come up with a plan to root out criticism and plant the virtues of charity and humility, with the help of our guardian angels.

Cover and decorate the box. Label it "C&H Box" and make sure everyone knows what that means. Look up charity and humility in the dictionary and brainstorm ways to practice these virtues. Write down the favorites and put into the box. At the end of the day, or early in the morning, choose one paper out of the box and put that action into practice all day. After a week or so, evaluate the family's growth in virtue and add or take away ideas as needed.

Angel on My Shoulder

You'll need blank stickers or labels; glitter; and gold and/or silver crayons or markers.

Draw a picture of your guardian angel on a blank label (ask him to help you!). Decorate with glitter and cut out the white part around the edges so the shape of the sticker matches your picture. Wear your guardian angel on your collar or shirt-pocket and be open to explain to friends who he is and what he does.

Our guardian angels are special friends sent to us by God. They help us and protect us. Sometimes our friends here on earth can act like "guardian angels."

My Best Friends

You'll need paper plates; crayons and/or markers; and tape.

Each person thinks of one person not in the family who is a good friend, then shares the reasons why. Share a time when this friend was a helper or protector to you. Using the paper plates, make a likeness of the friend and hang it above the dinner table. Spend some time before or after the meal to pray for the person and thank God for the gift of such a friend.

Sharing Vocations

The apostles answered the call to the first vocations in the Church. Your children will be called to one of three vocations: religious life, married life, or consecrated single life. Spend time today sharing *your* vocation with your children. Any one of the following ideas would be fun and educational:

Spend the evening looking at wedding pictures and/or videos and discussing God's plan for marriage and what it means to you. You and your spouse could spend some time discussing or studying the subject beforehand.

• Take one or more of the children to work for the day (or an hour). Show them around and introduce them to colleagues. This would be a good opportunity to practice manners when meeting adult strangers.

• If a trip to work is not possible, bring a tape recorder or video camera and document a typical work day.

• Let older children take on some more difficult household tasks for a day, in order to fully appreciate the vocation of parent and spouse.

Praying and Talking to Your Guardian Angel

"Beside each believer stands an angel as protector and shepherd leading him to life" — St. Basil.

Remind the family that our guardian angels are there always and say a special prayer today to your guardian angel. This week try to get in the habit of talking to your guardian angel. It is also an old custom to greet another's guardian angel, silently, as you greet the person aloud. Learn the St. Michael the Archangel Prayer, found on page 70.

Discuss the great hero St. Michael and his battle with his brother-angel Lucifer, who refused to serve God and had to be thrown out of heaven into the abyss.

Tuesday

The apostles are the focus on Tuesdays. This is an opportunity to get to know the men that our priests and bishops have followed. Their lives and personalities are revealed in the Gospels.

1. Read about them. Skim the gospels for any reference.

2. Memorize their names.

3. Mark their feast days with a celebration.

4. Choose one as an intercessor for your priests, pastor, and bishop, and pray often for them.

The three theological virtues — faith, hope, and charity — are the foundation of Christian moral activity. They are infused by God into our souls making us capable of acting as children of God and meriting eternal life (see CCC 1813). "Faith is the theological virtue by which we believe in God and believe all that he has said and revealed to us. . . ." (CCC 1814). Today would be a good day to learn the Act of Faith and pray it as a family. You might add it to your morning prayers for the week.

Act of Faith

O my God, I firmly believe that you are one God in three divine Persons, Father, Son and Holy Spirit; I believe that your divine Son became man and died for our sins, and that he shall come to judge the living and the dead. I believe these and all the truths that the holy Catholic Church teaches, because you have revealed them, who can neither deceive nor be deceived.

SUPPLIES

construction paper
tag-board or
 heavy poster-
 board (for the
 cover)
string and/or yarn
hole-punch
markers and/or
 crayons

Apostles Book

Fold construction paper in half to make pages. Use six pieces for small pages and 12 for larger pages. Punch two or three holes along the folded edge, being careful to match the holes on all pages. Do the same for one piece of poster-board, cut to the size of your construction paper and folded in half to make a front and back cover.

Tie string in a bow through the holes. When book is assembled, you may begin writing and drawing the information on each apostle. Be sure to include a picture, famous writings (from the Bible), favorite stories in his life, and any other interesting facts. The best way to get the information would be from the Gospels and the Acts of the Apostles. Read some favorite parts at the dinner table.

The Conversion of Saul
Acts 9:1-19

Using the book format above, make a book that tells the story of Saul's conversion. Include his presence at the stoning of Stephen. Take this time to discuss conversion and what it means.

The Story of Cornelius, the Centurion
Acts 10:1-48

You'll need a large piece of construction paper (old wrapping paper with one side that's white will work, cut in a large rectangle about 11"x 17"); and markers and/or crayons.

Make a story-board by folding the paper in half matching the two longer sides, once. Open and fold in half matching the shorter sides, twice. This should result in two rows of four squares. Number them one through eight, starting in the top-left corner, so that numbers one through four are on top and five through eight on the bottom. Now choose the eight most important or interesting parts of the story and illustrate them. Captions can be added on the bottom, or conversation in bubbles (like in a comic book).

The apostles were called to be "fishers of men" and bring

MY
APOSTLES
BOOK

others to Christ by their word, example, and preaching. We share in that call! Today invite a friend over that may be in need of evangelizing. They could come for dinner and thus witness the family praying together, or play a game with the family and thus witness Christian charity. Or maybe you could rent a good Christian movie and watch and discuss it with them. Whatever you choose, it should be done humbly and with charity.

Study Prudence

Prudence is right reason in action, says St. Thomas Aquinas, following Aristotle. This moral virtue disposes practical reason to determine our true good in every circumstance and them choose the right means of achieving it (see CCC 1806).

This virtue is very difficult for young children, since it takes a certain degree of intellectual development. The most prudent thing a young child can choose to do is listen to his parents and other authoritative adults. However, as children get older they can begin to develop the virtue of prudence with a three-step plan: 1) Size up the situation. 2) Know the standards which should guide judgment (i.e., the Church's teaching informing your conscience). 3) Make decisions in line with those judgments. Discuss this plan and practice it with your adolescent children.

Writing Epistles

Some of the apostles were known to have written "epistles," or letters, to the various communities in the early Church. They wrote to encourage, praise, and sometimes admonish their fellow brothers and sisters in Christ. The Second Letter of Paul to the Thessalonians is a good example. Note especially the greeting and closing. These letters to the early Christians were also written for us and contain the encouragement, praise, advice, and admonishment that we need.

Children can paraphrase the greeting and closing in a letter to a friend or relative that encourages the friend's Christian love and actions. For example: 1 Peter 1:1 might read "Johnny, a disciple of Jesus Christ, to the elect who dwell at 23 Main Street, Wintersville, Ohio, chosen and destined by God the Father and sanctified by the spirit of obedience to Jesus Christ and for sprinkling with His blood: May grace and peace be multiplied to you."

Parents can paraphrase the actual epistle so that it seems to speak directly to a child in need of support or direction. For example: 1 Peter 1:4 and the following verses can be simplified and to speak directly to a child with a seemingly heavy cross to bear.

Secret Buddies Game

"Love of one's neighbor is the only door out of the dungeon of self."

— G.K. Chesterton

Talk about this quote. Play the "Secret Buddies Game": Put each family member's name (including parents) in a hat and let each person draw a name secretly. Spend the week playing "secret buddy" to that person. Try to do little things for your buddy, anonymously (i.e., carefully hide anonymous notes, compliments, and gifts; fix or clean something secretly).

At the end of the week you could give prize for "best deeds" and another for "best secrecy."

Wednesday

St. Joseph is honored on Wednesdays. He is patron of families and especially fathers. Great topics for discussion are fatherhood, being a hard worker, and knowing Jesus intimately. On Wednesdays you could:

1. Honor St. Joseph in prayer.
2. Honor your father today in small way.
3. Fathers work on projects with children, such as woodworking.
4. Have lunch with Dad.
5. Go to work with Dad.
6. Pray for Dad daily.

St. Joseph was a carpenter. Dad could lead a woodworking project today, such as making a crucifix or a stable for next year's nativity scene. This may mean spending some time in the library with some simple woodworking books (*Woodworking for Kids* by Kevin McGuire, Sterling Publishing Co., Inc., New York, is a possibility), and could be spread over a couple of weeks. However, the emphasis should be on St. Joseph's life and his role in Jesus' life. So dads, keep it simple, and leave lots of time to talk in between hammering and sawing.

"Hope is the theological virtue by which we desire the kingdom of heaven and eternal life as our happiness, placing our trust in Christ's promises and relying not on our own strength, but on the help of the grace of the Holy Spirit" (CCC 1817). Today, talk about hope and what a gift it is. Learn the prayer below and add it to your midday prayer time for the week.

Act of Hope

O my God, relying on your almight power and infinite mercy and promises, I hope to obtain pardon for my sins, the help of your grace, and life everlasting, through the merits of Jesus Christ, my Lord and Redeemer.

Dad's Day

Dad cooks his favorite meal for the family. This could be anything from PB&J to filet mignon! Eldest son could lead prayer invoking St. Joseph for the intentions of the father.

Remember to work on woodworking project with the kids.

In honor of St. Joseph: Thank God for Dad

You'll need construction paper; lined paper (age appropriate for your children); pencils, markers, and/or crayons; and scissors and tape.

Make a crown and/or button out of construction paper and decorate with the words "We love Dad" or "Dad is great." Each person (even Mom!) can draw a picture and/or write a letter stating why Dad is so great (younger children can dictate to older ones). Put these in a folder for Dad to read on lunch breaks at work or on business trips.

Learn Temperance

Temperance moderates the attraction of pleasures and provides balance in the use of created goods. Practice temperance by limiting pleasurable foods and activities. This will help to ensure the will's mastery over instincts and help to keep desires within the limits of what is honorable, which is very important for adolescents struggling with chastity (see CCC 1809).

Discussion

"To live well is nothing other than to love God with all one's heart, with all one's soul and with all one's efforts; from this it comes about that love is kept whole and uncorrupted (through temperance). No misfortune can disturb it (and this is fortitude). It obeys only [God] (and this is justice), and is careful in discerning things, so as not to be surprised by deceit or trickery (and this is prudence)" — St. Augustine (*De moribus eccl.* 1, 25, 46: PL 32, 1330-1331).

Discuss Obedience

St. Joseph was obedient to the words of God spoken through the angels. We must be obedient to God's words spoken through His Church. Today would be a good day to discuss obedience and how children are obedient to their parents, as parents are obedient to God. How do we as parents act as an example of this? (Words to look up in the *Catholic Encyclopedia*: magisterium, pope, papal infallibility, conscience.) Read section 2197 and those following in the *Catechism*.

SUPPLIES

bare tree limb
(spray-painted if
you wish)
large, plastic
margarine tub
filled with plaster
of Paris (from
hardware store)
or clay
decorative paper
or tissue
ribbon
wooden or plastic
loops (such as
shower-curtain
hooks)
scissors
glue or tape
snapshots of family
members
holy cards of
patron saints

Pray a St. Joseph Prayer

Glorious St. Joseph, spouse of the immaculate Virgin, Foster-father of Jesus Christ, obtain for me a pure, humble, and charitable mind, and perfect resignation to the Divine Will. Be my guide, my father, and my model through life that I may merit to die as you did in the arms of Jesus and Mary. Patron of families, patron of fathers, patron of the Universal Church: St. Joseph, pray for us (adapted from the "Novena in Honor of St. Joseph").

Write the prayer in large letters on poster board and challenge the older children to memorize it. Come up with a small reward for those who do, such as a small St. Joseph medal, statue, or holy card.

Family Tree Centerpiece

St. Joseph is the patron of families. Today would be a good day to remind ourselves that our family is bigger than those who live in our house. It also includes those who have passed away (including infants and miscarried babies) and the communion of saints, especially our particular patrons.

See the list of supplies on this page.

Stick branches securely in wet plaster or clay, then wait for plaster to harden. Cover the container with bright paper and ribbon. Attach ribbon to the tops of the loops and glue or tape photos to the back of them. Hang the pictures on the Family Tree and use as a centerpiece at dinner. Can be used also on sacrament days and added to as often as you wish.

Thursday

We focus on the Holy Eucharist on Thursdays. The Eucharist is at the center of our faith and should be the center of our lives. God allows His people to meet Him face-to-face in this sacrament. It is said that if one understands the Eucharist, all other truths will fall in line. Activities might include:

1. Attend Mass as a family.

2. Spend some time in adoration in front of the Blessed Sacrament.

3. Make a spiritual communion — see the "Prayers and Devotions" chapter.

4. Develop a love for Christ in the Blessed Sacrament through prayer and conversation in His presence.

Food for Our Bodies — Food for Our Souls

You'll need: a healthy dinner; posterboard; and markers and/or crayons.

Cook an especially healthy dinner. Explain to the children that these foods help our bodies to grow and to be healthy. After dinner make a chart on the poster board, with "Food for the Body" listed on one side and "Food for the Soul" listed on the other. Under the "Body" side write the things discussed at dinner, such as:

• food makes us strong

• helps us grow

• can keep us healthy

• keeps us alive.

A "Family Tree Centerpiece."

On the other side list the ways in which the Holy Eucharist is nourishment for the soul. For example:

• must have it to live God's life

• makes us strong to resist temptation

• helps us become saints

• helps us to do what is right. (Adapted from *Faith and Life Series*, Grade 2.)

Learn the Act of Love

Charity (love) is the virtue by which we love God above all things and our neighbor as ourselves. Through this virtue we do this for the love of God not our own gain. Today remember this virtue by treating all people with charity for the love of God. Learn the prayer and add it to your evening prayer time for this week.

Act of Love

O my God, I love you above all things, with my whole heart and soul, because you are all-good and worthy of all love. I love my neighbor as myself for the love of you. I forgive all who have injured me and ask pardon of all whom I have injured.

Attend Mass

If you can, attend Mass this day; if it is not possible, make an act of spiritual communion, such as this one attributed to St. Francis of Assisi:

"I believe that you, O Jesus, are in the most holy sacrament. I love you and desire you. Come into my heart. I embrace you. Oh, never leave me. May the burning and most sweet power of your love, O Lord Jesus Christ, I beseech you, absorb my mind that I may die through love of your love, who were graciously pleased to die through love of my love."

Spiritual Reading

Paul's epistles (letters) to the Thessalonians were written to the new Christians in Thessalonica to answer questions that they had regarding Christ's second coming and stressing the need to be spiritually vigilant.

Write an Epistle

Moms and dads can write epistles to the children stressing their need to be spiritually vigilant. Personalize the letters so that specific household issues can be addressed, such as getting ready for bed on time so that prayer-time is not rushed.

Spend Time with the Blessed Sacrament

Many saints drew their strength and endurance from hours of adoration in front of the Blessed Sacrament. Spend some time in front of the Tabernacle or find a local church with Perpetual Adoration (the Blessed Sacrament exposed on the altar twenty-four hours a day for adoration). If a trip to church is not possible, set up a prayer corner for members of the family to spend quiet time in front of a picture or statue of our Lord.

This time should be spent telling Him you love Him and asking help to love Him better, but most importantly, it should be spent listening. Rules should be set to minimize distractions, such as no TV or stereo on in the room and only interruptions that are absolutely necessary. Don't even answer the phone!

Read the Acts

Read about the philosophers of Athens in Acts 17:16-34. Paul tells the philosophers that there is one God that created us and He does not inhabit any image of gold or silver or stone made by human hands. This might be a good time to check the children's understanding of the various representations of Christ and the saints that they are familiar with. Make sure they understand that they are reminders of the figures they symbolize (see CCC 2110-2117). Make the distinction concerning the Eucharist. In this case, God Himself replaces the bread and wine, keeping only the appearance of these elements (see CCC 1373-1381).

Make a Spiritual Communion

"Our Lord does not come from Heaven every day to stay in a golden ciborium. He comes to find another Heaven, the Heaven of our soul in which He loves to dwell" — St. Thérèse of Lisieux.

Today, ask Jesus to dwell in the heaven of your soul.

Spiritual Communion: Say an Our Father, Hail Mary, and Glory Be three times each. Then say, "I wish, Lord , to receive you with the purity, humility, and devotion with which your most holy Mother received you, with the spirit and fervor of the saints."

God's Temple

Jesus, present in the Eucharist, is kept in a tabernacle. When we receive the Eucharist, our bodies become His tabernacle in a very real way. St. Paul tells us in 1 Corinthians 3:16-17 that we are to always see ourselves as God's holy temple. Discuss the obligation to God to keep His temple clean and healthy. Evaluate family hygiene, eating, and sleeping habits. Determine where can you improve. Set one family goal and make a chart to measure when and how it is reached.

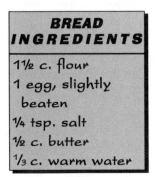

BREAD INGREDIENTS

1½ c. flour
1 egg, slightly beaten
¼ tsp. salt
½ c. butter
⅓ c. warm water

The Last Supper

Reread the story of the Last Supper, then bake unleavened bread using the ingredients at left.

Mix salt, flour, and egg. Add water, mix dough quickly with a knife, then knead on board, stretching it up and down to make it elastic until it leaves the board clean. Toss on a small, well-floured board. Cover with a hot bowl and keep warm ½-hour or longer. Then cut up into squares of desired size and bake in 350° oven until done.

Review Unselfishness

Today is a good day to discuss unselfishness, or selflessness. Christ is the perfect example of selflessness when He gives His body and blood for our salvation. How can we be selfless? How can we learn to be more "extra-centered," more concerned with others needs?

One activity to help teach this concept to small children is "Turns and Timers":

Small children playing together will inevitably want the same toy at the same time. Take the time to sit down with them (over and over) and explain sharing. Help them notice how happy they make the other person when they share with him. Praise even feeble attempts to share.

On occasion use a timer (or an oven clock or alarm clock) that rings when one child's turn is over and it is time to let the other child have his or her turn.

Bedtime Chats

Continue practicing selflessness. Try "Bedtime Chats." This is a good time to really listen to your children. Give them time to think and respond. Talk about selfishness and its ramifications. Help them to see where in their lives they have been selfish and where they have been unselfish. End with an act of contrition.

Attend Mass as a Family

Talk about the time immediately following reception of the Eucharist. His presence is in you in that way only as long as the host remains undigested. What do you say to Jesus in that short time? It helps children to imagine that they live in the time period in which Jesus was walking and talking to His disciples. If you had a chance to have a private meeting with Him, what would you say? Make a practice of staying after Mass for a few minutes, as a family, and giving thanks in silent prayer.

Friday

This day we remember the Passion of our Lord. This emphasis is so essential to Holy Mother Church that she asks us to make some sort of sacrifice on this day (even outside of Lent). Traditionally, abstinence from meat has been that sacrifice, but others may be more appropriate to your family. For instance: abstinence from sweets, TV, videos, or other forms of entertainment. Here's a couple of other suggestions:

Encourage the family to make a sacrifice together. First, decide if abstinence from meat is truly a sacrifice in your family. If not, decide on something that is.

Encourage family members to make an additional sacrifice that is just between themselves and the Lord.

Make a Small Sacrifice

Today, make a small sacrifice, such as abstaining from meat or desserts. Pray one or all of the Sorrowful Mysteries after dinner. They are:

Sorrowful Mysteries

Agony in the Garden — Mark 14:32-36
Scourging at the Pillar — John 18:28-38
Crowning with Thorns — Mark 15:16-20
Carrying of the Cross — John 19:12-17
Crucifixion — Mt. 27:33-56; Mark 15:22-41; John 19:16-30

Recognize the Sacrifices of Others

On Fridays we remember how Christ sacrificed His life for us. There are many people here on earth who have sacrificed for us in imitation of Christ. Today would be a good day to recognize them. Write a letter to a grandparent, neighbor, or family friend, letting them know you have not forgotten their sacrifices. Invite them over for dinner if possible and say a special prayer in thanksgiving for them.

Religious Art Fair

You'll need books containing religious art (for example, *Faith and Life* series student texts), and/or calendars, Christmas, or Easter cards; paper; markers, crayons, pencils, and/or paint; and a place to hang the finished product.

In the past, many artists have portrayed the Passion of Our Lord and other events of His life in paintings inspired by their own faith and prayers. Spend some time looking at and discussing various famous pieces of religious art. Decide whether to copy the style of the artist or the subject of the painting and then start drawing. Display the finished products in a prominent place and invite friends or relatives to view the art. The children can act as museum guides, explaining the different pictures and how they were inspired.

Bearing a Cross

In His passion and death Christ carried a cross for us, for our sins. He asks us to pick up our cross daily and walk with Him. Talk about the crosses we bear as children and parents. How can we carry them as Christ did? When do we allow others to help? Is complaining and whining part of bearing a cross? Using the directions from the Apostles Book (page 73), make a book that tells a true or fictional story about someone bearing a cross for Christ. Many saints have wonderful, real-world examples of crosses to bear: for example: death of spouse, rejection of family — St. Elizabeth Ann Seton; wayward child — St. Monica. (Resource: *The Saints And Our Children*, Mary Reed Newland, TAN.)

Study the Virtue of Fortitude

The moral virtues are acquired by human effort and are the fruit and seed of morally good acts. Four virtues play a key role and are thus called "cardinal" virtues. One is *fortitude*, which ensures firmness in difficulty and constancy in the pursuit of good (CCC 1804,1805, 1808). Over the next week discuss fortitude and try to practice this virtue. Dinner-time discussions each night with the children will help. Try to include examples of fortitude from real life or stories. (Try *The Saints And Our Children*, mentioned above.)

Review the Stations of the Cross Books

If you didn't make them in Lent, now would be a good time. If you did, you can remake or refurbish the old ones.

You'll need eight pieces of construction paper per book (any colors); yarn; markers and/or crayons; and a prayer book with responses for each station.

Fold all eight pieces of paper in half at once. Tie a piece of yarn around the fold to hold the pieces together. Close book and write "Stations of the Cross" on the front. On each page, draw a picture of the station and write the response or prayer to be said. Using the books, do the Stations of the Cross at a local church.

SUPPLIES

large pictures of each station, drawn yourself and covered with clear contact-paper
15 stakes to stick in the ground
14 spots in yard (can use front- and backyards)
heavy-duty staples or tape

Stations of the Cross Trail

Build this trail in your backyard using the supplies listed at left.

Attach pictures to the stakes with heavy duty staples or tape. The first one should mark the beginning of the trail and give instructions. Place the remainder in various spots throughout the yard, creating a meandering trail. When done, take the trail yourselves and pray the stations.

PANCAKE INGREDIENTS
2 c. flour
2 tbs. sugar
1 tsp. salt
2 tbs. baking powder
2 eggs
1½ c. milk
½ c. vegetable oil
1 tbs. cinnamon

Abstain from Meat

Bev's Secret Pancake Recipe

(For "buttermilk" pancakes: add one tablespoon vinegar; substitute two *teaspoons* of baking powder for the two *tablespoons*; add one teaspoon of baking soda.)

Mix with all ingredients together with a fork. For best results, let wet ingredients stand at room temperature before mixing.

— *Recipe compliments of the Grab family*

Family Service Chart

You'll need poster board and markers and/or crayons.

Make a list of household chores and assign each child one or more chores according to his or her age and ability. Write the names next to the chores on your chart. Use a pencil so that the chores can be changed periodically. Discuss how we sometimes need to sacrifice things we want in order to do the things we should. Christ gave His life to save us from our sins, we can imitate Him by giving our time for the good of our family.

Banishing Bickering

Meditating on the Stations of the Cross is most fruitful when it relates to our everyday lives. One example is the importance of silence, as in the silence on the part of Christ when He was condemned to death, when He was tormented by the soldiers, or when He fell under the weight of the cross. Bickering is one child's tormenting of another child. The one who holds out the longest in pecking at the other is the perceived "winner."

It might sound like this:

"You pig, you took the biggest."

"I'm not a pig."

"Yes, you are!"

"No, I'm not!" and so on. . . .

Silence can be the answer to this. If one of the children would just stop and remain silent in spite of the fact of the untruth of the other child's words, just as Christ did in the face of the soldiers, the bickering stops. We can explain to children that this is difficult, but with Christ's help and example we can do it. We can teach them Christ's words: "Whatever you did for one of these least brothers of mine, you did for me" (Matthew 25:40, NAB). Remind them that provoking a sibling is provoking Jesus and remaining silent under provocation is to be silent with Jesus.

Reader's Theater

Read aloud each Scripture reference. Split the parts up like a play so that everyone reads. (The entire passion is too long for one day, so we have split the reading over the next few Fridays.)

- Jesus condemned to death: Matthew 27:11-26
- Jesus accepts his cross: Mark 15:16-20
- Jesus falls the first time: Psalm 5

- Jesus meets his mother: Luke 2:25-35
- Simon helps Jesus: Matthew 27:32
- Veronica wipes the face of Jesus: Isaiah 53:4-5
- Jesus falls the second time: Acts 3:17-26

For best effect read in low light and dim to candles at the end. Spend some time in silence and finish by reading together John 11:25-26.

PRETZEL INGREDIENTS

1 tbs. honey or sugar
1½ c. lukewarm water
1 envelope active dry yeast
1 tsp. salt
4 c. flour
coarse or kosher salt
1 egg, beaten

Make Pretzels

Add the honey to the water (100° to 110°); sprinkle in the yeast and stir until dissolved. Add one teaspoon salt. Blend in the flour, and knead the dough until smooth.

Cut the dough into pieces. Roll them into ropes and twist into pretzel shapes. You can make small pretzels with thin ropes or large ones with fat ropes, but remember that to cook at the same rate, each batch of pretzels needs to be all the same size.

Place the pretzels on lightly greased cookie sheets. Brush them with beaten egg. Sprinkle with coarse salt. Bake at 425° for 12 to 15 minutes, until the pretzels are golden brown.

— Recipe from A Continual Feast, *Ignatius Press*

Prayer — Hidden Treasure

The four ends of prayer can be remembered by this acronym: ACTS.

A (adoration) — giving praise and honor to God.

C (contrition) — repenting of our sin.

T (thanksgiving) — giving thanks for all God gives to us.

S (supplication) — asking for God's help .

Make a sacrifice today as a family.

Read About the Fall

Together as a family, read Genesis 3:1-24. Discuss sin and how it separates us from God. You can also discuss original sin and how Baptism erases this, leaving only the consequence of original sin, which is called "concupiscence." This simply refers to the tendency to do wrong and is something we need to fight. The children should be very familiar with that urge within them to do things they know are wrong. We can help them to fight this through prayer, discipline, and the development of the virtues. Read verses 14 and 15 again. God promises that the serpent (Satan) will be crushed by the seed of the woman. Who might this be? Review the Ten Commandments.

Saturday

This day is dedicated to Our Blessed Mother. Pope Paul VI's apostolic exhortation *Marialis Cultus* (56) states: "The Church's devotion to the Blessed Virgin is intrinsic to Christian worship." At Fátima, Mary asked all people to honor on the first Saturdays of five consecutive months by attending Mass and confession, saying the Rosary, and meditating for fifteen minutes on one or more of the mysteries of the Rosary. Even if you are unable to make this devotion, any special remembrance of Our Blessed Mother would be a step in the right direction. Fresh flowers at a central image, a decade of the Rosary after dinner, or any offering, will be gladly accepted by Our Mother, who longs for our love and affection.

Some suggestions:

• Make a pilgrimage to a nearby Marian shrine or cathedral.

• Do a sacrifice in her honor for reparation.

• Read about Our Lady of Fátima, Our Lady of Lourdes, or another apparition of Our Lady.

• Following Mary's requests in her appearances in Fátima, follow the guidelines of the First Saturday Devotion: On five consecutive first Saturdays, attend Mass and confession, meditate on some part of the mysteries in front of the Blessed Sacrament, and say a Rosary. (See May, Mary's month.)

An example of a "Marian Shrine."

• Read about the history of St. Dominic and the Rosary. How did it start and why?

• Research the Brown Scapular and the promises that go with it.

Make a Marian Shrine

You'll need an empty shoebox; picture or small statue of the Blessed Mother; and plant clippings or colored paper.

Set the shoebox on its side, inside the lid. Paste an image of the Blessed Mother inside the box and decorate around her using colored paper, or real flowers and greenery. This can become a centerpiece for dinner and be used as a focal point during your family's "after-dinner decade" of the Rosary.

Marian Pancakes

You'll need an empty mustard or ketchup squeeze-bottle; pancake batter; blueberries; and pictures of Marian symbols to copy (such as a lily; crown with twelve stars; heart encircled by roses, thorns, and pierced by sword; rose without thorns; morning star; sun and/or moon with monogram; letter M). You might want to include blue food coloring.

Squeeze the batter out in shapes on the griddle, then cook. Use leftover blueberries or whipped cream for decoration. The pictures will need a child's imagination to be understood, but the image will be set in their mind's eye!

Start a Novena

Start a novena today to the Blessed Mother (choose one from the novena section). First decide on an intention (mothers, women, families, or a related specific issue), then choose a time of day for the rest of the week that would be best for all participating. Ideally everyone should be able to participate. Use your Marian shrine as a focal point during prayer, or a picture of Our Lady.

Make Mom Queen for Today!

One title for the Blessed Mother (found in litanies) is "Queen of the Angels and Saints." Our earthly mothers are "queens," too. You'll need paper; tape; crayons and/or markers; and scissors.

Make a crown for mom that says "Queen of the (Smith) House" and a heart to pin on her blouse listing all of the family names. Plan to take care of all of mom's chores for the day (including dishes after dinner!). A special prayer and/or blessing should be given before dinner by the eldest child or the father.

Thank a Spiritual Mother

All women are called to motherhood, whether it be physical or spiritual. Often there are many spiritual mothers in a child's life, and it is important for both the child and the spiritual mother to be aware of and thankful for this relationship. A spiritual mother might be a babysitter, a teacher, a family friend, an aunt, grandmother, confirmation sponsor, neighbor, or any woman that fulfills a nurturing role in the child's life.

You'll need construction paper; markers and/or crayons; glue; large envelope. You might want to include pictures of spiritual mothers.

Help your children identify the spiritual mothers in their lives (pictures would be useful for this). Each child should choose one person for whom to make a thank-you card. Write a thanksgiving prayer for the inside and invoke the Blessed Mother to help and guide the spiritual mother.

Prepare for Sunday!

Clean house and bake *Edelweiss Coffeecake* for tomorrow's brunch. It's a delectable coffeecake traditionally served with coffee to guests on Sunday afternoons:

Dissolve yeast in the warm water (100°-110°) in large bowl. Stir in one tablespoon of sugar. Let sit until frothy. In saucepan, scald the milk. Add the butter, remaining sugar, and the salt. Stir until butter is melted. Cool to lukewarm. Add the lemon rind and cinnamon and beat in eggs. Add to yeast mixture. Stir in two cups of the flour and beat with wooden smooth until smooth. Gradually add enough of remaining flour to make a soft, non-sticky dough.

Turn the dough out onto a lightly floured surface and knead for about 10 minutes, until dough is smooth and elastic and blisters form on the surface. Place dough in a greased bowl, turning to grease the top. Cover with towel or plastic wrap and let rise in draft-free spot until doubled in bulk, about 1½ hours.

EDELWEISS COFFEECAKE INGREDIENTS

2 packages dry yeast
½ tsp. cinnamon
½ c. warm water
2 eggs
½ c. sugar
about 6 c. flour
1½ c. milk
1 c. confectioner's sugar
1 stick (¼ lb.) sweet butter
⅔-1 c. butter at room temperature
1 tsp. salt
1 tsp. vanilla
grated rind of 1 lemon
1 c. chopped or ground blanched almonds

Preheat oven to 350°. Punch dough down, divide into two or three parts (depending if you prefer two large or three small cakes). Grease two baking sheets or three pie pans. Form the dough into two large, round, flat coffeecakes on the baking sheets, or pat into pie pans.

Prepare the topping: Cream the confectioner's sugar with the butter. Stir in the vanilla and almonds. Sprinkle onto the dough. Let rise again until doubled in bulk, about 45 minutes.

Bake at 350° for about 45 minutes, or until golden brown. Yields: Two large or three small coffeecakes.

P.S. These coffeecakes freeze well. You can add raisins or currants, or substitute other nuts for the almonds. For tomorrow's menu, you may also make quiche, cut fruit, and bake muffins today. If possible, all preparations should be done today.

Discuss Justice

Justice is the moral virtue which consists in the constant and firm will to give due to God and neighbor. The just man, spoken of in the Sacred Scriptures, is one who habitually thinks rightly and whose conduct is upright towards his neighbor.

"You shall not be partial to the poor or defer to the great, but in righteousness shall you judge your neighbor" (Leviticus 19:15).

Discussion: Since justice has to do with one's actions, more so than one's thoughts, discuss just actions. What do we owe God, in justice? (Everything!) What do we owe our neighbor, in justice? What would Christ say?

Movie Time

Rent the movie *Song of Bernadette*, or get a children's movie about the Blessed Mother such as *The Day the Sun Danced* or *Bernadette* from CCC Video. Watch as a family.

"The Most Important Person on earth is a mother. She cannot claim the honor of having built the Notre Dame Cathedral. She need not. She had built something more magnificent than any cathedral — a dwelling for an immortal soul, the tiny perfection of her baby's body. . . . The angels have not been blessed with such a grace. They cannot share in God's creative miracle to bring new saints to Heaven. Only a human mother can. Mothers are closer to God the Creator than any other creature; God joins forces with mothers in performing this act of creation. . . . What on God's good earth is more glorious than this: to be a mother?"

— Cardinal Joseph Mindszenty

Honor Mary

Do a small sacrifice in honor of Mary today such as: saying a Memorare, three Hail Marys, and the Angelus at noon.

Attend Mass as a Family

One of the titles of the Blessed Mother, found in the Litany of Loreto, is "Health of the Sick." After Mass today would be a good time to visit a nursing home or any housebound parishioners. Ask your pastor for information on these. Bring flowers to cheer the day of the sick and housebound!

Make a Rosary Shrine

Set up a special shrine inside or outside your home at which to say the Rosary together. Say the Rosary (Joyful, Sorrowful, or Glorious Mysteries) as a family. Look up the Bible references for the mysteries and read them before each decade.

Joyful Mysteries

Annunciation — Luke 1:26-38

Visitation — Luke 1:39-47

Nativity — Matthew 1:18-25; Luke 2:1-7

Presentation — Luke 2:22-40

Finding in the Temple — Luke 2:41-52

Mystical Rose

You'll need any number of fresh roses in various colors (if not possible, then a picture or two will do); watercolor paints in the colors of the roses; and watercolor paper or construction paper.

One title of the Blessed Mother is "Mystical Rose." Using a pencil, sketch one or more roses, then paint them to look "mystical." Hang the pictures near a statue or shrine of the Blessed Mother. Put the fresh roses in vases around the statue or picture.

Review Your Week and Celebrate

Review this week of imitating Mary. How did you do? Celebrate with a special dessert called *Scrumptious Sundaes.* It used to be that this ice cream dessert was only eaten on the Lord's day, thus the name "sundae."

You'll need one or more kinds of ice cream and/or sherbet; chocolate, hot fudge, butterscotch, and/or marshmallow sauce; fresh or frozen fruit; and various toppings, such as nuts or candy.

Let everyone concoct their favorite combination in fancy cups or bowls, and serve.

Weekend Retreat

Plan to spend a weekend together at home or away. Come up with a theme that relates to your family's own spiritual journey. This is an especially good time to have discussions with your children on things that concern them deeply and intimately, such as the mysteries of childbirth, or, for older children, dating and marriage. Whatever the topics of discussion, the atmosphere should be prayerful, reflective, and somewhat structured.

A sample schedule might be:

7 a.m.	Mass
8:15 a.m.	Breakfast (together)
9:15 a.m.	Introduction to the plan and purpose; father leads
9:45 a.m.	Discussion of "Family Motto"(see "Love is a Decision?"); mother leads
10:30 a.m.	Write family motto on poster board and decorate (all)
11:30 a.m.	Silent prayer and reflection (in church if possible): How do I live the family motto? How can I?
Noon	Angelus

12:30 p.m.	Lunch
2 p.m.	Split into groups: boys with Dad, girls with Mom (if all children same sex, one parent gets further reflection time). Discuss the parent's particular role as men or women in the family.
3 p.m.	One-on-one time with parents to talk about each child's particular spiritual/moral life
4 p.m.	Silent prayer and reflection
5 p.m.	Dinner
6 p.m.	Rosary
6:30 p.m.	Family reading
7 p.m.	Inspirational movie such as *The Miracle of Marcelino* or *A Man For All Seasons* (older children and adults).

Sunday — Continue your family retreat following morning Mass. Sunday's schedule can be less intensive and more celebratory. Be sure to give closure to the family motto and individual discussions. Set family and individual goals and plan when to check on them, such as during a family meeting.

Memorize a Mary Prayer

Memorize a new prayer to Mary such as the Memorare or the Hail Holy Queen:

Memorare

Remember, O most gracious Virgin Mary, that never was it known that anyone who fled to your protection, implored your help, or sought your intercession was left unaided. Inspired with this confidence, I fly unto you, O Virgin of virgins, my Mother. To you I come, before you I stand, sinful and sorrowful. O Mother of the Word incarnate, despise not me petitions, but in your mercy hear and answer me. Amen.

(The Memorare is attributed to St. Bernard of Clairvaux.)

Perform an Act of Charity

Remember the Visitation, when the Blessed Mother visited her cousin Elizabeth in her time of need. Is there anyone you know who would appreciate a visit and some help?

Write a Mary Poem

As a creative family project, write poetry together in honor of Our Lady. A poem written in the cinquain style is constructed as follows:

Cinquain

Line 1 — Consists of a noun with two syllables

Line 2 — Uses adjectives totaling four syllables

Line 3 — Words ending in "ing" totaling six syllables

Line 4 — Sentence or phrase using eight syllables

Line 5 — Synonym of line one, also with two syllables

Example:

Mary

Pure and gentle

Waiting, loving, giving

Let us honor and imitate
Mother

Now, in your family time, try to write some of your own.

Role-Playing

Try role-playing different situations in which one would need to exercise respect. Some suggestions: respect for life, for property, for parents, for elders, for nature, and for the beliefs and rights of others. Courtesy, politeness, and manners. Self-respect and the avoidance of self-criticism (a different form of self-reflection!). Discuss this in a family meeting.

Some Ideas for Exploring Scripture with Children

New Testament — The Gospels

Read a chapter out loud and let the children act out the parts as you read. They can take turns being Jesus. This is a good time to discuss Jesus' actions and how we might imitate Him.

The children can illustrate the scenes. You might have them make a booklet of the Gospels.

Some examples of Gospel stories to start with:
• The infancy narrative: Luke 1-2
• The Good Samaritan: Luke 10:29-37
• The Parables: Matthew 13:18ff and 23-35
• The Zaccheus: Luke 19
• Jesus feeds five thousand and walks on water: Mark 6ff
• Parable of the lost sheep, lost coin, and lost (prodigal) son: Luke 15

The Book of Acts

• The young church: Acts 2:42-47; 4:32-33. Discuss how it must have been to live then. Compare to your own lives.

• The apostles before the Sanhedrin: Acts 5:12-42. Read the verses. Talk about Gamaliel and his warning to the men of Israel. Does it make sense? What do you think Gamaliel thought when the apostles continued to preach and the Christians grew in number?

• Baptism and confirmation in Samaria: Acts 8:4-25. Talk about the sacraments of baptism and confirmation. If you have not already begun, this may be a good time to find out the dates of these events in family member's lives, write them on the calendar, and plan how to celebrate them.

• "Tabitha, Rise!": Acts 9:32-43. Draw a picture of St. Peter healing Tabitha. Older children can do this too, or simply read the passage on their own.

• The first missionary journey of Paul: Acts 13:2 to 14:27. Using a map of biblical times (check your family Bible) trace Paul's trail. Or, write a travel diary for Paul. What might he have thought? What things would have been most important to him?

• Paul travels to Europe: Acts 16:7-16. Locate Europe on a map. Make a poster that could have been used at the time to announce Paul's arrival and tell why he has come to Europe.

• Thessalonians: Paul's epistles (letters) to the Thessalonians were written to the new

Christians in Thessalonica to answer questions that they had regarding Christ's second coming and stressing the need to be spiritually vigilant. Moms and dads can write epistles to the children stressing their need to be spiritually vigilant. Personalize the letters so that specific household issues can be addressed such as getting ready for bed on time so that prayer time is not rushed.

• Paul as tentmaker in Thessalonica: Acts 17:1-13. Set up a tent in the backyard and read the story. Pretend it is Jason's house and have friends come to hear the Gospel of Jesus Christ. Practice explaining the Faith to these "new Christians."

• Leave-taking in Miletus: Acts 20:17-38. In verse 24 Paul says that his life is of no matter unless he accomplishes the course and the ministry which he received from the Lord Jesus. We all receive a ministry from Christ. Each one is unique and nothing in our lives matters if we have not done His will. Discussing this can help put things in perspective for adults and children alike.

• The storm at sea: Acts 27:2-26. Create a skit, outside, using real props (such as water!). Find a copy of Rembrandt's painting for inspiration and draw your own pictures of the storm at sea.

Old Testament

There are many events in the Old Testament to explore. Here are a few examples that might be enjoyable.

• Genesis: Make a creation wall-mural, a seven-day project. You'll need a large strip of poster paper (the back side of old wrapping paper can be used); a wall (outside or inside, depending on weather and your own courage! Hallways, family rooms, or play rooms work well); markers and/or crayons and/or poster paints; and a ruler.

Separate the paper into seven equal parts using a crayon or marker and a ruler. After reading each day's section of Genesis, decorate each part of the mural accordingly. The seventh day might show paradise with Adam and Eve resting.

1. The First Day — Genesis 1:1-5
2. The Second Day — Genesis 1:6-8
3. The Third Day — Genesis 1:9-13
4. The Fourth Day — Genesis 1:14-19

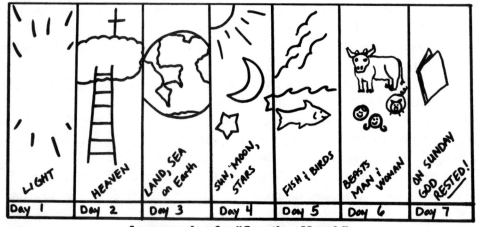

An example of a "Creation Mural."

5. The Fifth Day — Genesis 1:20-23

6. The Sixth Day — Genesis 1:24 to 2:4 (day of rest)

7. Paradise — Genesis 2:8-25

Finish the mural. Leave it up for awhile and take turns retelling the story. At night, turn the lights off and tell the story using a flash light to light up the appropriate parts.

• Cain and Abel: Genesis 4:1-16. Discuss: What did Cain do wrong? Do you think he was sorry for what he did? What makes you think so? What do you think Cain will teach his children about God?

• The Great Flood: Genesis 5:3-4; 7:1-23.

• The rainbow: Genesis 7:24-9:17. Review original sin and the story of Cain and Abel. Discuss how things might have gotten so bad. What did God promise Noah? What was the sign he gave? Draw a picture.

• The Tower of Babel: Genesis 11:1-9. Make a list of all the languages your family can think of. Are there more? Does this make it hard to communicate? Can God speak all of these languages?

• Abraham's call: Genesis 12:1-8; 15:5-6. Discuss: What did God promise Abraham? Why was this promise like a miracle? (Abraham had no children.) Add Abraham to your book.

• Abraham's spirit of sacrifice: Genesis 21: 2-7; 22:1-19. Discuss: Who did God ask Abraham to sacrifice? Was he willing to do this? Who else sacrificed his only son? Add Abraham to your book.

• Moses is called by God: Exodus 2:11-15; 3:1-18; 4:10-16. What was Moses asked to do? Did God promise Moses anything? Add Moses to your book.

• Departure from Egypt and the passage through the Red Sea: Exodus 12:37-41; 13:1-3, 6, 10, 18ff; 14:5ff. Older children can read this part and retell the story to the younger children. Have a contest to see who remembers how they got to Egypt in the first place. (Hint: Find the story of Joseph and his coat.)

• The Ten Commandments: Exodus 19:1-20:21; Deuteronomy 5:1ff; 18:15-19. Review the commandments. Who can still recite them by heart?

Psalms

• Psalm 33 (32): Choose a favorite part and sing to a well known or favorite tune. How is the woodworking project coming along? (From Week 2, Wednesday.)

• Psalm 46 (45):1-7. Discuss. Who do you think might need to hear these words? Why? If you know someone who needs to hear these words, write to them.

• Psalm 82 (83):1-4. Find a favorite verse to memorize or set to music. Sing or recite at dinner.

• Psalm 139 (138):7-12. Discuss how it relates to the story of Cain and Abel.

• Psalm 51 (50). Read aloud in parts. Separate the family into men and women and altarnate verses (or every three or four verses). This can be the prayer before or after dinner.

PART TWO
Celebrating the Liturgical Year

We mention the color of the season in case one wants to match a tablecloth at dinner. Also, if one attends a weekday Mass, the color of the priest's vestments will indicate what type of day it is: a memorial, feast, or ordinary, and can be coordinated with home colors. We have tried to give a brief description for each month and saint, as well as some notable quotes and recipes that symbolize certain nationalities of some of the saints. We hope this acts as a springboard for the reader to better celebrate the liturgical year in the home.

Feasts of the Saints

January

January is dedicated to the Holy Name of Jesus. The English letters "IHS" are equivalent to the Greek letters that represent Christ's name. It is an old tradition to inscribe "IHS" over the doorways of Christian homes. "Therefore God has highly exalted him and bestowed on him the name which is above every name, that at the name of Jesus, every knee should bow, in heaven and on earth and under the earth, and every tongue confess that Jesus Christ is Lord. . . !" (Philippians 2:9-11)

1 January
White — Feast
Solemnity of Mary the Mother of God

"Father, / source of light in every age, / the virgin conceived and bore your Son / who is called Wonderful God, Prince of Peace. / May her prayer, the gift of a mother's love, / be your people's joy through all ages. / May her response, born of a humble heart, / draw your Spirit to rest on your people" (Opening Prayer from the Liturgy for January 1, the Solemnity of Mary, Mother of God).

Make this a day of hospitality. Honor godparents with a card, phone call, or visit. Make a family resolution to get to know Mother Mary better.

2 January
White — Memorial
St. Basil the Great (379), Bishop, Doctor of the Church

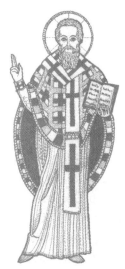

St. Basil was born of a Christian family at Caesarea in Cappadocia (modern-day Armenia) in 330. He lived as a hermit before being made a bishop in 370. He fought against the heresy of Arianism. In an attempt to describe Jesus as the God-man, the Arians taught that Christ was only *similar* to God and not *truly* God. They also mistakenly taught that Christ was *similar* to man but not *truly* man. St. Basil wrote many admirable works, especially his monastic rule, which many Eastern monks still follow. He was a very learned and virtuous man. He is the patron saint of hospital administrators, bishops, and Doctors of the Church. His symbol is a scroll. He once said: *"If everyone would take only according to his need, no one would be rich, no one poor, no one in misery."*

St. Basil the Great

St. Gregory Nazianzen (390), Bishop, Doctor of the Church

St. Gregory was also born in 330. Traveling as a youth in the pursuit of learning, he joined his friend Basil as a hermit and was later ordained a priest and bishop. He was elected Bishop of Constantinople (modern-day Istanbul), but because of factions dividing the Church, returned to his homeland where he died. He was called "Theologus" because of his outstanding teaching and eloquence. He is known as the "supreme theologian of the Trinity." See January 3 for a special activity in memory of St. Basil.

3 January
White
St. Basil's Cupcakes

If you lived in Greece, on New Year's Day you would make *Basilopitta* — a flat, round cake that resembles shortbread and requires an hour of hand-mixing! Before it's baked, coins and other symbolic items are hidden within it, and after it's baked, a hole is cut in the center. (That's St. Basil's portion!) The cake is hidden under a napkin while it is being sliced, since no one must see the divisions. Guests are served from eldest to youngest.

This tradition is based on a legend about St. Basil. He supposedly persuaded the terrified citizens of a cruel, tax-collecting governor to go to the city gates and meet the governor with their jewels, which the governor was planning to confiscate. The governor was so impressed, he refused the treasures and spared the city. It was up to St. Basil to return the heaps of jewels to the owners, so he baked small cakes, hiding a jewel in each one. After saying a Mass of thanksgiving, he distributed the cakes, and miraculously, every person received his own property back!

• To save time and effort, bake cupcakes from your favorite cake recipe or mix. After cooling, cut the top of each cupcake and scoop out enough of the center to accommodate a small "treasure" (such as a candy). Replace the tops, frost, and serve.

4 January
White — Memorial
St. Elizabeth Ann Seton (1821), Widow

Born in 1774 into a wealthy and distinguished American family, St. Elizabeth was baptized in the Episcopal faith. She married and became the mother of five children. Her husband died after a long illness when they were in Italy. She made her profession of faith in the Catholic Church in Italy. Upon her return to the United States, she established Catholic schools and founded the Sisters of Charity of St. Joseph, a religious community of teaching sisters based in Emmitsburg, Maryland.

She sincerely loved her family life, once writing, "[My husband] is quietly writing by my side in as perfect health as he has ever enjoyed — my chicks quiet in bed and my father smiling. . . . For myself, I think the greatest happiness of this life is to be released from the cares and formalities of what is called the world. My world is my family, and all the change to me will be that I can devote myself unmolested to my treasure."

Today, take time to ponder the gift of your family. Pray that children be properly educated and that parents and teachers receive direction and insight to teach the Faith.

5 January
White — Memorial
St. John Neumann (1860), Bishop

St. John was born in Bohemia in 1811. He had a great desire to dedicate himself to the American missions, so he came to the United States as a cleric and was ordained in New York in 1836. He entered the Redemptorists in 1840 and worked in Pennsylvania, Ohio, and Maryland. In 1852, he was consecrated Bishop of Philadelphia. There he worked establishing parish schools and erecting churches for the numerous immigrants. He was beatified in 1963.

John Neumann

Tomorrow is the feast of the Epiphany, so after the children are in bed is a good time to move the figures of the three kings right up to the Nativity scene. You could also raise the manger to a throne, draping it in red and gold paper and leaving tiny gold crowns on each Christ Child figure. In the morning the children can check to see whether the kings visited, and what they did when they visited!

6 January

White

Epiphany (normally celebrated in parishes on the first Sunday after Christmas)

"Epiphany" means the revelation of the Messiah's coming to the Gentiles, whom the Magi represent. Epiphany marks the day the three kings — Casper, Melchior, and Balthasar— brought gifts to the Christ Child. Some families exchange gifts on this day rather than Christmas, so that Christ's birth will be the complete focus on December twenty-fifth. Other families save one gift for Epiphany.

Also, on this day, families traditionally bless their homes by marking the doors with blessed chalk. They write the year with the initials of the three kings in the middle, like this: 19+C+M+B+95. The children could dress as the three kings and "journey" to Bethlehem for the day.

Blessing of Chalk: *Bless, O Lord God, this creature chalk to render it helpful to men. Grant that they who use it in faith and with it inscribe upon the entrance of their homes the names of the saints, Casper, Melchior and Balthasar, may through their merits and intercession enjoy health of body and protection of soul. Through Christ our Lord. Amen.*

Blessing of Homes: *Bless O Lord, Almighty God, this home that it be the shelter of health, chastity, self-conquest, humility, goodness, mildness, obedience to the command-ments, and thanksgiving to God the Father, Son and Holy Spirit. May blessing remain for all time upon this dwelling and them that live herein. Through Christ our Lord. Amen.*

7 January

White

St. Raymond of Peñafort (1275), Priest, Patron of Canonists

St. Raymond was born near Barcelona around 1175. He became a canon of that diocese and joined the Dominicans. At the command of Pope Gregory IX, he produced a collection of canon law, but his most noted work was on the Sacrament of Penance. He was elected general of his order and directed it wisely. St. Raymond was also devoted to the conversion of Muslims and Jews. He lived to be about one hundred years old. He is the patron of canonists.

12 January

Green

St. Marguerite Bourgeoys (1700), Religious

Born in 1620, this French foundress became a missionary to the Americas and settled in Canada, where she founded the Congregation of Notre Dame in 1658.

• In honor of St. Marguerite Bourgeoys, see the delicious recipe for crêpes, French-Canadian style, on page 97.

13 January

Green

St. Hilary of Poitiers (367), Bishop, Doctor of the Church

St. Hilary was born at Poitiers at the beginning of the fourth century. Born to a pagan family, he converted upon realizing that "if the present life is not given us to set us on the road to eternal life then it isn't a benefit to God." He was made a bishop and fought against Arianism, a heresy which denied the divinity of Christ. He was exiled by the Emperor Constantine.

17 January
White
St. Anthony the Abbot (356)

St. Anthony was born to a rich family around 250 in Egypt. As a young man, he gave up riches to live a life of simplicity and poverty in the desert. He endured many years of spiritual trials and eventually became well-known for his sanctity and virtue. People came from miles around to seek guidance. He is the founder of monasticism.

"He who can love himself, loves all men." — St. Anthony the Abbot

20 January
Green
St. Fabian (250), Pope, Martyr

St. Fabian was elected bishop of the Church of Rome in 236. In 250, at the beginning of the persecution of Christians by Decius, a Roman emperor, he won the crown of martyrdom. He was buried in the cemetery of St. Callixtus.

St. Sebastian (third century), Martyr

St. Sebastian was a young and handsome man who died a martyr at Rome in the beginning of the Emperor Diocletian's persecution of the Christians. Legend has it that he was pierced by many arrows by fellow soldiers. The faithful have long venerated his tomb in the catacombs in Rome, on the Appian Way. He is the patron of athletes and soldiers.

FRENCH-CANADIAN CRÊPES

1 c. flour
pinch of salt
½ c. milk
shortening
1 egg

Mix the above ingredients, except the shortening, to form a batter of medium consistency. Put enough shortening in a skillet so that when melted it is about ¼-inch deep. Heat, watch, and when the blue smoke curls over the shortening, drip the batter into it with a perforated spoon.

When the crêpe is golden brown on one side, turn it over.

You may sprinkle powdered sugar, cinnamon, maple syrup, or another favorite topping. Delicious!

If you double the recipe, use two cups of flour; one egg will still be sufficient, but increase the milk to one cup.

— *Recipe from the kitchen of Lillian Romanowsky (nee Drapeau)*

St. Agnes

21 January
Red — Memorial
St. Agnes (304), Virgin, Martyr

St. Agnes died a martyr at Rome during either the second half of the third century or, more probably, at the beginning of the fourth century. Pope Damascus adorned her tomb with sacred poetry, and many of the Fathers of the Church, following St. Ambrose, have honored her in their writings. She is the patroness of the children of Mary.

"Christ made my soul beautiful with the jewels of grace and virtue. I belong to Him whom the angels serve." — St. Agnes

22 January
Green
St. Vincent the Deacon (304), Martyr

St. Vincent was deacon of the church of Saragossa and after suffering tortures, died as a martyr at Valencia in Spain during the Diocletian persecution. Devotion to Him spread immediately throughout the Church.

Blessed Laura Vicuña (1904), Virgin, Martyr

Blessed Laura was born in 1891 in Santiago, Chile. At ten years old, Laura offered her life for the conversion of her mother, whom she realized was in danger of losing her eternal life with God because she had left the Church. Laura's teachers, the Salesian Sisters, modeled the loving service to God and others that Laura imitated. Laura died a martyr's death at age thirteen, at which time her mother returned to the Faith.

24 January
White — Memorial
St. Francis de Sales (1622), Bishop, Doctor of the Church

Born at Savoy in 1567, St. Francis became a priest and worked diligently for the restoration of Catholicism in his country. Chosen Bishop of Geneva, he showed himself as a true pastor toward his clerics and the faithful, strengthening their faith by his writings, works, and example. His most renowned work for laity is *Introduction to the Devout Life*, which he wrote for St. Jane Frances de Chantal. He died at Lyons in France. St. Francis de Sales is the patron of writers.

"The past must be abandoned to God's mercy, the present to our fidelity, the future to divine providence." — St. Francis de Sales

• Make Wheatless Fruit Bread for tomorrow's feast day; see page 99.

25 January
White — Feast
Conversion of Paul, Apostle

Read the account in Acts 9:1-31 at dinner and have a feast to celebrate the conversion of this great apostle. Serve Wheatless Fruit Bread for dessert in remembrance of the story of

Paul fleeing to the desert. The story says that after he dwelt for many years there, living on dates from a palm tree, a raven came one day, bringing him a half-loaf of bread. Thereafter the raven came every day with fresh bread.

26 January
White — Memorial
Saints Timothy and Titus, Bishops

Saints Timothy and Titus were disciples and assistants of the apostle Paul. Timothy had charge of the church at Ephesus and Titus of the church at Crete. The biblical letters written to them are called the pastoral epistles, for they contain excellent advice for the instruction of both pastors and laity.

"Aim at righteousness, godliness, faith, love, steadfastness, gentleness. Fight the good fight of faith, take hold of the eternal life to which you were called. . . ." — 1 Timothy 6:11-12

27 January
Green
St. Angela Merici (1540), Virgin

Born in 1470 in Desenzano in the territory of Lombardy (now in Italy), St. Angela took the Franciscan habit of the Third Order Regular and called together a group of girls, whom she instructed in charitable works. In 1535, under the patronage of St. Ursula, she founded a congregation of women who instructed poor girls in the Christian life.

"You will effect more by kind words and a courteous manner, than by anger or sharp rebuke, which should never be used but in necessity." — St. Angela Merici

---

BETH'S WHEATLESS FRUIT BREAD

2½ c. rye flour
1 tsp. salt
2 tsp. baking powder
½ c. sliced figs
⅓ c. raisins
3 soft prunes, sliced
½ tsp. baking soda
1½ c. warm water
¼ c. molasses or honey
2 tbs. oil or melted butter

Combine flour, salt, baking powder, figs, raisins, and prunes. Mix soda, water, and honey in a one-pint measuring cup. Add oil. Blend and pour gradually into flour mixture. Mix and spoon into greased and floured 8"x4"x2½" loaf pan. Bake at 350° for 50 to 60 minutes until done. Loosen with a knife, cool on a rack.

28 January
White — Memorial
St. Thomas Aquinas (1274), Priest, Doctor of the Church

St. Thomas was born in 1225 into the family of the Count of Aquino. He first studied at the monastery of Monte Cassino and later at the University of Naples. Afterward, he joined the Friars Preachers and completed his studies at Paris and Cologne under the tutelage of St. Albert the Great. He became a teacher himself and wrote many learned volumes and philosophical and theological studies. One of his best-known works is the *Summa Theologica*. Ironically, he was nicknamed "The Dumb Ox"! The Church considers him one of the most important theologians of all time.

"Three things are necessary for the salvation of man: to know what he ought to believe; to know what he ought to desire; and to know what he ought to do." — St. Thomas Aquinas

St. Thomas Aquinas

31 January
White — Memorial
St. John Bosco (1888), Priest

St. John was born near Castelnuovo in the diocese of Turin in 1815. His early years were very difficult, so after becoming a priest, he dedicated himself to the education of the young, founding congregations which would instruct youth in both the arts and the Christian life. He also composed pamphlets for the support and defense of religion. He possessed mystical gifts and the ability to foretell future events.

"You can do nothing with children unless you win their confidence and love by bringing them into touch with oneself, by breaking through all the hindrances that keep them at a distance." — St. John Bosco

February

This month is devoted to the Passion of Our Lord. Sometime during February, consider prayerfully walking the Stations of the Cross with your family. Meditate on Jesus' walk to Calvary. Let us be reminded of how much God loves us — He sent us His only Son, to suffer and die at the hands of sinners! Offer your sufferings and difficulties to Jesus, joining it to His passion and death.

The Church is the mystical body of Christ and we mysteriously *"make up in our bodies what is lacking in the sufferings of Christ."* — Colossians 1:24

2 February
White — Feast
Presentation of Our Lord

This is the fourth Joyful Mystery of the Rosary, when Mary and Joseph brought baby Jesus to Jerusalem to present Him to God in the temple. A holy and devout man named Simeon was waiting to set eyes on the Redemption of Israel. The Holy Spirit was with

Simeon and when he saw Jesus, he knew that this baby was the long-awaited Messiah. Simeon also spoke a prophetic word to Mary, foretelling her future sorrow. Read Luke 2:22-40 to better understand what happened on that day.

• At dinner, light a blessed candle or your Christ Candle from Christmas in honor of Baby Jesus, Who was called *"a light for the revelation to the Gentiles"* (Luke 2:32) by Simeon.

3 February
Green — Blessing of Throats
St. Blase, Bishop (circa 316), Martyr

St. Blase was the bishop of Sebaste in Armenia during the fourth century. His followers spread throughout the entire Church in the Middle Ages. Priests usually bless throats on this day because St. Blase had a special ministry of healing ailments of the throat. He is also invoked for the protection of animals and for fine weather.

St. Ansgar (865), Bishop

St. Ansgar was born in France at the beginning of the ninth century and educated in the monastery. In 826 he preached the Faith in Denmark with little success, but his later efforts had great effect in Sweden, where he eventually became bishop.

5 February
Green — Memorial (Commemoration in Lent)
St. Agatha (circa 249-251), Virgin, Martyr

Agatha suffered martyrdom at Catania in Sicily, probably during the persecution of Decius, for refusing to give up her vow to chastity. From antiquity, her followers spread throughout the Church; her name was therefore inserted into the Roman Canon. She is the patroness of nurses.

6 February
Red — Memorial (Commemoration in Lent)
St. Paul Miki and Companions (1596), Martyrs

St. Paul Miki was born in Japan between 1564 and 1566. Entering the Jesuits, he preached the Gospel to the Japanese with great success. When persecution against Catholics became oppressive, he was arrested along with twenty-five others, including at least four boys between the ages of ten and nineteen. After enduring torment and derision, they were finally taken to Nagasaki, where they suffered crucifixion. It is said that they preached the whole way to their deaths and went to the crosses singing praise to God. This inspired many Christians and in the years after that over thirty-one hundred Christians were killed in Japan for their faith.

8 February
Green (Commemoration in Lent)
St. Jerome Emiliani (1537), Founder

St. Jerome was born at Venice in 1486. He first embraced the military life but later dedicated himself to helping the poor, distributing to them his own possessions. He founded the Order of Clerks Regular of Somascha, which supported orphan boys and the poor. Jerome died at Somascha in the Bergamese District.

10 February
White — Memorial
St. Scholastica (547), Abbess and Founder

Scholastica, a sister (possibly a twin) of St. Benedict, was born in Nursia, Italy, about the year 480. She made vows to God and followed her brother to Monte Cassino, where she died.

11 February
Green (Commemoration in Lent)
Our Lady of Lourdes

In 1858, the Virgin Mary appeared to Bernadette Soubirous near Lourdes in France within the cave of Massabielle. Through this humble girl, Mary's message called sinners to conversion and enkindled within the Church a great zeal for prayer and charity, especially service to the sick and poor. It was during this apparition that Mary said of herself, "I am the Immaculate Conception," a doctrine of the Church defined by Pope Pius IX. There are many books available about St. Bernadette and Our Lady of Lourdes if you would like to read more. *The Song of Bernadette* is a well-known movie about Our Lady of Lourdes.

14 February
White — Memorial (Commemoration in Lent)
Saints Cyril (869), Monk, and Methodius (885), Bishop

St. Cyril was born in Thessalonica and educated in Constantinople. He accompanied his brother Methodius to Moravia to preach the Faith. In order to make the Scriptures and the Mass more available to people, they prepared Slavic liturgical texts into what would subsequently be known as the Cyrillic alphabet. Both were summoned to Rome, where Cyril died, while Methodius was consecrated bishop and went to Pannonia, where he tirelessly preached the Gospel. He died in Velehrad, Czechoslovakia.

17 February
Green (Commemoration in Lent)
Seven Holy Founders of the Servite Order

Seven men, born at Florence, began a life on Monte Senario with a particular veneration of the Blessed Virgin Mary. Later they preached throughout Tuscany and founded the Order of Servites of the Blessed Virgin Mary, approved by the Holy See in 1304. Alexis Falconieri, one of the seven, died on this day in 1310.

21 February
Green
St. Peter Damian (1072), Priest

St. Peter Damian was born at Ravenna in 1007. After completing his studies he began to teach, but soon abandoned this and entered the hermitage of Fonte Avellana where, once elected prior, he promoted the religious life with such fervor that all of Italy was affected by his renewal.

During calamitous times he helped the Roman pontiffs through his works and writings and by various missions on behalf of Church reform. He was made bishop and cardinal of Ostia by Pope Stephen IX. Peter Damian was venerated as a saint shortly after his death.

22 February
White — Feast
The Chair of St. Peter the Apostle

Since the fourth century, the feast of the Chair of Peter has been celebrated at Rome as a sign of the unity of the Church founded upon that apostle. This is a good time to discuss with your family why Catholics believe that the Holy Father has a special grace from the Holy Spirit to teach in the Church on Faith and morals infallibly.

"You are Peter, and on this rock I will build my church, and the powers of death shall not prevail against it. I will give you the keys of the kingdom of heaven, and whatever you bind on earth shall be bound in heaven, and whatever you loose on earth shall be loosed in heaven." — Matthew 16:18-20

Christ and the Apostles

23 February
Red — Memorial
St. Polycarp (circa 155), Bishop, Martyr

St. Polycarp, the bishop of Smyrna, was a disciple of the apostles, and a friend of St. Ignatius of Antioch. He went to Rome to confer with Pope Anicetus concerning the celebration of Easter. About the year 155 he suffered martyrdom by burning at the stake in the amphitheater of Smyrna.

March

This is the month to honor St. Joseph, the husband of Mary and foster-father of Jesus. In March, let us especially reflect on family life, of which St. Joseph is the patron. Perhaps families could offer a novena to St. Joseph for the husband and father of the home. Think of St. Joseph, the head of the Holy Family — he was responsible for Mary, the only sinless human being, and for Jesus, the God-man — yet Joseph was like us! His humility, chastity, tenderness, strength, courage, and his example of responsible fatherhood are a model for all men.

3 March
Violet
Blessed Katherine Drexel (1955), Founder

Born in 1858 into a wealthy family in Philadelphia, Pennsylvania, Katherine eventually devoted her wealth to founding schools and missions for Native American Indians and African-Americans. She founded the Sisters of the Blessed Sacrament for Indians and People of Color.

4 March
Violet
St. Casimir (1484), Patron of Poland and Lithuania

St. Casimir, son of the King of Poland, was born in 1458. He embodied the Christian virtues with special regard to chastity and kindness to the poor. He was zealous in the Faith, particularly in his devotion to the Holy Eucharist and the Virgin Mary. Casimir died of consumption.

7 March
Violet — Memorial
Saints Perpetua and Felicity (203), Martyrs

Perpetua, a young pregnant wife, and Felicity, the young servant of Perpetua, were fed to wild beasts in a coliseum, suffering martyrdom in the persecution of Septimus Severus at Carthage. A most accurate account of their death still exists, derived partly from their own testimonies at their death, from a writer of the period.

On the way to their martyrdom, St. Perpetua said, *"We are not in our own power, but in the power of God."*

8 March
Violet
St. John of God (1550), Founder

St. John of God was born in Portugal in 1495. After a hazardous period in the military service, he decided to devote himself entirely to the care of the sick. Founding a hospital in Granada, Spain, he selected assistants who later formed the Order of Hospitallers of St. John of God. He was most distinguished for his charity to the needy and the sick. St. John died in Granada.

"Just as water extinguishes a fire, so love wipes away sin." — St. John of God

9 March
Violet
St. Frances of Rome (1440), Founder

St. Frances was born at Rome in 1384. While still young, she married and had three sons. Though living at a difficult time, she gave her goods to the poor and looked after the needs of the sick. She was remarkable in this active work for the destitute and also in cultivating the virtues of humility and patience. In 1425 she founded the Congregation of Oblates, under the rule of St. Benedict.

16 March
Violet

Today, prepare an Irish dish for tomorrow — St. Patrick's Day. His feast day usually falls in Lent, a time of fasting. In Ireland, cooks add raisins or currents to Lenten bread to mark the special day. Below is a recipe for beer bread. Before baking, make a cross on the top of the bread.

DEE DEE'S BEER BREAD

3 c. self-rising flour	1 12-oz. can of beer
2 tbs. sugar	1/2 c. butter

Mix flour sugar with a wooden spoon. Blend in beer, one-third at a time, and turn batter into three well-greased 6"x9" loaf pans.

Drizzle butter over the top of each and bake at 350° for 50 minutes.

---

17 March
Violet
St. Patrick of Ireland (461), Bishop

St. Patrick was born in Great Britain about the year 385. As a young man he was captured and sold as a slave in Ireland, where he had to tend sheep. After escaping slavery, he chose to enter the priesthood, and later, as a bishop, tirelessly preached the Gospel to the people of Ireland, where he converted many to the Faith. His efforts established the Church in Ireland. He died at Down in 461.

"I was like a stone lying in the deep mire; and He that is mighty came, and in His mercy, lifted me up, and verily raised me aloft and placed me on top of the wall." — St. Patrick

18 March
Violet
St. Cyril of Jerusalem (386), Bishop

St. Cyril was born of Christian parents in 315. He succeeded Maximus as bishop of Jerusalem in 348. He was involved in the dispute over Arianism, which denied Christ's divinity, and was more than once punished with exile. His catechetical writings, explaining the true teachings of the Faith and of Scripture, and also the Traditions of the Church, reveal his pastoral zeal.

19 March
White
St. Joseph, Husband of Our Lady

St. Joseph was the foster-father of Jesus. We know from the Scriptures that he was a just and upright man. We should go to St. Joseph often and ask for his guidance in our own trials of family life and in following the will of God, especially when we don't seem to understand. St. Joseph is the patron of the Universal Church and of family life. According to centuries-old custom, the best dishware, cutlery, and serving trays were used to serve fine foods on this day. Below is a recipe for a special dessert, a simpler version of the traditional "St. Joseph *Sfinge*."

23 March
Violet
St. Turibius of Mogrovejo (1606), Bishop

St. Turibius (also called St. Toribio Alfonso de Mogrovejo) was born in Spain around the year 1538. He taught law at the University of Salamanca, and in 1580 he was chosen as bishop of Lima, Peru. He journeyed to the Americas. Burning with apostolic zeal, he called together many councils and synods that successfully promoted the reform of religion throughout the whole region. He vigorously defended the laws of the Church. He devoted much of his time and attention to the care of the native Indian population.

25 March
White — Solemnity
The Annunciation of Our Lord

This is the great day on which the Archangel Gabriel appeared to the Blessed Virgin Mary and told her of God's great plan for salvation. Her response was the Magnificat. Read about this momentous event in Luke 1 and 2.

For centuries this day has been celebrated with cakes, coffee rings, and wreath-shaped cookies. In Sweden, waffles are served with a lingonberry sauce.

ST. JOSEPH'S CREAM PUFFS

For the cream puffs:

1 c. water	¼ lb. butter
¼ tsp. salt	1 c. sifted flour
4 eggs	1 tbs. sugar

1 tbs. each grated lemon peel and grated orange peel

For the filling:

1 lb. cottage cheese	2 tbs. grated chocolate
1 tbs. grated orange peel	2 tbs. almond extract
3 tbs. milk	sugar to taste
maraschino cherries	½ c. glazed orange peel

Boil water and butter. Add flour and salt. Keep stirring until mixture leaves sides of pan or forms a ball in the center. Cool. Beat in eggs, one at a time. Add sugar and grated peel. Drop tablespoons of dough every three inches on a greased cookie-sheet or fill muffin tins half-full. Bake in a hot oven (400°) for 10 minutes. Reduce heat to 350°, and continue baking until light brown. Remove from oven. Open puff in the center of top to let steam escape. Cool.

Mix cottage cheese with chocolate and orange rind. Add flavoring, milk, and sugar to taste. Beat until smooth and custard-like. Fill puffs.

Chill until ready to use. Before serving, top with cherry and orange peel. This recipe makes about 18 cream puffs.

---

26 March
Violet

In honor of the Annunciation, see the recipe for pound cake below.

April

This is the month of the Holy Eucharist. The Eucharist is at the center of our Faith. Receiving the body and blood of our Lord and Savior Jesus Christ strengthens us and makes us one with Christ. He Himself says in Scripture that if we do not eat His body and blood, we will "have no life within us." That life is Christ Himself, veiled in bread and wine. At the moment we receive Him, we are united with Him and we become a literal tabernacle for the Lord! It is important to meditate on this reality, which is such a great mystery. This month, you might make a commitment to go to Mass a little more frequently or to spend some extra time praying before the Blessed Sacrament. Jesus waits for us in every tabernacle of every Church, so go to Him. A great book that suggests ways to better focus at Mass is *When Your Mind Wanders at Mass*, by Thomas Howard (Franciscan University Press).

HELEN'S GERMAN POUND CAKE

3 c. sifted flour
½ lb. butter
1 c. sugar
3 tsp. baking powder
1 tsp. vanilla
3 eggs
1 c. milk

Cream butter with sugar, add eggs, and beat five minutes. Add flour a little at a time with the milk. Beat well and add baking powder and beat well. Batter will be very thick. Bake in a well-greased angel food pan for two hours at 325°. Sprinkle powdered sugar on top.

2 April
Violet
St. Francis of Paola (1507), Hermit

St. Francis was born at Paola in Calabria in 1416. He founded a congregation of hermits, which was later entitled the Order of Minims, and approved by the Apostolic See in 1506. He died at Tours in France.

"The recollection of an injury is in itself wrong. It adds to our anger, nurtures our sin and hates what is good. It is a rusty arrow and poison for the soul. It puts all virtue to flight." — St. Francis de Paola

4 April
Violet
St. Isidore of Seville (636), Bishop and Doctor

St. Isidore was born around 560 at Seville in Spain. After his father's death he was raised by his brother Leander. Although he had a difficult time with his studies, Isidore persisted and became a very learned man. He eventually wrote a history of the world and an encyclopedia. This Doctor of the Church also encouraged the reading of Sacred Scripture. However, it wasn't these accomplishments that won St. Isidore heaven. It was his love of God and others!

"The whole science of the saints consists knowing and following the will of God." — St. Isidore

5 April
Violet
St. Vincent Ferrer (1419), Teacher and Preacher

St. Vincent Ferrer was born in Valencia in Spain in 1350. He joined the Dominican Order and taught theology. As a preacher, he traveled through many regions and instructed many people to observe the true teachings of their Faith and to reform their lives. Although he lived in a confusing time, filled with schisms and heresies, Vincent was ever faithful to Christ and His teachings. On his deathbed he asked for the Passion (the story of Christ's crucifixion) to be read.

"Whoever will proudly dispute and contradict will always stand outside the door. Christ, the master of humility manifests his truth only to the humble and hides himself from the proud." — St. Vincent Ferrer

7 April
Violet
St. Jean Baptist de la Salle (1719), Founder

St. John was born at Rheims in France in 1651. After ordination to the priesthood, he devoted himself to the education of boys and the founding of schools for the poor. He brought his companions together as a religious congregation, for the sake of which he endured many sufferings. He died at Rouen.

"Would we wish that our own hidden sins should be divulged? We ought, then, to be silent regarding those to others." — St. Jean Baptiste de la Salle

11 April
Violet
St. Stanislaus (1097), Bishop and Martyr

St. Stanislaus was born in the town of Szczepanow in Poland around the year 1030. He studied in Paris and was ordained to the priesthood.

In 1071 he succeeded Bishop Lambert at Cracow. In this post he ruled as a good shepherd by helping the poor and visiting his clerics every year. He courageously rebuked King Boleslaus, who put him to death.

13 April
Violet
St. Martin I (656), Pope and Martyr

St. Martin was born at Todi in Umbrai, Italy. He became a member of the clergy of Rome and was elected pope in 649. He convened the council that condemned the heresy of the Monothelites.

In 653 he was taken prisoner by the Emperor Constans and detained in Constantinople, where he was forced to suffer many indignities. He died in exile in Kherson (Crimea). He was the last pope to die a martyr.

21 April
White
St. Anselm (1109), Bishop and Doctor

St. Anselm was born at Aosta, Italy, in 1033. He entered the Benedictine Order at the monastery of Bec in France. While he quickly progressed in the spiritual life, he taught theology to his fellow students.

Eventually, Anselm went to England, where he was appointed archbishop of Canterbury. He fought vigorously for the freedom of the Church, and for this he was twice exiled. He has achieved fame for his writings, especially those on mystical theology.

Anselm's holiness, patience, and love of the Church were well-respected by many. The Church encourages the faithful to live as Anselm did — loyal to God at whatever cost.

"Faith seeks understanding. I do not seek to understand that I may believe, but I believe in order to understand." — St. Anselm

23 April
White
St. George (circa 300), Martyr, Patron of England

The veneration of St. George began as early as the fourth century in Lydda in Palestine, where a church was built in his honor. From antiquity this veneration has spread throughout both East and West.

George was probably a soldier in the third century around the time of the persecution under Diocletian. He suffered martyrdom at the hands of this emperor due to he courageous public defense of the Faith.

Although the stories of St. George slaying a dragon are courageous, none could be more heroic than dying for Christ!

24 April
White
St. Fidelis of Sigmaringen (1622), Priest and Martyr

St. Fidelis was born in the town of Sigmaringen in Germany in 1578. He entered the Order of Friars Minor Capuchins and led an austere life of penance, vigils, and prayer. Continuously engaged in preaching the Word of God, he was commissioned by the Sacred Congregation for the Propagation of the Faith to preach in the canton of the Grisons, Switzerland.

In 1622 he was attacked by a band of heretics, a group who fought against what the Church teaches, and suffered martyrdom at Seewis in Switzerland. His life of courage, faith, and deep love of God is a beautiful example to all Christians.

"It is because of faith that we exchange the present for the future. What made the holy apostles and martyrs endure fierce agony and bitter torments, except faith, and especially faith in the resurrection?" — St. Fidelis of Sigmaringen

25 April
Red
St. Mark, the Evangelist

St. Mark, a cousin of Barnabas, accompanied St. Paul on his first missionary journey and later went with him to Rome. He was a disciple of St. Peter, whose teaching was the basis for Mark's Gospel. In his Gospel he shows Jesus to be the suffering Son of God. Although it is easy to be a disciple (one must only decide to follow Christ), Mark knew that it meant accepting the cross. After all, Christ was glorified in His willingness to suffer and die for our salvation.

"And he called to him the multitude with his disciples and said to them, 'If any man would come after me, let him deny himself and take up his cross and follow me.'" — Mark 8:34

28 April
White
St. Peter Chanel (1841), Priest

St. Peter Chanel was born in the town of Cuet, France, in 1803. After ordination to the priesthood, he was engaged in pastoral work for a few years. He then joined the Marists and journeyed to Oceania to preach the Gospel. Despite many hardships, he converted some of the natives to Christ. A band of native warriors hostile to the Faith killed him on the island of Futuna.

29 April
White
St. Catherine of Siena (1380), Virgin and Doctor of the Church

St. Catherine was born in Siena in 1347. While still a young girl, she sought "the way of perfection" and entered the Third Order of St. Dominic. On fire with love of God and neighbor, she established peace and concord between cities, vigorously fought for the rights and freedom of the Roman pontiff, and promoted the renewal of religious life. She also composed works of doctrine and spiritual inspiration.

"There is no sin nor wrong that gives a man such a foretaste of hell in this life as anger and impatience. O lovely Compassion, You are the balm that snuffs out rage and cruelty in the soul." — St. Catherine of Siena

30 April
White
St. Pius V (1572), Pope

St. Pius V was born near Alexandria, Italy, in 1504. He entered the Dominican Order and taught theology. After being ordained a bishop and named a cardinal, he became pope in 1566. He vigorously implemented the reform of the Church begun at the Council of Trent, promoted the spread of the Faith, and renewed divine worship.

May

This month is dedicated to the Blessed Virgin Mary. In May it's spring in North America, and the flowers are beginning to bloom and the earth is fresh and new, symbolizing new life. Mary's "yes," her "fiat" to bear Jesus to the world, gave us new life. She is the New Eve of the new creation. This month, as Mother's Day is celebrated, remember not only your earthly mother, but honor Holy Mother Mary.

1 May
White — Feast
St. Joseph the Worker

St. Joseph is the husband of Mary and foster-father of Jesus. He was by trade a carpenter, devoted to the care of his family. He is the patron of laborers, the Universal Church, family life, and Canada.

"When Joseph woke from sleep, he did as the angel of the Lord commanded him. . . ." — Matthew 1:24

2 May
White — Memorial
St. Athanasius (373), Bishop, Doctor of the Church

Born at Alexandria in 295, he accompanied Bishop Alexander to the Council of Nicaea, and succeeded him as bishop of Alexandria. Known as the "Father of Orthodoxy," he fought the Arian heresy, which denied the divinity of Christ.

He suffered many hardships and was exiled several times. His writings explaining and defending the Faith are outstanding.

3 May
Red — Feast
Saints Philip and James, Apostles

St. Philip was born at Bethsaida and was a disciple of John the Baptist before he followed Christ. James, a cousin of Jesus and son of Alphaeus, ruled over the Church at Jerusalem, wrote an epistle, and converted many of the Jewish people to the Faith.

He suffered martyrdom in the year 62.

12 May
White
Saints Nereus and Achilleus (100), Pancratius (304), Martyrs

Nereus and Achilleus were Roman soldiers who refused to serve the Emperor after becoming Christians. They were exiled and put to death for their faith. Their sepulcher is preserved in the cemetery on the Ardeatine Way, where a basilica was constructed in their honor.

Pancratius (also called Pancras) died a martyr as a young teenager in Rome. His tomb, over which Pope Symmachus built a church, is preserved on the Aurelian Way.

He is the patron saint of children receiving their first communion.

14 May
White — Feast
St. Matthias, Apostle

Since he was a witness to the Lord's resurrection, and due to his good and holy life, St. Matthias was chosen by the other apostles to take the place of Judas. Tradition links him with the country of Ethiopia, where he is believed to have met his martyrdom.

Not much is known of St. Matthias, but it is known is that he loved Christ and that he lived and died to spread the Good News as far as possible.

• Read Acts 1:15-26.

15 May
White
St. Isidore the Farmer (1170), Miracle Worker

Born in Spain, Isidore began to work with the soil as soon as he was old enough. As he plowed, planted, and harvested, he also prayed. His three great loves in life were God, his family, and the soil.

He and his wife, St. Mary de la Cabeza (who is also honored as a saint), proved to all their neighbors that poverty, hard work, and sorrow (their only child died as a little boy) cannot destroy human happiness if we accept them with faith and in union with Christ.

Having been credited with miracles such as feeding hungry people with baskets of food that never seemed to run out, Isidore is considered the patron of farmers and of the seriously ill.

• In honor of St. Isidore the Farmer, make a vegetable dish. Use the recipe on page 113.

18 May
White
Pope St. John I (526), Martyr

St. John was born in Tuscany and elected bishop of the Church of Rome in 523. He lived at a time when the Arian heresy was still troubling the Church, and the Emperor of Constantinople, in his zeal for the Faith, was oppressing the Arians. John went to Emperor Justin, at the request of the king of the Arians, and was able to moderate Justin's zeal. King Theodoric was not satisfied and had St. John thrown in jail, where he eventually died a martyr. Out of the twenty-three popes named John, St. John I is the only saint so far!

20 May
White
St. Bernardine of Siena (1444), Priest

Born at Massa Marittima in Tuscany in 1380, he entered the Friars Minor and, after being ordained to the priesthood, traveled on foot preaching throughout Italy. He began using the Greek monogram "IHS" on a badge, as a symbol for Christ. The letters IHS are

---

HEARTY VEGETABLE SOUP

1 lb. peeled and cut potatoes
1 lb. chopped leeks
1 lb. peeled and cut carrots
8 oz. of peeled and cut sweet apples
3 bay leaves
10 c. of water
1 tsp. coriander seeds
¼ tsp. peppercorns
2 cloves peeled and chopped garlic
2 c. fresh parsley
½ c. olive oil

Place the vegetables, apples, bay leaves, and water in a large pot and heat. Place coriander and peppercorns in a cheesecloth sack and add to the pot. Add one tablespoon of salt and reduce to medium heat, cover, and cook for 45 minutes.

In a small bowl, mix finely minced parsley, chopped garlic, and olive oil and stir well.

When the vegetables are soft, remove them from the broth. Remove the cheesecloth sack and bay leaves as well. Reserve the broth. Next, puree the vegetables and apples, and transfer to another soup pot. Add enough broth to make the soup thick, about 2½ cups total. Reheat the soup to almost boiling. To serve the soup, ladle it into heated soup bowls and add one tablespoon of the parsley mixture, swirling it on the top. Serve immediately. Serves six to eight.

— A Martin family recipe for Lent

the equivalent of the Greek letters for Jesus. Bernadine wrote theological treatises and also assisted at the Council of Florence.

Have the children draw or paint symbols for Christ, including the IHS symbol. Display them or send them to relatives.

25 May
White
St. Gregory VII (1085), Pope

Gregory was born in the early part of the eleventh century, at a time when the Church was battling several internal, evil practices such as "lay investiture," the practice of laity, such as kings and emperors, appointing bishops and abbots. As pope, Gregory preached against these practices courageously, even in the face of exile by Henry IV. Although he did not totally defeat these evil practices, St. Gregory was responsible for beginning the long fight that eventually did.

St. Mary de Pazzi (1607), Virgin

Born Catherine de Pazzi, in Florence, Italy, St. Mary was quite wealthy and many expected her to be a woman of high society. She surprised them all when she became a nun at age sixteen! After many years of growth in holiness, she was given the gift of reading minds, which she used only for the good of her sisters in the Carmelite convent. It was her deep prayer, humble use of the talents God had given her, and great charity that made her a saint.

Venerable Bede (735), Priest and Doctor

Bede was born in the neighborhood of the Wearmouth, England, monastery in 673. Trained by St. Benedict Biscop, he later entered the monastery, was ordained to the priesthood, and spent his ministry teaching and writing.

"All the ways of this world are as fickle and unstable as a sudden storm at sea." — St. Bede

26 May
White — Memorial
St. Philip Neri (1595), Priest, Founder

Philip Neri was born in Florence in 1515. He went to Rome and began working with young men, among whom he fostered Christian life and formed an association for the poor and sick. He founded the Oratorians, where reading,

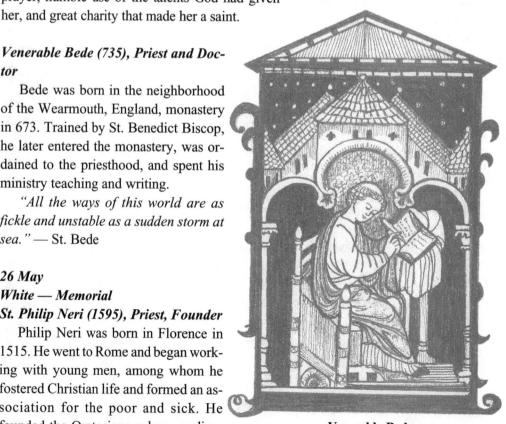

Venerable Bede

singing, and charitable works were practiced. He encouraged frequent confession and preached the path of perfection for the laity. Although friends with all the popes of his time, he was also a humorist. St. Philip was remembered for his cheerfulness, his ability to bring out the best in people, and his joyful spontaneous love of God.

"Cast yourself into the arms of God and be very sure that if he wants anything of you, He will fit you for the work and give you strength." — St. Philip Neri

27 May
White
St. Augustine of Canterbury (605), Bishop
Augustine was sent in 597 from St. Andrew's monastery in Rome by St. Gregory the Great to preach the Gospel in England. He was aided there by King Ethelbert and chosen bishop of Canterbury. He converted many to the Faith and established many dioceses.

31 May
White — Feast
Feast of the Visitation
The Visitation is the second Joyful Mystery of the Rosary. On this day we remember Mary's visit to her cousin Elizabeth. Read the Gospel story in Luke 1:39-56.

• Today, pray the Joyful Mysteries of the Rosary.

June
This month is dedicated to the Sacred Heart of Jesus. In 1693, Sister Mary Margaret Alacoque had the first of four visions of Jesus, with his heart exposed, burning with love for His people. Consecrate yourself and your family to the Sacred Heart of Jesus this month and place or hang an image of the Sacred Heart in your home. This indicates and reminds us that Jesus Christ is indeed the King and Lord of our homes and lives. See the the "Prayers and Devotions" chapter for information on the Enthronement of the Sacred Heart.

1 June
White — Memorial
St. Justin (165), Martyr
St. Justin was born at Flavia Neapolis in Samaria at the beginning of the second century. Though he was born of pagan parents, he became the most important apologist of his time. He opened a school in Rome where public debates were held. A philosopher and writer, he was beheaded with some companions when he refused to sacrifice to pagan gods.

2 June
White
Saints Marcellinus and Peter (304), Martyrs
Pope Damasus is our authority for the martyrdom of these two men during the persecution of Emperor Diocletian. He received this information from the executioner himself.

Marcellinus (a priest) and Peter were captured for baptizing Christians and when they would not worship the Roman idols, they were tortured and sentenced to death. The two men were beheaded in a grove, but their bodies were moved and buried in the cemetery. Once peace was restored, the Church built a basilica over their tombs.

3 June
Red — Memorial
St. Charles Lwanga and Companions (1887), Protomartyrs of Equatorial Africa

King Mwanga killed many Christians in Uganda during the years 1885-87, even his own relatives. Charles and his companions, all young men, adhered steadfastly to the Faith and were put to death by sword and burning because they wanted to be baptized and practice their Christian faith.

• On a map, find the continent of Africa and locate Uganda. Pray for the peoples of that nation.

5 June
Red — Memorial
St. Boniface (755), Bishop, Martyr

Boniface was born in England about the year 673. He became a monk and went to preach the Gospel in Germany. There he converted many to the Faith and was made a Bishop, ruling over the church at Mainz. With companions, he founded and restored dioceses in Bavaria, Thuringia, and Franconia, convened councils, and promulgated laws. While preaching the Gospel to the Frisians, he was killed by pagans.

"The Church is like a great ship being pounded by the waves of life's different stresses. Our duty is not to abandon ship, but to keep her on her course." — St. Boniface

6 June
Green
St. Norbert (1134), Bishop

Born in the duchy of Cleves around the year 1080, this nobleman underwent a conversion at age thirty-five, after narrowly escaping death. He was ordained a priest, preaching mostly in France and Germany. With some companions, he laid the foundations for the Premonstratensian Order. Attempts were made on his life by those who despised his vigor. Elected Archbishop of Magdeburg in 1126, he reformed the Christian life and spread the Faith to nearby pagan nations.

9 June
Green
St. Ephrem of Syria (373), Deacon, Doctor of the Church

St. Ephrem was born of a Christian family at Nisibus around the year 306. Ordained a deacon, he exercised this office throughout the country and in Edessa (in present-day Iraq), where he founded a theological school. He is famous for his writings, homilies, and hymns, and was hailed as a great teacher in the Syrian churches.

• Locate Syria and Iraq on a map or globe. Pray for peace in the Middle Eastern nations.

11 June
Green — Memorial
St. Barnabas (first century), Apostle, Martyr

Born in Cyprus, Barnabas is numbered among the first of the faithful at Jerusalem. He preached the Gospel at Antioch and Cyprus and, as a companion of St. Paul, accompanied him on his first journey. He was also present at the Council of Jerusalem. Upon returning to his own country, he continued to spread the Gospel and eventually died there.

13 June
White — Memorial
St. Anthony of Padua (1231), Priest, Doctor of the Church

Born in Lisbon, Portugal, near the end of the twelfth century, Anthony was a strong and fearless man. As a Franciscan Friar he was sent to work among the Muslims of Morocco. The crowds who came to hear his preaching and teaching could not be contained in the churches and had to gather in the marketplaces. He was chosen by St. Francis to teach theology to the friars and later converted many heretics from the Albigensian heresy. He had great success preaching in France and Italy and gained quite a reputation as a miracle-worker. He died young, at age thirty-six. His shrine is a place of pilgrimage and many miracles are attributed to him. He is the patron of the poor and of lost articles.

19 June
Green
St. Romuald (1027), Abbot

A hermit, Romuald was born at Ravenna, Italy, in the middle of the tenth century. He traveled in various lands preaching on solitude and establishing small monasteries, while directing himself to a life of perfection by the practice of virtues. He fought strenuously against the depraved habits of monks of his day.

21 June
White — Memorial
St. Aloysius Gonzaga (1591), Religious

Aloysius was born into the princely family of Castiglione in 1568 near Mantua in Lombardy. Although his father wanted him to be a soldier, he wanted to be a missionary and, at age seventeen, entered the Society of Jesus. A model novice, he contracted the plague while nursing hospitalized patients and died at the young age of twenty-three. His writings show his holiness and strength. He is hailed as the patron of Catholic youth.

• Today, pray for the youth in your family and community. Have teenage children lead grace or other family prayers today.

22 June
Green
St. Thomas More (1535), Martyr

St. Thomas More was born in 1477 and was educated at Oxford. He married and had

four children. A friend and right-hand man to King Henry VIII, he opposed the Lutheran reforms and was charged with treason for upholding the validity of the King's marriage.

He was beheaded in front of his family and countrymen. He is a patron of lawyers.

St. John Fisher (1535), Bishop, Martyr

St. John Fisher, a learned and holy bishop, was also beheaded for upholding the authority of the Church on the matter of King Henry VIII's divorce and remarriage.

He was also famous for his writings, and was a gifted theologian and scholar whose writings were used at the Council of Trent.

24 June
White — Solemnity
Solemnity of the Birth of John the Baptist

John the Baptist is the only saint for whom we celebrate both his birth and death. He was the cousin of Jesus, the son of Elizabeth and Zechariah.

St. John preached a baptism of repentance, preparing the people for Christ. He baptized Jesus in the River Jordan and was later jailed for denouncing Herod's marriage to his sister-in-law.

- Read about St. John the Baptist in Luke 1:5-80 and Luke 3:1-20.
- Find the Jordan River on a globe or map.

26 June
Green
Blessed Josemaría Escrivá de Balaguer (1975), Priest

This founder of Opus Dei and the Priestly Society of the Holy Cross (1975) was born on January 9, 1902, in Barbasto, Spain. On the Feast of the Guardian Angels, October 2, 1928, Josemaría received a grace from God to understand the mission of his calling.

He was to be dedicated to opening "a way," a spirituality, to all the faithful, in which they could be sanctified in the midst of the world by living and fulfilling their daily duties for the love of God.

He died in Rome on June 26, 1975.

"Blessed be the hardships of this earth! Poverty, tears, hatred, injustice, dishonor. . . . You can endure all things in him who strengthens you." — Josemaría Escrivá, *The Way*

27 June
Green
St. Cyril of Alexandria (444), Bishop, Doctor of the Church

This saint was born in 370 and lived a monastic life. He was ordained a priest and succeeded his uncle as bishop of Alexandria. He had a preeminent role at the Council of Ephesus and wrote many works defending the Catholic Faith.

St. Cyril fought bravely against the doctrines of Nestorius, a heresy which erroneously taught that Jesus was both a human person and a divine person, instead of one divine person with both a human and divine nature, as the Church teaches.

"The root of all good works is the hope of the resurrection; for the expectation of the reward moves the soul to good works." — St. Cyril of Alexandria

28 June
Red — Memorial
St. Irenaeus (202), Bishop, Martyr

Born around the year 130, he became a disciple and successor of Polycarp. He was ordained a priest at Lyons in France and shortly thereafter was made bishop.

St. Irenaeus fought against Gnosticism, one of the earliest heresies that denied the goodness of God's creation and separated the unity of the Holy Trinity. He is considered one of the most important theologians of the second century.

"With God nothing is empty of meaning, nothing without symbolism." — St. Irenaeus

29 June
Red — Solemnity
Solemnity of Saints Peter and Paul, Apostles (first century)

Peter, a fisherman, was chosen by Christ as the first pope (see Matthew 16:13-20). He is the apostle always mentioned first and the one to walk on water. He was also the one to preach at Pentecost, when all the people understood him in their own language. Peter was crucified, probably about 64 A.D.

Paul (called Saul until his conversion) was a well-educated, devout Jew who thought it was his responsibility to persecute Christians. One day, while traveling to Damascus, he had a vision and was converted.

A great missionary, writer (many of his letters are in the New Testament), and preacher, Paul traveled all over the Roman Empire, converting people to Christ. Paul was finally beheaded in Rome.

• Read Matthew 16:13-20 and Acts 9:1-31.

He wrote to the Christian community in Rome:

"For I am sure that neither death, nor life, nor angels, nor principalities, nor things present, nor things to come, nor powers, nor height, nor depth, nor anything else in all creation, will be able to separate us from the love of God in Christ Jesus our Lord." — Romans 8:38-39

30 June
Red
First Martyrs of the Church of Rome (64)

In the first persecution against the Church, begun by the Emperor Nero after the burning of Rome in 64, many of the faithful were tortured and slain. The pagan writer Tacitus testifies to these events in his *Annales* (15, 44) as does Clement, Bishop of Rome, in his letter to the Corinthians (Chapters 5-6).

July

This month is dedicated to the Most Precious Blood of Jesus Christ. We remember and revere the blood Christ spilled on Calvary by attending Mass and receiving the Eucharist. Christ's very own body and blood is veiled in His Eucharistic presence. In prayer, we can place our sins and sufferings into the wounds of Christ, and be washed, renewed, and healed through the power of His Precious Blood.

1 July
Green
St. Junípero Serra (1713-1784), Priest

This newly canonized Franciscan priest is responsible for most of the missions that began the evangelization of California. He is known for taking "El Camino Real" or "the royal road." If you visit California or live there, visiting the missions is a marvelous experience for all ages. There are many books out now on St. Junípero Serra and the California missions.

". . . We shall fulfill our Christian law which commands us to forgive injury and not to seek the sinner's death, but his eternal salvation." — Blessed Junípero Serra

3 July
Red — Feast
St. Thomas (74), Apostle, Martyr

Thomas is remembered for his incredulity concerning Christ's resurrection from the dead. When confronted by the risen Lord, his disbelief gave way to belief as he proclaimed the Easter faith of the Church: "My Lord and my God!"

He is said to have preached the Gospel in India. Since the fourth century, the celebration of the transference of his body to Edessa has been commemorated on this day. In Spain, lamb is often served on the Feast of St. Thomas.

Thomas the Doubting Apostle

4 July
Green
St. Elizabeth of Portugal (1336), Queen

St. Elizabeth was born of the Aragonese royal family in 1271. She married the King of Portugal and had two children. She endured her many trials, including an unfaithful husband, by prayer and charitable works. She founded hospitals, women's shelters, and orphanages. At her husband's death, she gave her property to the poor, joined the Third Order Franciscans, and devoted herself to God and the needy.

Blessed Pier Giorgio (1925), Student

Blessed Pier was born in Turin, Italy, in 1901. A young, handsome student, he was active in Catholic organizations, defended chastity, and united students to peacefully demonstrate for Christian values. An athlete and leader, he loved to socialize with friends and was an avid mountain climber. He had great devotion to the Blessed Sacrament and service to the poor. The son of a rich, political family, Pier mingled with all classes, spent his money on the needy, and regularly visited the sick. He died suddenly of an illness at age twenty-three and was beatified in 1990. Pope John Paul II has called him the saint for modern youth.

• Tell your teenagers about Blessed Pier Giorgio. Encourage discussion about ways they too can increase their faith.

5 July
Green
St. Anthony Zaccaria (1539), Priest

Born at Cremona in Lombardy in 1502, Anthony studied medicine at Padua. He was ordained a priest and founded the Barnabites, the Society of Clerics of St. Paul, which did much to reform the morals of the faithful.

6 July
Green
St. Maria Goretti (1902), Virgin, Martyr

Maria was born in 1890 to a poor family in Corinaldi, Italy. She worked hard at chores to assist her family in their farming duties. Maria was only eleven when a teenage farmhand, who worked with her family, attempted to rape her. After trying to fight him off, she was stabbed fourteen times, preferring to die than have him commit mortal sin. She forgave her attacker and died in the hospital. She is the patroness of chastity.

• Read about St. Maria Goretti and the amazing conversion of the man who murdered her.

"I forgive Alessandro. I forgive him with all my heart; and I want him to be with me in heaven." — St. Maria Goretti

11 July
White — Memorial
St. Benedict (543), Abbott

St. Benedict was born at Nursia in Umbria about the year 480. Educated at Rome, he began the eremic (hermit-like) life at Subiaco, where he gathered disciples, then departed for Monte Cassino. There he established the famous monastery and composed the Benedictine Rule. Because this rule was subsequently adopted throughout Europe, he received the title of Patriarch of Western Monasticism.

13 July
Green
St. Henry II (1024), Emperor

This sovereign was born in Bavaria in 973. He married St. Cunegunda, and is most remarkable for his work in Church reform and fostering missionary activity. He is the patron of the childless and the handicapped.

14 July
White
Blessed Kateri Tekakwitha (1680), Virgin

When she was only four, Kateri's Native American father and Christian mother died from smallpox. The disease left Kateri scarred and half-blind for life. As a child, her one desire was to be baptized as a Christian, but her chieftain uncle and relatives despised Christians. Because Kateri refused to marry or to watch the torture of captives, she was neglected and abused by her people. Kateri eventually escaped to Sault St. Louis, a village of Christian Indians near Montreal, where she prayed and suffered for God until she died during Holy

Bl. Kateri Tekakwitha

Week. Upon death, the pockmarks on her face disappeared, leaving her "radiant and lovely." She is known as the "Lily of the Mohawks."

APPLE FRITTER AND CARAMEL SUNDAES

½ apple per person	¼ c. milk
¼-½ c. flour	2-3 tsp. cinnamon
1-2 tbs. sugar	vanilla ice cream
jar of caramel sauce	whipped cream or whipped topping
nuts to taste	

Core, peel, and slice apples, and set aside. In a shallow bowl, mix flour, sugar, and cinnamon, and set aside. Pour milk into another shallow bowl. Make an assembly line to allow for an easy process. (In this order: apples, milk, flour mixture, frying pan.) First, dip apples into milk, then place in cinnamon/sugar/flour mixture, making sure to coat each slice completely. Next, gently place the apples into the frying pan and lightly fry in oil. Place the fried apples on top of vanilla ice-cream and top with caramel sauce, whipped cream, and nuts. Yum!

15 July
White — Memorial
St. Bonaventure (1274), Bishop, Doctor of the Church

This Franciscan priest was born around 1218 at Bagnorea in Tuscany. He studied philosophy and theology in Paris and, having earned the title Master, he taught his fellow members of the order of Friars Minor with great success. He was elected Minister General of the order. He was known for his prudence, wisdom, and personal simplicity. After being made Cardinal-Bishop of Albano, he died at the Council of Lyons in 1274. His writings did much to illumine the studies of theology and philosophy.

"Since happiness is nothing other than the enjoyment of the highest good and since the highest good is above, no one can be happy unless he rise above himself, not by ascent of the body, but of the heart." — St. Bonaventure

16 July
Green — Feast
Our Lady of Mt. Carmel

Sacred Scripture celebrated the beauty of Carmel, where the prophet Elijah defended the purity of Israel's faith in the living God. In the twelfth century, hermits withdrew to that mountain and later founded the order devoted to the contemplative life under the patronage of Holy Mother Mary. For information on devotion to the Brown Scapular, see the the "Prayers and Devotions" chapter. In Mary's honor, make a delicious dessert from the recipe on page 122.

21 July
Green
St. Lawrence of Brindisi (1619), Priest, Doctor of the Church

Mary Magdalene

St. Lawrence was born in 1559 and became a Capuchin Friar. He taught theology to his fellow religious, and was chosen to fill positions of leadership in his order. He became famous throughout Europe as an effective preacher. He spoke six languages, had remarkable knowledge of the Bible, and was a writer and diplomat. St. Lawrence was known for his goodness, prudence, simplicity, and devotion to the Blessed Mother.

22 July
White
St. Mary Magdalene (77)

Mary Magdalene was one of Christ's disciples and was present when he died. According to St. Mark, she was the first to see our risen Lord. Devotion to St. Mary Magdalene was widespread in the western Church by the twelfth century.

• Read Mark 16:1-9.

23 July
Green
St. Bridget (1373), Religious

Bridget was born in Sweden in 1303. She married and bore eight children, to whom she was a devoted mother. After her husband's death, she continued to live in the world but became a Third Order Franciscan. She founded a religious order, journeyed to Rome for penance, and became a great model of virtue to all. She also wrote many books in which she related her mystical experiences. She died in Rome.

"The time will come when there will be one flock and one shepherd, one faith and one clear knowledge of God." — St. Bridget

24 July
Green

• See the recipe below to help celebrate the feast day of St. James.

25 July
Red — Feast
St. James (42), Apostle

James, the son of Zebedee and brother of St. John the apostle, was born at Bethsaida. He

---

SEA SCALLOP SUPPER

2-3 lbs. fresh (or frozen) scallops
6 baking potatoes
½ c. butter
2 tsp. instant minced-onion
½ c. flour
2 tsp. salt
⅛ tsp. tabasco sauce
1 tsp. Worcestershire sauce
3 c. milk
1 tsp. dry mustard
2 c. green peas, cooked

Defrost scallops if necessary. Cover with boiling salted water; cook gently 12 to 15 minutes; drain; save broth. Scrub potatoes, rub with butter, and bake at 450° for 50 to 60 minutes. Meanwhile, melt ½-cup butter; add instant minced onion; cook five minutes, but do not allow to brown. Combine flour, salt, and dry mustard; blend in. Add tabasco and Worcestershire sauces. Add milk and one cup scallop broth. Stir over low heat until smooth and thick. Add peas and scallops; heat over hot water 10 minutes. Serve on buttered baked potato halves. (You may serve scallops over pasta instead of potatoes.) Serves six.

— *Recipe from* The Cook's Blessings, *Random House*

was present at most of Christ's miracles and was killed by Herod. He is especially honored in Spain, where a famous church is dedicated to his name. Because of his association with the sea, the cockle shell is regarded as St. James's symbol. Today, make Sea Scallop Supper, using the recipe fon page 124. Any kind of shellfish is fitting for St. James's feast.

26 July
White — Memorial
Saints Ann and Joachim, Parents of the Blessed Virgin

From an ancient tradition going back to the second century, the parents of the Virgin Mary are known as Joachim and Ann. Devotion to St. Ann is found in the sixth century in the East, and by the tenth century it was widespread in the West. St. Joachim was honored at a later date. Brittany, France, which lies on the seashore, is the place which claims to be the birthplace of St. Ann.

29 July
White — Memorial
St. Martha, Virgin

Martha was a sister of Mary and Lazarus. She received the Lord as a guest in Bethany and looked after him with devoted attention. She begged the Lord to raise her brother Lazarus from the dead.

Read Luke 10: 38-42. Let us learn from the lesson Martha was taught and plan a dinner that will place little strain on the cooks, requiring little time to prepare.

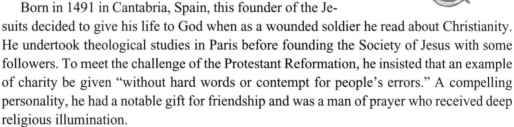

31 July
White — Memorial
St. Ignatius of Loyola (1556), Priest

Born in 1491 in Cantabria, Spain, this founder of the Jesuits decided to give his life to God when as a wounded soldier he read about Christianity. He undertook theological studies in Paris before founding the Society of Jesus with some followers. To meet the challenge of the Protestant Reformation, he insisted that an example of charity be given "without hard words or contempt for people's errors." A compelling personality, he had a notable gift for friendship and was a man of prayer who received deep religious illumination.

"As too great care for bodily things is reprehensible, so reasonable care is to be commended to preserve health for the service of God." — St. Ignatius of Loyola

August

August is devoted to honoring the Immaculate Heart of Mary. The Feast of the Immaculate Heart is officially celebrated on the Saturday following the Feast of the Sacred Heart of Jesus in June. Nevertheless, August is the month to re-consecrate yourself and your family to the Immaculate Heart. Mary's heart, so pure and grace-filled, loves us with a mother's love and desires for all to be united with her Son, Jesus. (See the the "Prayers and Devotions" chapter for information on consecration to Mary.)

1 August
White — Memorial
St. Alphonsus Liguori (1787), Bishop, Doctor of the Church

Alphonsus was born at Naples in 1696. Though renowned as a doctor of both canon and civil law, he left the legal profession and entered the priesthood, subsequently founding the Redemptorist Order. He preached simple sermons and opposed Jansenism, a heresy that overemphasized human sinfulness and was disrespectful of God's grace. He desired to win back sinners by patience and moderation rather than repelling them with severity and fear. Alphonsus wrote books on moral theology, a subject on which he was considered a master.

2 August
Green
St. Eusebius of Vercelli (371), Bishop, Martyr

Born at the beginning of the fourth century in Sardinia, Eusebius became a priest and was elected first Bishop of Vercelli. He spread the Faith by his preaching and established the monastic life in his diocese. He was the first bishop to live with his clergy in an organized community. Because of his faith, he was driven into exile by the emperor and endured much suffering. Upon returning to his country, he worked tirelessly against the Arians.

John Baptist Vianney

4 August
White — Memorial
St. Jean Marie Vianney (1859), Priest

John Vianney was born at Lyons in 1786. He was a devout man, and after being ordained became a parish priest of a lonely, neglected village called Ars, where he lived the rest of his life. He was a great preacher and became renowned as a confessor, spending up to eighteen hours a day in the confessional as tens of thousands flocked to him for counsel. He could read hearts and many miracles of healing were credited to him. St. John Vianney is the patron of parish priests.

• Make a decision to go to confession this week. See the the "Prayers and Devotions" chapter for an examination of conscience. Consider inviting your parish priest for dinner.

"Love of our neighbor consists of three things: to desire the greater good of everyone; to do what good we can when we can; to bear, excuse, and hide others' faults." — St. John Vianney

5 August
Green
Dedication of the Basilica of St. Mary Major (Rome)

After the Council of Ephesus (431), at which Mary was acclaimed "Mother of God," Pope Sixtus III erected a basilica in Rome in her honor. It is the oldest church in the West dedicated to the Blessed Virgin.

6 August
White — Feast
The Feast of the Transfiguration

Today we remember and celebrate the day the Lord appeared radiant in the company of Moses and Elijah. Jesus had taken Peter, James, and John to the top of Mount Tabor. While they watched, Jesus' face began to shine more brightly than the sun and His clothes became white as snow. Suddenly, Moses and Elijah appeared on either side of Jesus. The three spoke for a time with each other about Jesus' coming death and resurrection. When Peter said he wanted to build tents on the spot of this miracle, a voice from heaven said, "This is My beloved Son, with Whom I am well pleased; listen to Him." The apostles were frightened, but Jesus touched them and told them not to fear. As they descended the mountain, the Lord asked them not to tell of their experience until after He had risen from the dead.

• Read the accounts of the Transfiguration: Matthew 17:1-8, Mark 9:2-8, Luke 9:28-36.

7 August
Green
St. Sixtus II (258), Pope and Martyr, and Companions

St. Sixtus II is one of the most revered martyrs in the early Roman Church. A year after he became pope, while celebrating the sacred liturgy in the cemetery of St. Callistus, he was arrested by soldiers carrying out the edict of the Emperor Valerian. He was put to death on the same day with four deacons and buried in the same cemetery.

St. Cajetan (1547), Priest

St. Cajetan was born at Vicenza in 1480. He studied law at Padua, and after being ordained a priest, founded the Congregation of Clerks Regular at Rome to foster the Church's mission. He was prominent among Catholic reformers before the Council of Trent, noted for his earnest prayer and love of neighbor.

8 August
White — Memorial
St. Dominic (1221), Priest

This saint was born in Calaruega, Spain, around the year 1170. He studied theology at Palencia and was made canon of the church at Osma. He is the founder of the Order of Preachers, known as the Dominicans. Through preaching and good example, he fought against the Albigensian heresy, which viewed people as good spirits trapped in evil bodies. He upheld the great importance of women's help in his work and was a man of amazing character, vision, and compassion. His emblem is a star or a dog with a torch in its mouth.

"A man who governs his passions is a master of the world. We must either command them or be enslaved by them. It is better to be a hammer than an anvil." — St. Dominic

Edith Stein

10 August
Red — Feast
Blessed Teresa Benedicta (Edith Stein) (1942), Convert and Religious

Edith Stein was born to a Jewish family. She was an atheist intellectual. She converted to the Catholic Church, became a nun, and was killed by the Nazis in 1942.

"In three ways, woman can fulfill the mission of motherliness: in marriage, in the practice of a profession which values human development . . . and under the veil as the Spouse of Christ." — Edith Stein

St. Lawrence (258), Martyr

A deacon of the church of Rome, Lawrence was martyred on a grill-iron four days after Pope St. Sixtus II. When ordered by the city's prefect to hand over the Church's treasures, he presented them to the poor and sick people. He is the patron of the poor.

In Italy, St. Lawrence's day is celebrated with lasagna. In Spain, duck is served.

11 August
White — Memorial
St. Clare of Assisi (1253), Virgin

Born in Assisi, Italy, in 1193, and hailing from a noble family, Clare was inspired by St. Francis of Assisi and, at age eighteen, followed him in a life of poverty. She is the foundress of the "Poor Claires," the sister order of the Franciscans. St. Clare is depicted in art carrying a monstrance.

14 August
Red
St. Maximilian Mary Kolbe (1941), Priest, Martyr

St. Maximilian was born "Raymond" in 1894 in Poland. When he was only ten, Mary appeared to him and he chose the two crowns she offered him: purity and martyrdom. He had many talents, and after becoming a Franciscan priest, founded entire cities of monk-printers who published many magazines designed to spread devotion to Mary and love for Jesus. In 1941, Maximilan was arrested and sent to Auschwitz, where he offered his life in place of a husband and father who was condemned to die. St. Maximilian was starved to death and died from a lethal injection on the vigil of the Assumption of Mary. He is the patron of media.

15 August
White — Solemnity
Solemnity of Our Lady's Assumption
Holy Day of Obligation — Catholics are to attend Mass today.

Today is the celebration of the fourth Glorious Mystery of the Rosary. The Church infallibly teaches that Mary was assumed — taken up — body and soul into heaven at the end of her life.

• Celebrate with a summer truffle from the recipe below.

16 August
Green
St. Stephen (1308), King of Hungary

Stephen was born at Pannonia around the year 969. After his baptism, he was crowned the King of Hungary in 1000. He married St. Henry II's daughter, Gisela, and worked energetically for the conversion of his people to Christianity. He was just, peaceful, and pious, and founded many dioceses and monasteries.

18 August
Green
St. Jeanne Frances de Chantal (1641), Religious

Happily married, St. "Jane" was left a widow with four children and went to live with her father-in-law. She then met St. Francis de Sales, who became her spiritual director.

CYNTHIA'S SUMMER TRUFFLE

Buy a prepared pound cake.
Make two large packages of vanilla pudding and place in the refrigerator to chill.
Soak the following fruits (or seasonal fruits of your choice) in ¼-cup of brandy:

strawberries
blueberries
raspberries
blackberries
peaches
kiwi
etc. . . .

Whip one pint of heavy whipping cream.
In a tall truffle bowl, layer cake, pudding, berries; cake, pudding, and berries.
Top with whipped cream and berries.

— From the kitchen of Cynthia Hashbarger

Their friendship was very deep and came to be highly regarded by the Church. She eventually took charge of his first convent. St. Francis de Sales said of her, "She is one of the holiest people I have ever met on this earth." *Introduction to the Devout Life* was written for St. Jane by St. Francis de Sales.

"Hell is full of the talented, but Heaven of the energetic." — St. Jeanne de Chantal

19 August
Green
St. John Eudes (1680), Priest

John was born in the diocese of Seez in France in 1601. He gave missions and founded congregations dedicated to improving priestly formation. He also worked with prostitutes, encouraging them to live Christian lives. He took the first step in bringing the devotion to the hearts of Jesus and Mary into the public worship of the Roman Catholic Church.

20 August
Green
St. Bernard of Clairvaux (1153), Abbot and Doctor

Born in 1090 near Dijon, France, Bernard had a religious upbringing and joined the Cistercians in 1111. He was later chosen abbot of the Clairvaux monastery and directed his companions in the practice of virtue by his own good example. In response to the schisms which had arisen in the Church during that time, he traveled around Europe restoring peace and unity. He wrote many spiritual and theological works.

St. Bernard

"If Christ is with us, who is against us? You can fight with confidence where you are sure of victory. With Christ and for Christ victory is certain." — St. Bernard de Clairvaux

21 August
White
Our Lady of Knock (1879)

On the evening of August 21, 1879, in a humble little Irish village known as Knock, a priest's housekeeper, Mary McLoughlin, and thirteen others saw the moving figures of the Blessed Virgin Mother, St. Joseph, and St. John the Evangelist along the south wall of the local church. St. John was standing near an altar with a young lamb upon it, clutching a book, and preaching. Although the onlookers could not hear anything and there was no vocal message, they witnessed the miracle for about one hour. Many were skeptical about the vision but soon after, a little girl was cured of her deafness when her mother touched to the child's ears a piece of concrete from where the Virgin Mother appeared.

St. Pius X (1914), Pope

St. Pius X was born in 1835 in the village of Riese in the province of Venice to a large, poor family. He became a priest and performed his duties with distinction. After becoming bishop of Mantua and patriarch of Venice, he was elected pope in 1903. He fought against modernism, a heresy which denies the unchangeable nature of truth. St. Pius X was noted for his single-mindedness, courage, simplicity, and miracles of healing. He is the most recently canonized pope.

His motto was *"to renew all things in Christ."*

22 August
White — Memorial
Queenship of Mary

Today is the celebration of Mary's coronation — Mary's being crowned queen of heaven and earth. This is the fifth Glorious Mystery of the Rosary. Let us proclaim with the whole Church: *"Blessed are you for your firm believing that the promises of the Lord would be fulfilled."*

• After dinner or before bedtime, pray a litany to Mary as a family. See the the "Prayers and Devotions" chapter for litanies.

POTATOES A LA HUANCAINA

½ c. cottage cheese
1 tsp. onion, finely grated
½ oz. lemon juice
1 small can evaporated milk
10 medium potatoes, boiled
1 tsp. salt
1 tsp. ground chili, no seeds
juice of 1 large orange
2 hard-boiled yolks
½ c. oil

Blend cheese and milk to thick cream, season with chili, onion, salt, egg yolks, lemon juice, and orange juice. Mix together with oil. Cover chopped boiled potatoes with sauce and garnish with olives, radishes, hard-boiled eggs, minced parsley, and lettuce.

— *Recipe courtesy of Carlota Morel*

23 August
Green
St. Rose of Lima (1617), Virgin

St. Rose was born at Lima, Peru, in 1586. At age twenty, she became a lay Dominican and lived in a small hut on the family property. She loved nature, was prayerful, and lived a life of severe penance and contemplation. Her sympathy and service to the poor, the sick, the Indians, and the slaves earned her credit for being the originator of social service in Peru.

St. Rose was the first saint of the Americas to be canonized and she is patroness of South America.

Potatoes *a la Huancaina* is a delicious Peruvian dish to make in honor of St. Rose. See the recipe on page 131.

24 August
Red — Feast
St. Bartholomew (72), Apostle

Born at Cana, Bartholomew was brought to Jesus by the apostle Philip. After our Lord's ascension, he is said to have preached the Gospel in India, where he received the crown of martyrdom.

• Make an Indian recipe called "Chick Pea Curry," shown below.

CHICK PEA CURRY

1 can chick peas
1 tsp. garlic ginger paste (see below)
½ tsp. turmeric powder
1 tsp. Indian chili powder
1 tsp. coriander powder
4 fresh tomatoes, chopped (or 2 cans)
2 small onions, chopped
2 green chilis, chopped
¼ tsp. sugar
1 tsp. cumin powder
¼ tsp. pepper
cilantro for garnish

In olive oil, fry onions until lightly brown. Continue frying, adding spices and chiles. Add tomatoes, then chick peas. Sprinkle with lime or vinegar. Add cilantro.

For the garlic-ginger paste: In a food processor, blend together two peeled garlic cloves with the same amount of fresh ginger-root. Add one to two teaspoons of apple-cider vinegar to keep moist. Store in refrigerator until use.

— *Recipe from* Feasting and Fasting, *Christmas*

---

25 August
Green
St. Louis (1270), King of France

St. Louis was born in 1214 and became king at age twelve. He married and had eleven children, whom he instructed well in the Faith. He was just, merciful, prayerful, and had a love for the poor. King Louis had a high regard for peace, the good of his subjects, and their spiritual welfare.

St. Joseph Calasanz (1648), Priest

St. Joseph was born at Aragon in 1557. Well-educated, he became a priest and founded a society dedicated to the education of poor boys. His schools were set up in four countries. He endured many trials at the hands of those who were jealous of his success. He died in Rome.

27 August
Green — Memorial
St. Monica (387), Mother and Witness

Monica was born of a Christian family at Tagaste in Africa in 331. As a young woman, she married Patricius and had children, one named Augustine. She was a virtuous mother and witness to the Faith by her prayers and good deeds. She cried many tears and prayed constantly for the conversion of her son Augustine (who became the famous saint) and husband, Patricius. Eventually, both men were converted to Christ.

• Today, women should ask St. Monica to join them in praying for their husbands, children, and loved ones to become more deeply converted to the Lord.

28 August
White
St. Augustine (430), Bishop, Doctor of the Church

The son of St. Monica, Augustine was born at Tagaste in Africa in 354. He lived a rebellious life, but searching for truth, he eventually converted to the Faith at Milan, where he was instructed and baptized by St. Ambrose. Returning to his homeland, he became a bishop and for thirty-four years guided his flock with pastoral authority and compassion. He lived under strict rule, preached, prepared catechumens, fought bravely against errors of his time, and explained the Faith carefully and clearly through his writings. He is the patron of theology. Read his *Confessions* for more information on his life and conversion.

"Too late have I loved Thee, O Beauty of ancient days, yet ever new! Too late have I loved Thee! And lo! Thou wert within and I abroad searching for Thee. Thou wert with me, but I was not with Thee." — St. Augustine

29 August
Red — Memorial
The Beheading of St. John the Baptist, Martyr

St. John the Baptist prepared the way for Christ (his cousin) by preaching repentance and baptizing in the Jordan River. After baptizing Jesus, John was imprisoned by Herod for preaching against Herod's marriage to his brother's wife, Herodias. Herod's fear of John was overcome by his need to please Herodias's daughter, whose wish he had promised to grant after she danced for him. At the advice of her mother, she asked for the head of John the Baptist on a platter. John was beheaded in jail.

• Read the account in Mark 6:14-29.

September

September is the month of Our Lady of Sorrows. We remember Mary's suffering and her broken heart as she watched her innocent son be ridiculed, misunderstood, and put to death. She is our model for uniting our suffering to Christ and the cross. Mary also gave birth to the Church by standing by her son and accepting the will of the Father. This month, take some time to contemplate the seven sorrows of Mary, shown on page 38.

3 September
Green — Memorial
St. Gregory the Great (604), Pope and Doctor

St. Gregory was born around the year 540 in Rome. He entered monastic life, was ordained a deacon, and became pope in 590. He proved to be a true shepherd by carrying out his office, helping the poor, and spreading and strengthening the Faith. He wrote extensively on moral and theological subjects.

He said:

"There are some who wish to be humble, but without being despised, who wish to be happy with their lot, but without being needy, who wish to be chaste, without mortifying the body, to be patient without suffering. They want both to acquire virtues and to avoid the sacrifices those virtues involve: they are like soldiers who flee the battlefield and try to win the war from the comfort of the city." — St. Gregory the Great

8 September
White — Feast
Birth of the Blessed Virgin Mary

Today, celebrate the birth of our Holy Mother Mary! There are many symbols that represent the purity and virtue of the Blessed Mother. Some of the most popular are: a lily of the valley, a crown with twelve stars, a Rosary, or a rose without thorns. There are many others, too. Can you think of more?

• Make a special dinner, since it is a feast day. You might prepare a birthday cake in honor of Mary's birth.

9 September
White
St. Peter Claver (1654), Priest

It was St. Alphonsus Rodriguez who encouraged the young Jesuit Peter Claver to concentrate on the needs of the New World. In 1610, Peter landed in what is now Colombia (then called Cartagena). He witnessed the great injustice to the African victims being sold into slavery, and vowed to be "the slave to the black people forever."

He also cared for the imprisoned and hospitalized. He is remembered for his great compassion for those suffering, and people of all colors and walks of life.

13 September
White
St. John Chrysostom (407), Bishop, Doctor of the Church.

St. John was born in Antioch around 349. Well-educated, he became a priest and was elected bishop of Constantinople in 397. Envied by his enemies, he was forced into exile twice by the hatred of the imperial court. He was renowned for his preaching and writing, in which he explained Catholic doctrine and the Christian life. *Chrysostom* means "golden mouth." He is the patron of orators.

14 September
Red
The Triumph of the Holy Cross (629)

There are over sixty styles of crosses used in art and culture throughout history. A crucifix is a cross with the image of the suffering Christ, nailed to the cross with arms outstretched. Since crucifixions were still frequent during the first three centuries of the early Church, the crucifix was not used in art until the fourth century. Since the eleventh century, crucifixes have been placed on or above the altar to remind the faithful of Christ's great sacrifice and triumph. The true cross was excavated by St. Helena around 326 A.D.

• It might be fun to plan an evening activity of processing around the house with the youngest child holding a crucifix and the family following while singing a Christian song.

15 September
White — Memorial
Our Lady of Sorrows

Review the seven sorrows of Mary on page 38. See the section on the sixth Friday in Lent. Simeon said to Mary, *"And thy own soul a sword shall pierce. . . ."* — Luke 2: 35

16 September
Red — Memorial
St. Cornelius (253), Pope, Martyr

St. Cornelius became pope in 251. With the help of Cyprian, he fought against the Novatian schismatics, a group that taught that no one who left the Faith could ever be reconciled with the Church. Driven into exile by the Emperor Gallus, he died at Civitavecchia. His body was brought to Rome and buried in the cemetery of St. Callistus.

St. Cyprian (258), Bishop, Martyr

St. Cyprian was born of pagan parents in Carthage around 210. He was converted, ordained, and subsequently made bishop of that city.

He guided the Church through difficult times with his writings and actions. In the Valerian persecution, he was exiled, then martyred.

17 September
St. Robert Bellarmine (1621), Bishop, Doctor of the Church

St. Robert Bellarmine

Born in 1542 in the town of Montepulciano in Tuscany, Robert Bellarmine was the third of ten children in a family where prayer and serving others were priorities. He became a Jesuit and distinguished himself by brilliant defenses of the Faith. He was advisor to five different popes. He was involved in all sorts of controversies, including the teachings of Galileo the scientist, who was a friend of St. Robert. He became a cardinal and was named Bishop of Capua.

"The school of Christ is the school of charity. In the last day, when the general examination takes place. . . . Charity will be the whole syllabus." — St. Robert Bellarmine

19 September
Green
St. Januarius (Gennaro) (305), Bishop, Martyr

Little is known about St. Januarius, except that he was a bishop of Benevento (near Naples, Italy) and was probably martyred during the persecutions under Diocletian around 305. Today he is especially venerated in Naples, where he is the patron. There, in a church, it is reported that every year on his feast day, St. Januarius's blood liquefies. His protection is sought when there is the danger of volcanic eruption.

20 September
Red
St. Andre Kim Taegon (1839), Priest, Martyr
St. Paul Chong Hasang and Companions (died between 1839-1867)

Known as the "Korean martyrs," these missionaries were put to death for their refusal to renounce the Faith. The companions of Paul Chong Hasang numbered one hundred three. The presence of Catholicism in Korea is due to the unfailing courage of these zealous Christians.

• Find Korea on the map and pray for all those who live there.

21 September
Red
St. Matthew (65), Apostle and Evangelist

St. Matthew was born at Capernaum and was working as a tax collector when he was called by Jesus. Most tax collectors were hated by the Jews because they worked for the Romans, who had conquered the land. The temptation to riches was great and many tax collectors were dishonest. Matthew, also known as Levi, was called by Jesus to go out and spread the Gospel to others. Matthew wrote the Gospel of Matthew in Hebrew and is said to have preached in the East. His shrine is in Salerno, Italy, and he is the patron of bankers.

"[Jesus] saw a man named Matthew sitting at the tax office; and he said to him 'Follow me.' And he rose and followed him." — Matthew 9:9

24 September
Green
Our Lady of Ransom (1218)

"Only he who ponders things in his heart with a true Christian spirit can discover the immense riches of the interior world, the world of grace, that hidden treasure which is within us all. . . . It was by pondering things in her heart that Mary, as time went on, grew in her understanding of the mystery, in sanctity and in unity with God." — F. Suarez, *Mary of Nazareth*

26 September
Green
Saints Cosmas And Damian (circa 303), Martyrs

Not much is known about these two saints except that they suffered martyrdom for their faith in Syria sometime during the persecution of Diocletian. Supposedly, Cosmas and Damian were twin brothers who were born in Arabia and studied and practiced medicine in Syria. They brought their belief in Christ to those they ministered to.

According to ancient documents the tombs of Cosmas and Damian is at Cyrrhus in Syria. There a basilica stands in their honor. Devotion to these martyrs spread to Rome and from there through the whole Church. They are the patrons of pharmacists and doctors.

27 September
White
St. Vincent de Paul (1660), Priest

St. Vincent de Paul was born in Gascony (France) in 1580, the son of peasant farmers. He was educated by the Franciscans and became a priest at age twenty. Planning for a life of security and ease in his priesthood, it took the help of a wise friend to make him understand what true Christianity meant. After working in a poor, small parish, he organized charitable confraternities, groups who would provide the poor with clothes and food on a regular basis. St. Vincent also organized priests to go to the poor sections of town and preach to the people so they would be spiritually fed. At night he would search the city for abandoned babies and find homes for them. He cared for prisoners, began hospitals and homes for orphans and the aged, and found the Congregation of the Daughters of Charity. He remained good friends with many of the rich and influential and involved them in the work for the needy.

He was canonized by Pope Clement XII in 1737. He died in Paris and is the patron of charitable societies.

"Extend mercy toward others, so that there is no one in need whom we meet without helping. For what hope is there for us if God should withdraw his mercy from us." — St. Vincent

28 September
Green
St. Wenceslaus (935), King of Bohemia, Martyr

St. Wenceslaus was born in Bohemia (modern-day Czechoslovakia) around the year 907. After his father's death when he was young, his mother ruled the kingdom, favoring the anti-Christian factions. He was brought up as a Christian by his grandmother, and he began his rule around the year 925. Making peace with his mother, he worked in close cooperation with the Church, ended the persecution of Christians, brought back exiled priests, and built churches. Known as the "Good King," he gave alms, was just to the poor and rich, visited prisoners, and promoted the Faith. Eventually, he was betrayed by his brother Boleslaus and killed by assassins. He was immediately recognized as a martyr and is venerated as the patron of Bohemia.

The Holy Angels: Saints Michael, Gabriel, and Raphael, the Archangels ("Come Let Us Worship the Lord in the Company of His Angels!")

St. Raphael the Archangel

Revelation reveals that the angels are grouped into nine choirs and form three hierarchies around the throne of God:

First Hierarchy: the Seraphim, the Cherubim, and the Thrones.

Second Hierarchy: the Dominations, the Virtues, and the Powers.

Third Hierarchy: the Principalities, the Archangels, and the Angels.

The archangels are entrusted with the more important missions to mankind. In times of temptation and for protection, people pray to Michael. For safety in travel and to do God's will, people turn to Gabriel. For healing of sickness and finding a spouse, people turn to Raphael. These angels help to ensure us that God cares and is with His people.

30 September
White
St. Jerome (420), Priest, Doctor of the Church

St. Jerome was born at Striden in Dalmatia (Italy) around the year 340. He studied the classical authors at Rome, and was baptized there. He embraced a life of asceticism and went to the East, where he was ordained a priest. Returning to Rome, he became a secretary to Pope Damasus. At Rome he began to translate the entire Scriptures into Latin and to promote the monastic life. Eventually he settled in Bethlehem, where he served the needs of the Church. He wrote many works, but one of his greatest services was translating the Bible so more people could read it. St. Jerome had a great love of the Church. He died in Bethlehem and is hailed as the patron of librarians.

October

This is the month of the Holy Rosary. The Universal Church celebrates the Feast of the Holy Rosary this month to highlight this beautiful prayer form, which dates back to the Virgin Mother's appearance to St. Dominic in 1214. Traditionally, Catholics have honored Mary by observing the Fátima devotion: attending Mass, going to confession, meditating for fifteen minutes on one of the mysteries, and the recitation of the Rosary on the first Saturday of five consecutive months. Reacquaint yourself with the beautiful message, story, and miracle of Fátima. Remind your children that Lucia, Francesco, and Jacinta were only ten, nine, and seven years old when Our Lady appeared to them, yet they were brave and faithful. *The Day the Sun Danced* is a good video for children about the Fátima story. If you do nothing else this month, pray for a love of the Rosary, because it is undoubtedly a powerful prayer for family life, peace, and unity. Mary's intercession is the most powerful of all the angels and saints.

"Hail Mary, full of grace, the Lord is with thee. Blessed art thou among women and blessed is the fruit of thy womb, Jesus. Holy Mary, Mother of God, pray for us sinners now and at the hour of our death. Amen."

1 October
Green
St. Thérèse of Lisieux (1897)

Thérèse Martin was born in Alençon, France, in 1873. When she was only four years old, her mother died and she took the Blessed Virgin Mary as her mother. While still a young girl, she joined two of her sisters at the Carmelite monastery at Lisieux, and took the name Thérèse of the Child Jesus. There she lived a life of humility, evangelical simplicity, and trust in God. By word and example she taught these virtues to the novices of the community. Offering her life for the salvation of souls and the growth of the Church, she died at the age of twenty-four. She is the patroness of missions and is known as the "Little Flower." Before she died, she said that she would "spend her Heaven doing good on earth."

• Today, place a rose or fresh flowers in your home in honor of St. Thérèse.

"Our Lord does not come down from Heaven every day to lie in a golden ciborium. He comes to find another heaven which is infinitely dearer to Him — the heaven of our souls."
— St. Thérèse of Lisieux

2 October

White

Feast of the Guardian Angels

"Come Let Us Worship the Lord, Whom the Angels Serve."

Angel means "messenger." St. Jerome wrote that the human soul is so valuable that everyone has a guardian angel from the moment they come into being. Guardian angels assist us in our work or study. In times of temptation, these spiritual beings direct us to do good. They are best known for protecting us from physical danger, but their main role is to care for our salvation. The angels also offer prayers to God for us. Let us love our guardian angels and ask for their help every day.

"Behold, I send an angel before you, to guard you on the way and to bring you to the place which I have prepared. Give heed to him and harken to his voice. . . ." — Exodus 23:20-21

"Get into the habit of praying to the Guardian Angel of each person you are concerned about. His angel will help him to be good, faithful and cheerful." — Josemaría Escrivá, *The Forge.*

4 October

White

St. Francis of Assisi (1226), Founder of the Franciscan Orders and Poor Clares

Francis was born at Assisi in 1182, the son of a wealthy cloth merchant and devout, loving mother. He learned to enjoy life and dreamed of being a noble knight. After becoming a soldier, he realized it was not what he had expected and eventually he heard God's call to him to "rebuild the Church." He led a life of evangelical poverty and preached the love of God to all. He found his heavenly Father in everyone and every creature, as well as in nature itself. He established a rule which a number of his companions followed and which gained approval of the Holy See. Subsequently, he founded an order of nuns and a society of lay people. His energy, cheerfulness, playfulness, and liveliness were supported by a life of deep prayer and penance. He is the patron of peace and unity, animals, and nature.

St. Francis

Prayer for Peace of St. Francis of Assisi:

Lord, make me an instrument of your peace.
Where there is hatred, let me sow love.
Where there is injury, pardon.
Where there is doubt, faith.
Where there is despair, hope.
Where there is darkness, light.
Where there is sadness, joy.
O Divine Master,
grant that I may not so much seek
to be consoled as to console;

to be understood as to understand;
to be loved as to love.
For it is in giving that we receive;
it is in pardoning that we are pardoned;
and it is in dying that we are born to eternal life.

6 October
Green
St. Bruno (1101), Priest

St. Bruno was born at Cologne about the year 1035. He was educated at Paris and, after ordination to the priesthood, he taught theology for eighteen years. St. Hugh of Grenoble and Pope Urban II were two of his disciples. He desired a solitary life, however, and, with six companions, built a small chapel and hermitage where they could live a quiet life of prayer. He was summoned to Rome by Pope Urban II, where he aided the pontiff in meeting the needs of the Church. He showed a talent for friendship. He is considered the founder of the Carthusian monks and is the patron of those possessed by evil spirits.

7 October
White
Our Lady of the Rosary

This feast was established by St. Pius V, who was able to unite Spain, Venice, and the Church States in a naval expedition to fight the troublesome, anti-Christian Ottoman Turks. The battle took place in 1571 at the same time that the Rosary Confraternity of Rome was meeting at the Dominican headquarters. They recited the Rosary for the special intention that the Christians would win the battle. The Turks were defeated and the credit was given to the intercessory prayer of Our Lady. Pope Pius V dedicated the day as one of thanksgiving to Our Lady of Victory. Later, Pope Gregory XIII changed the name of the feast to "Our Lady of the Rosary." Mary accepted the will of God perfectly. Mary's intercession is powerful and we should go to her with all our needs, as she is our spiritual mother. Meditating on the mysteries of the Rosary unites us with Christ.

• Pray a family Rosary. If time is short, pray a decade.

9 October
Green
St. Denis (95), Bishop, Martyr, and His Companions, Martyrs

St. Gregory of Tours relates that St. Denis came to France from Rome in the middle of the third century. He preached and organized the Church in Paris and became the first bishop there. During a persecution, he was beheaded. He became a popular saint and France took him as its patron. An abbey was built in his honor and many miracles were attributed to his intercession. St. Denis is invoked against demons.

141

St. John Leonardi (1609), Priest

St. John was born at Lucca in Tuscany in 1541. He was originally a pharmacist and later became a priest. In 1574 he founded the Order of Clerics Regular of the Mother of God, an undertaking which caused him many hardships. He was also associated with the founding of the first society of priests dedicated to working in foreign missions. Under subsequent popes this small order grew into the Society for the Propagation of the Faith, and for this reason John is often called the founder. In addition to these efforts, he restored discipline in different religious congregations by his charity and wisdom. He died in Rome.

14 October
Green
St. Callistus (222), Pope, Martyr

St. Callistus was a slave to a Christian master who noticed that he was skilled at finance and put him in charge of a bank. He tried to escape Rome when he was falsely accused of embezzlement, and after being caught was condemned to working in the mines. Once he obtained his liberty, he was ordained a deacon by Pope Zephyrinus and actually succeeded him as pope. Hippolytus and his followers were shocked that Callistus had been chosen and the group elected Hippolytus as pope, making Hippolytus the first anti-pope. This schism went on for eighteen years. He fought against the Adoption and Modalist heretics. The Adoption heretics viewed Christ as a good man "adopted" by God, and the Modalists wrongly defined the Trinity as one Divine Person acting in three various ways. He was crowned with martyrdom in 222 and was buried on the Aurelian Way.

15 October
Green — Memorial
St. Teresa of Ávila (1582), Virgin, Doctor of the Church

St. Teresa was born in Ávila, Spain, in 1515. She joined the Carmelite Order, made great progress in the way of perfection and enjoyed mystical revelations. When she reformed the order, she met with much resistance, but she succeeded with undaunted courage. She also wrote books filled with sublime doctrine, the fruit of her own spiritual life. She died at Ávila.

She is the patroness of headache sufferers.

When the cart she was riding in overturned during a journey to found a Carmelite convent, St. Teresa was heard to say to God, *"No wonder you have so few friends, since this is the way you treat them!"*

16 October
Green
St. Margaret Mary Alacoque (1690), Religious

St. Margaret Mary was born in 1647 in the diocese of Autun, France. She joined the Sisters of the Visitation at Paray-le-Monial, where she advanced in the life of perfection, and was favored with mystical revelations. She was especially devoted to the Sacred Heart of Jesus and was responsible for spreading the devotion throughout the Church.

St. Hedwig (1243), Religious

St. Hedwig was born in Bavaria around the year 1174. She married a prince of Silesia and had seven children. She led a most devoted life, looking after the poor and sick, and founding hospitals for them. When her husband died, she entered the monastery of Trebnitz, where she died.

Today, make heart-shaped cookies or cakes in honor of the Sacred Heart of Jesus, the devotion started by St. Margaret Mary.

17 October
Red — Memorial
St. Ignatius of Antioch (107), Bishop, Martyr

St. Ignatius was a successor of St. Peter as bishop of Antioch. He was condemned to death and brought to Rome for execution, where he was martyred on the order of Emperor Trajan by being thrown to wild animals. On the journey to Rome he wrote seven letters to different churches. In these he discussed Christ, the structure of the Church, and the Christian life in a manner at once wise and learned. At Antioch, this day was observed in his memory as early as the fourth century.

"Be eager for more frequent gatherings for thanksgiving to God and His glory. For when we meet thus, the forces of Satan are annulled and his destructive power is canceled in the concord of your faith." — St. Ignatius of Antioch

18 October
Red
St. Luke, Evangelist, Martyr

St. Luke was born of a pagan family. Converted to the Faith, he became a fellow-worker of the apostle Paul. From St. Paul's preaching he compiled one of the Gospels. He handed down an account of the beginning of the Church in another work, the Acts of the Apostles,

---

BANBURY TARTS

1 c. sugar	2 tsp. cornstarch
1 c. raisins	1 egg
2 saltine crackers	grated peel and juice of 1 lemon
2 packages pie crust mix	

Combine sugar and cornstarch; add raisins. Beat egg slightly; add to mixture. Crumble saltine crackers; add lemon juice and peel. Cook over hot water, stirring constantly, until thick.

Prepare pie crust according to directions on package; roll out ⅛-inch thick on floured board. Cut into four-inch squares. Place a spoonful of raisin mixture on each square. Fold over to make triangle. Press edges together with fork. Prick tops with design. Bake on cookie sheet at 425° for 10 to 15 minutes or until golden brown. Makes 12.

— *Recipe from* The Cook's Blessings, *Random House*

---

which tells of events up to the time of St. Paul's first sojourn in Rome. He is the patron of doctors and painters.

• Some of the great friars of England were placed under St. Luke's patronage, so the famous Banbury Tarts, which rank high in British culinary, can be served today. See the recipe on page 143.

19 October
Red
Saints Isaac Jogues (1647), John de Brébeuf (1648), and Companions (1649), Priests, Martyrs of North America

Between the years 1642 and 1649, eight members of the Society of Jesus were killed in North America, after fearful torture by members of the Huron and Iroquois tribes. These men were dedicated to working among and bringing God's word to these tribes. After being tortured, Isaac Jogues returned to the area where he had tried so hard to bring the natives to the true Faith.

20 October
Green
St. Paul of the Cross (1775), Priest, Founder of the Passionists

St. Paul of the Cross was born at Ovada in Liguria (Italy) in 1694. As a young man he helped his father, who was a merchant. However, aspiring to a life of perfection, he left all behind and brought together a group of associates who joined with him in caring for the poor and the sick. After he became a priest, he worked even more earnestly for the salvation of souls by founding homes, exercising apostolic zeal, and afflicting himself with harsh penances.

He is the founder of the Passionists. He died in Rome.

23 October
Green
St. John of Capistrano (1456), Priest

St. John was born in Capistrano in the Abruzzi (Italy) in 1386. He studied law at Perugia and for a time was governor of that city. He entered the Order of Friars Minor and, after ordination to the priesthood, he led an untiring apostolic life preaching throughout Europe both to strengthen Christian life and to refute heresy. He died at Villach in Austria.

24 October
Green
St. Anthony Mary Claret (1870), Bishop of Cuba

St. Anthony Claret was born at Sallent in Spain in 1807. After being ordained a priest he traveled many years through Catalonia, preaching to the people. He founded a society of missionaries and, after being named a bishop in Cuba, won renown for his pastoral seal. After returning to Spain, he continued to work for the Church. He died at Fontfroide in France in 1870.

28 October
Red
St. Simon snd St. Jude, Apostles

The name of St. Simeon usually appears eleventh in the list of apostles. Nothing is known of him except that he was born at Cana and is surnamed "The Zealot." St. Jude, also called Thaddeus, was the apostle who asked the Lord at the Last Supper why he had manifested himself only to his disciples and not to the whole world. Read John 14:22.

31 October
Green
All Saints Day Eve

Instead of a Halloween party, have an All Saints Day party! Have the children dress up as saints and biblical characters. Play "guess the saint." Players have to ask questions in order to find out who person is dressed as. This is a great way for children to have fun and appreciate what the real celebration is all about.

November

This month is dedicated to the Holy Souls. The Church has always prayed for the dead and we must remember to pray for those who have gone before us, especially our loved ones and those souls in purgatory who are waiting to enter the fullness of God's glory. Our prayers and sacrifices can help them to gain heaven faster, because all believers in Christ are part of His body and are joined in the communion of saints.

1 November
White — Solemnity
The Solemnity of All Saints — Holy Day of Obligation

Make a special attempt to really celebrate this solemnity for the saints. Have an especially nice dinner with linens and candles. Explain how we owe so much to the great saints, known and unknown. Perhaps during or after dinner, each member of the family can share a favorite saint story.

2 November
White
Feast of All Souls

This is a great day to pray for the dead. Catholics believe that prayer helps souls in purgatory obtain heaven. A great tool to explain the concept of purgatory is the *Catechism of the Catholic Church*: ". . . After death they undergo purification, so as to achieve the holiness necessary to enter the joy of heaven. The Church gives the name *Purgatory* to this final purification of the elect [those on the way to heaven], which is entirely different from the punishment of the damned [Cf. Council of Florence (1439): DS 1304; Council of Trent (1563): DS 1820; (1547): 1580; see also Benedict XII, *Benedictus Deus* (1336): DS 1000]" (CCC 1030-1031). (See also the *Catechism* 1032; 1 Corinthians 3:15; 1 Peter 1:7; and 2 Maccabees 12:46 for scriptural references to purgatory.)

3 November
Green
St. Martin de Porres (1639), Religious

St. Martin de Porres was born in Lima, Peru, of a Spanish father and a Negro mother in 1579. As a boy, he studied medicine, which later, as a member of the Dominican Order, he put to good use in helping the poor. He led a humble and disciplined life and was devoted to the Holy Eucharist.

He is the patron of hairdressers and of South America.

• On your globe, find South America and name the countries.

4 November
White
St. Charles Borromeo (1584), Bishop

St. Charles Borromeo was born at Arona in Lombardy in the year 1538. After having taken honors in both civil and canon law, he was made cardinal and bishop of Milan by his uncle, Pope Pius IV.

A true pastor of his flock, he tirelessly promoted Christian life by the reform of his diocese, convocation of synods, and promulgation of regulations intended to foster the Church's mission. He is the patron of seminarians.

"If you wish to make any progress in the service of God we must begin every day of our life with new ardor." — St. Charles Borromeo

---

HORSESHOE COOKIES

1 c. butter
½ c. powdered sugar
2 tsp. vanilla
½ tsp. salt
1 c. quick-cooking rolled oats, uncooked
2 c. sifted all-purpose flour

Cream butter and sugar until fluffy. Stir in vanilla, flour, and salt. Blend in rolled oats.

Roll out to ¼-inch thick on floured board. Cut in strips six inches long and ½-inch wide. On ungreased cookie sheet, shape strips to resemble horseshoes. Bake at 325° for 20 to 25 minutes. Remove carefully, as they break easily. Makes three dozen.

— *Recipe from* The Cook's Blessings, *Random House*

---

9 November
White
Dedication of St. John Lateran Basilica

The anniversary of the dedication of the Lateran Basilica, which was erected by the Emperor Constantine, has been observed on this day since the twelfth century. This feast was at first observed only in Rome. Later, in honor of the basilica (which is called the mother church of Christendom), the celebration was extended to the whole Church. This action was taken as a sign of devotion to and of unity with the Chair of Peter which, as St. Ignatius of Antioch wrote, "presides over the whole assembly of charity."

Pope Leo the Great

10 November
White
St. Leo the Great (461), Pope, Doctor of the Church

St. Leo was probably born in Rome and was raised to the See of Peter in 440. He was a true pastor and father of souls. He labored strenuously to safeguard the integrity of the Faith and vigorously defend the unity of the Church. He pushed back or at least softened the onrush of the barbarians. He has then deservedly won the title "the Great."

11 November
White
St. Martin of Tours (397), Bishop

St. Martin of Tours was born in Pannonia (modern Hungary) of pagan parents around the year 316. Having became a soldier at age fifeen, he later gave up military life and was baptized. Soon after, he founded a monastery at Liguge in France, where he led a monastic life under the direction of St. Hilary. He was ordained a priest and chosen bishop of Tours. He provided an example of the ideal good pastor, founding other monasteries, educating the clergy, and preaching the Gospel to the poor. He is the patron of soldiers and the uncle of Ireland's St. Patrick.

In Poland, rich cookies are shaped like horseshoes to remember St. Martin's snow-white horse, on which he "comes riding through the snow" when one least expects him. See the recipe on page 146.

12 November
Green
St. Josaphat (1623), Bishop and Martyr

St. Josaphat was born in the Ukraine of Orthodox parents about the year 1580. Embracing the Catholic faith, he became a Basilian monk. Ordained to the priesthood and chosen bishop of Polock, he worked faithfully for the unity of the Church. Enemies plotted his death, and he was martyred in 1623.

13 November
White
St. Frances Xavier Cabrini (1917), Virgin

St. Frances Xavier Cabrini was born in Lombardy, Italy, in 1850. At Codogno, Italy, she founded the Missionary Sisters of the Sacred Heart in 1880. By 1887, she had established many schools, hospitals, and orphanages. With the encouragement of Leo XIII, she set out in 1889 for the United States, where for the next twenty-eight years she established many schools, hospitals, and orphanages. Her missionary spirit also led her to South America, where she founded schools in Argentina, Brazil, and Nicaragua. Mother Cabrini died in Chicago. On July 7, 1946, she became the first United States citizen to be canonized. She is the patroness of immigrants.

"Give me a heart as big as the universe!" — St. Frances Cabrini

14 November
Green
• In honor of St. Margaret Queen of Scotland, whose feast is this month, make scones. See the recipe below.

15 November
Green
St. Albert the Great (1280), Bishop, Doctor of the Church

St. Albert was born in Lauingen along the Danube about the year 1206. Having studied at Padua and Paris, he entered the Order of Preachers and excelled as a teacher. Ordained bishop of Ratisbon, he strove earnestly to establish peace among peoples and between cit-

---

SCONES

6 c. flour
6 tsp. baking powder
1½ tsp. salt
1½ c. milk
1 c. raisins (or currants)
1 c. sugar
1 rounded tsp. baking soda
1 c. margarine
2 large eggs

Mix dry ingredients. Cut in margarine until it has consistency of cornmeal. Add wet ingredients all at once. Knead 25 to 30 times. Pat out dough into large square about one-inch thick, then cut into squares or circles. Bake on greased cookie sheet at 450° for 10 minutes.

— Recipe from the kitchen of Maureen Coughlin

---

ies. He wrote brilliantly on many subjects to the advantage of sacred and secular sciences alike, and died at Cologne. He is the patron of scientists.

16 November
Green
St. Margaret of Scotland (1093), Queen

St. Margaret was born around the year 1046 in Hungary, where her father had been exiled. When she fled from her native country, her ship capsized during a bad storm along the shores of Scotland, where she was found by the king's men. King Malcolm III of Scotland fell in love with her; they married and had eight children. Queen Margaret was an ideal mother and queen. She died at Edinburgh in 1093. She is the patroness of large families and invoked for the death and dying of children.

St. Gertrude the Great (1301), Religious

St. Gertrude was born at Eisleben in Thuringia (Germany) in 1256. As a young girl she was received into the Cistercian nuns at Helfta and applied herself to her studies, concentrating on literature and philosophy. Devoting her life to God, she dedicated herself to the pursuit of perfection, and gave herself over to prayer and contemplation.

17 November
White
St. Elizabeth of Hungary (1231), Religious

St. Elizabeth, born in 1207, was the daughter of Andrew, king of Hungary. While still a young girl she was married to Louis the Landgrave of Thuringia, and gave birth to three children. She enjoyed a passionate and devoted marriage with her husband and, besides her family duties, devoted herself to prayer and meditation. After her husband died, she embraced a life of poverty, erecting a hospital in which she herself served the sick. She died in Marburg.

18 November
Green
Dedication of the Basilica of Saints Peter and Paul, Apostles (1626, 1854)

Anniversaries of dedication were celebrated in the Vatican Basilica of St. Peter and in the Basilica of St. Paul on the Ostian Way as early as the twelfth century. The two basilicas had been completed under popes Sylvester and Siricius in the fourth century. More recently this commemoration was extended to the entire Latin Rite. Just as the Maternity of the Virgin Mother of God is celebrated on the anniversary of the Basilica of St. Mary Major (August 5), so on this day we honor the two princes of Christ's apostles.

21 November
White
Presentation of the Blessed Virgin Mary

This feast commemorates the dedication of the Church of St. Mary, which was built in Jerusalem near the site of the Temple. With Christians of the East, the Latin Church also recalls on this day the tradition that Mary was presented as a small child to the Lord in the temple by her parents.

22 November
Red
St. Cecilia (230), Virgin, Martyr

In the fifth century a basilica dedicated to St. Cecilia was erected at Rome. From that time devotion to her spread, largely owing to accounts of her sufferings. She is praised as a great model for Christian women because of her virginity and the martyrdom she suffered for love of Christ. She is the patroness of musicians.

23 November
Green
St. Clement I (100), Pope

St. Clement I, the third pope to rule the Roman Catholic Church after St. Peter, reigned toward the end of the first century. He wrote the famous epistle to the Corinthians to strengthen and encourage peace and unity among them. He is the patron of marble workers.

St. Columban (615), Abbot

St. Columban was born in Ireland before the middle of the sixth century. He was well-trained in the classics and theology. He went to France and founded many monasteries, which he ruled with strict discipline. After being forced into exile, he went to Italy and founded the monastery of Bobbio.

EUGENIE'S JAMBALAYA

1 finely chopped large onion
½ finely chopped green pepper
4 cloves of garlic
1 12 oz. can of V8 tomato juice
1½ c. raw rice
3 tbs. chopped parsley
2 bay leaves
1 small can of tomato sauce
2-3 lbs. raw shrimp, cleaned and deveined
salt and pepper to taste

In a large deep skillet or Dutch oven, sauté onion and green pepper. Add garlic, parsley, and bay leaves. Drain off grease. Add small can of tomato sauce and cook for 10 minutes. Then add ¾ can of V8 juice. Add 1½ iced-tea glasses of water, salt, pepper, and shrimp. Cook about one hour. Add rice and bring to a boil. Lower fire and cover, stirring now and then. Takes about 45 minutes. Add the remaining V8 juice if it looks dry and rice is not yet cooked.

— *Recipe in loving memory of Eugenie Pagnac*

---

25 November
Green
St. Catherine of Alexandria (307), Virgin, Martyr, Patroness of Philosophers
St. Catherine Labouré (1870), Virgin, Saint of the Miraculous Medal

St. Catherine Labouré belonged to Daughters of Charity, an order founded by St. Vincent de Paul. On July 18, 1830, the Blessed Virgin appeared to her, encouraging her to be strong in the upcoming persecutions in France. On November 27, Our Lady appeared again, this time asking that a medal be made in the model of her image.

Catherine's spiritual director refused to believe her, but eventually the medals were made and the order of the "Children of Mary" was formed. In 1876, Mary came to her for the last time, this time to escort St. Catherine to heaven.

26 November
White
The Solemnity of Christ the King

In 1925, this feast was initiated by Pope Pius XI to counteract the growing secularism and atheism of the times. It was a bold proclamation in the face of Mussolini's (a dictator of the Italian states) attempt to make himself a grand king.

30 November
Red
St. Andrew, Apostle

Born at Bethsaida, Andrew was a disciple of John the Baptist before becoming a follower of Christ, to whom he also brought his brother Peter. With Philip he presented the Gentiles to Christ and, before the miracle in the desert, it was Andrew who pointed out to Christ the boy carrying the loaves and fishes. After Pentecost he preached the Gospel in many lands and was put to death by crucifixion at Ache. He is the patron of fisherman.

• Remembering St. Andrew's role at the miracle of the loaves and fishes, serve jambalaya from the recipe found on page 150.

December

This has traditionally been the month to reflect on the Divine Infancy. At this time, preparations are being made for the celebration of Christ's birth. Pray that all nations will come to respect life from conception to natural death, and that children will be cared for properly. For those struggling with financial difficulties, the Christ-child is often invoked.

This month, the Church celebrates the Feast of the Immaculate Conception. It is the day the Church remembers the great moment when Mary was preserved from original sin. This age-old belief was defined by Pope Pius IX in 1854 as an article of revealed truth. Mary was indeed redeemed by Jesus Christ, as we all are, but instead of being freed from original sin after contracting it, she was preserved from it. Jesus' saving act cuts through and across time. This act of God was most fitting for the Mother of the Redeemer.

Invocation: *"O Mary, conceived without sin, pray for us who have recourse to thee."*

3 December
Violet — Memorial
St. Francis Xavier (1552), Priest

Francis Xavier was born in Spain in 1506. While studying the liberal arts at Paris, he became a follower of Ignatius Loyola. In 1537 he was ordained at Rome and there devoted himself to works of charity. Francis went to the Orient in 1541, where for ten years he tirelessly proclaimed the Gospel in India and Japan, and through his preaching brought many to believe. He died near the China coast on the island of Sancian.

St. Francis Xavier is the patron of foreign missions.

"The better friends you are, the straighter you can talk, but while you are only on nodding terms, be slow to scold." — St. Francis Xavier

4 December
Violet
St. John Damascene (749), Priest, Doctor of the Church

John Damascene was born of a Christian family in Damascus in the latter part of the seventh century. Learned in philosophy, he became a monk in the monastery of St. Sabbas near Jerusalem, and was then ordained a priest. He wrote many doctrinal works, particularly against people who wanted to destroy all icons, statues, and paintings of our Lord, the saints, and Our Lady (iconoclasts). He died in the middle of the eighth century.

ST. NICHOLAS COOKIES

1 c. butter
1 c. lard
2 c. brown sugar
½ c. sour cream
½ tsp. baking soda
4 tsp. cinnamon
½ tsp. nutmeg
½ tsp. cloves
4½ c. sifted flour
½ c. chopped nuts

St. Nicholas Cookie

Cream butter, lard, and sugar. Add sour cream alternately with sifted dry ingredients. Stir in nuts. Knead the dough into rolls. Wrap the rolls in wax paper and chill overnight in refrigerator. Roll dough very thin and cut into shapes. The dough may be cut into different shapes — stockings, wreaths, trees, stars, anything representing the season. Bake at 375° for 10 to 15 minutes.

"Repentance is returning from the unnatural to the natural state, from the devil to God, through discipline and effort." — St. John Damascene

5 December
Violet

• Make your St. Nicholas Cookies (called *Speculatius* in the Netherlands) today or to-night! Before everyone goes to bed tell about the life of St. Nicholas and put a shoe outside each person's door. Fill the shoes with cookies and watch the delight on the morning of the sixth! See the recipe on page 152. I reshaped a metal cookie-cutter into the form of St. Nicholas (see the recipe), then decorated him with icing.

6 December
Violet
St. Nicholas (350), Bishop

St. Nicholas was the bishop of Myra in Lycia (now part of Turkey). He had a very generous heart and always gave to the poor and needy. It is said that he saved three girls from being put into slavery by giving them money for their father's debts. He did this and many similar acts anonymously. He is the patron of children for this reason. He died in the middle of the fourth century, and, particularly since the tenth century, has been honored by the whole Church.

• Enjoy the cookies in your shoes! St. Nicholas is the patron of children, bakers, pawn-brokers, and the country of Russia. It might be fun to look up and read aloud the life story of St. Nicholas after dinner.

7 December
White — Memorial
St. Ambrose (397), Bishop, Doctor of the Church

Ambrose was born of a Roman family at Trier about the year 340. He studied at Rome and served in the imperial government at Sirmium. In 374, while living in Milan, he was elected bishop of the city by popular acclaim and ordained on December 7. He devotedly carried out his duties and especially distinguished himself by his service to the poor and as an effective pastor and teacher of the faithful.

He strenuously guarded the laws of the Church and defended orthodox teaching by writings and actions against the Arians, who denied Christ's divinity. St. Ambrose died on Holy Saturday. He is the patron of candlemakers.

"Patient endurance is the perfection of charity." — St. Ambrose

8 December
White — Solemnity
Immaculate Conception of the Blessed Virgin Mary
Holy Day of Obligation — Attend Mass Today

This is the day that the Church celebrates the fact that Mary was conceived in St. Anne's womb without original sin. We honor her as sinless from her conception. It would be great to have w*hite* flowers as a centerpiece for your feast tonight, representing purity.

CORN TORTILLAS

2 c. masa harina (especially prepared flour, ground from cooked
 corn grain — obtainable at most grocery stores)
1½ c. water

Mix *masa harina* and water. The mixture should not be crumbly, but moist. Shape into 12 balls. To keep them from drying out, cover with plastic wrap and flatten in a tortilla press or with a heavy plate. Peel off the tortilla and place in a hot ungreased frying pan (cast iron works best). Cook about one minute on each side; the cooked tortillas should be soft. Wrap cooked tortillas in a clean towel and serve warm.

RITA'S FAJITAS

whole boneless chicken breasts
tomatoes
cheese
lettuce
olives
sour cream
guacamole
pica de gallo salsa (see recipe below)

marinade ingredients:
  juice of 1 lime
  ¼ c. olive oil
  1 onion
  oregano, to taste
  ½ c. red-wine vinegar
  1 tbs. soy sauce
  ½ c. red wine
  chopped fresh cilantro, to taste
  garlic powder, to taste

Combine the ingredients for the marinade. Marinate whole boneless chicken breasts in the sauce listed above for two hours or more in the refrigerator. Grill, then cut into strips. Fill warm tortillas (see above for recipe for homemade tortillas) with chicken, tomatoes, cheese, lettuce, olives, sour cream, guacamole, and pica de gallo salsa.

• Salsa instructions — Mix in bowl: two green onions, two diced tomatoes, one green pepper, finely diced fresh cilantro.

— Recipe from the kitchen of Rita Lee

For more information on the dogma of the Immaculate Conception, see the *Catechism of the Catholic Church*, sections 490-493. The Blessed Virgin Mary is the patroness of the United States.

9 December
Violet
St. Peter Fournier (1640), Priest
Blessed Juan Diego (sixteenth century), Layman

Blessed Juan Diego was an Aztec from Mexico who saw the Virgin Mary in the image of Our Lady of Guadelupe. See the brief story under December 12, when we celebrate this feast of Mary.

• In honor of Our Lady and her servant, Blessed Juan Diego, make the Mexican recipe for Rita's Fajitas on page 154.

10 December
Violet

• In preparation for the feast of Our Lady of Guadalupe, prepare a Mexican meal. See the recipe for corn tortillas on page 154.

11 December
Violet
St. Damasus I (384), Pope

Damasus was born in Spain around the year 305. He was admitted to the Roman clergy and in 366, during a period of upheaval in the Church, was ordained Bishop of Rome.

He summoned synods to work against those who attacked the Church's unity (schismatics) and those who attacked the Church's teachings (heretics) and widely promoted the cult of martyrs, whose burial places he adorned with sacred verse.

12 December
White — Memorial
Our Lady of Guadalupe (1531)

The shrine of Our Lady of Guadalupe, near Mexico City, is one of the most celebrated places of pilgrimages in the world. On December 9, 1531, the Blessed Virgin Mary appeared to an Aztec Indian, Juan Diego, and left him with a picture of herself impressed upon his cloak and a message for the bishop: She asked that a church be built in her honor on the hill of Tepeyac. The bishop refused to believe Juan Diego, until Juan showed him the cloak filled with beautiful Castilian roses — not native to Mexico — and the imprint of the beautiful lady herself.

Devotion to Mary under this title has continually increased, and today she is the patroness of the Americas. Because Mary's garb was the same as that worn by pregnant Aztec women, and the Aztecs were sacrificing babies in pagan worship, Our Lady of Guadalupe is also the patroness of the unborn. Because of the close link between the Church in Mexico and the Church in the United States, this feast was placed on the calendar of the United States dioceses. Your family might want to more about this story.

13 December
Red — Memorial
St. Lucy (304), Virgin, Martyr

St. Lucy died in Syracuse, probably during the persecution of Christians by Diocletian, a Roman emperor. From antiquity her following spread throughout the Church, and her name was therefore introduced into the Roman Canon. She is the patroness of the blind.

14 December
White — Memorial
St. John of the Cross (1591), Priest, Doctor of the Church

St. John of the Cross was born at Fontiveros, Spain, around 1542. After a number of years as a Carmelite, he was persuaded by St. Teresa of Ávila in 1568 to lead a reform movement among the brothers, which brought a new energy to the Carmelite Order. Renowned for his wisdom and sanctity, he died at Ubeda. His spiritual writings remain a fitting testimony to his life. One of his most popular mystical writings is called *The Dark Night of the Soul*.

"The soul of one who loves God always swims in joy, always keeps holiday, and is always in the mood for singing." — St. John of the Cross

17 December
Violet
O Sapientia ("O Wisdom")

Who issued from the mouth of the Most High
Reaching from beginning to end
Ordering all things mightily yet tenderly —
Come to teach us the way of prudence.
(Open the first window of your Advent House.)

ST. LUCY'S LIFE CAKES

1½ c. honey	¼ c. water
2 c. brown sugar	2 eggs
8 c. flour	½ tsp. baking soda
½ tsp. salt	¼ tsp. nutmeg
¼ tsp. cloves	1½ tsp. cinnamon
1½ c. shredded orange peel	1½ c. chopped citron
2 c. chopped blanched almonds	

Boil honey, sugar, and water for five minutes. Beat in eggs. Add sifted dry ingredients. Sir in fruit and almonds. Cover and let stand overnight to ripen. Roll ¼-inch thick. Cut into rectangles one-inch wide by three-inches long. Bake at 350° for 15 minutes. When cool, ice with: one cup powdered sugar, five teaspoons boiling water, and one teaspoon lemon juice.

— *Recipe from* Advent and Christmas in a Catholic Home, *St. Raphael Press*

18 December
Violet
O Adonai ("O Lord of Lords")

    Lord and Leader of the house of Israel,
    Who appeared to Moses in the bush's flaming fire
    And gave to him the Law on Sinai —
    Come to redeem us with outstretched arms.
    (Open the second window of your Advent House.)

19 December
Violet
O Radix Jesse ("O Root of Jessie")

    A standard to the peoples
    Before whom kings are mute,
    To whom all nations shall appeal —
    Come to deliver us; delay, please, no longer.
    (Open the third window of your Advent House.)

20 December
Violet
O Clavis David ("O Key of David")

    And Scepter of the house of Israel,
    You open and no man dares shut,
    You shut and no man dares open —
    Come, deliver from the chains of prison him
        who sits in darkness and in the shadow of death.
    (Open the fourth window of your Advent House.)

21 December
Violet — Commemoration
St. Peter Canisius (1597), Priest, Doctor of the Church

    Peter Canisius was born in Nijmegen, Holland, in 1521. He studied at Cologne, entered the Society of Jesus, and was ordained a priest in 1546. Sent to Germany, he worked strenuously for many years by his writings and teachings to safeguard and confirm the Catholic Faith.

    Of his numerous books, the *Catechism* is most renowned. St. Peter died in Fribourg, Switzerland.

O Oriens ("O Rising Dawn")

    Radiance of eternal light
    And Sun Of Justice,
    Come, enlighten those sitting in darkness
    And in the shadow of death.
    (Open the fifth window of your Advent House.)

22 December
Violet
O Rex Gentium ("O King Of Nations")

And their desired one,
Cornerstone who binds two into one —
Come, and save man
Whom you fashioned from the slime of the earth.
(Open the sixth window of your Advent House.)

23 December
Violet — Commemoration
St. John Kanty (1473), Priest

St. John was born at Kanty in the diocese of Crakow in 1390. After his ordination to the priesthood, he taught for many years at the academy in Cracow, then became pastor of the parish at Olkusz.

He distinguished himself as an orthodox teacher of the Faith, and by his piety and love of neighbor gave Christian example to his colleagues and students.

O Emmanuel ("O Emmanuel")

God-with-us,
Our King and Lawgiver,
The Awaited of the peoples and their Savior —
Come to save us, O Lord our God.
(Open the seventh window of you Advent House.)

24 December
Violet
Adam and Eve (First Age of the World)

On the eve of the birth of the Second Adam, Savior of the World, we prayerfully remember our first parents.

Open your Advent House door and see Jesus on Mary's knee!

ST. JOHN'S WINE

2 c. red wine
2 whole cloves
2" stick of cinnamon
1 cardamom seed
¼ tsp. nutmeg

Boil the spices in the wine for five minutes. Strain the wine and serve. Offer a toast!
— *Recipe from* Cooking for Christ, *National Catholic Rural Life Conference*

25 December
White — Solemnity
Christmas, the Birth of Jesus Christ, Lord and God!
Holy Day of Obligation — Attend Mass Today

As the angel said to the shepherds: *"I proclaim to you good news that will be for all the people. For today in the city of David a savior has been born for you who is Messiah and Lord"* (Luke 2:10-11 NAB). Alleluia!

26 December
Red — Feast
St. Stephen, First Martyr

St. Stephen was a deacon of the early Church and became the first martyr. He is the patron of stonemasons. You can read about his death in Acts 7:55-60.

Both Christmas and Easter, as our two major feasts, are preceded by an octave (eight days) of preparation, and followed by an octave of celebration. The first eight days (of the twelve) of Christmas constitute the octave of celebration following this great feast.

27 December
White — Feast
St. John, Apostle and Evangelist

FRAN'S FAMOUS ENGLISH TOFFEE

1½ c. butter
3 c. sugar
4 tsp. vanilla
¾ c. water
1 one-lb. jar of peanuts
6 Hershey candy bars (or chocolate chips if you prefer dark chocolate)

To prepare the dishes for candy, break up the peanuts and cover the bottom of the plates. Make sure that the dishes you are using will not burn or melt. Aluminum or recycled microwave dinner dishes are best.

Use a heavy pot and a metal spoon. In a large pot, melt butter and add sugar, vanilla, and water. Stir constantly. The mixture will become think and darker. When it is the color of a Kraft caramel (after 15 to 20 minutes) the mixture will not stick to the sides of the pot. At this stage pour IMMEDIATELY into prepared pans of peanuts. This recipe makes six to eight small dishes.

Wait for two to three minutes, then break up the candy bars and place the pieces all around the tops of the toffee. After a few minutes more you will spread the melted chocolate around to cover the toffee. Then sprinkle with chopped peanuts or almonds to taste.

— This recipe is from my wonderful mother, Frances Dudley.
The candy makes wonderful gifts, too.

St. John is known as "the disciple Jesus loved." He and his brother Andrew were fisherman. St. John is the author of the Gospel of John.

Serve St. John's Wine as you celebrate his feast day. (See the recipe on page 158.) In Ireland, each person toasts the other, saying, "I drink to you in the love of St. John." Then each person takes a sip and the next one does the same. An alternative to wine is hot apple-cider served with a cinnamon stick.

28 December
Red — Feast
Holy Innocents, Martyrs

This day marks the death of the seventy-two Jewish boys killed by Herod. They were the first innocent to die for Christ. Read the account of the death of the Holy Innocents in Matthew 2:7-19.

Make a dessert of vanilla pudding (white symbolizes innocence) topped with cherry pie-filling (red symbolizes martyrdom). Do something pro-life! For instance, put together a bag of baby items for an un-wed mothers' home.

You might also wear *red* clothes today, give a special blessing to the children, or allow the youngest be the leader for the day.

Thomas Becket

29 December
White — Commemoration
St. Thomas Becket (1170), Bishop, Martyr

Born in London in 1118, St. Thomas Becket became a cleric of the Canterbury diocese. He then became chancellor to the king and was chosen bishop. His tireless defense of the Church's rights against Henry II prompted the king to exile Thomas to France for six years. After returning to his homeland, he endured many trials and was murdered by agents of the king.

31 December
White — Commemoration
New Year's Eve

St. Sylvester added the *Kyrie* and Creed to the liturgy of the Mass in 314 at the Council of Nicaea. Today is a good day to reflect on these great prayers. Also take stock of the past year and make resolutions for the new year. It's a good opportunity to ask pardon for omissions and lack of love. It's also good to thank God for all He has given you. You may wish to pray for peace throughout the world, having family members name the countries of the world out loud.

Prayers and Devotions

Examination of Conscience

For Ages Seven to Ten

1. Do I say my morning and night prayers with real purpose, and do I try to think of God at different times throughout the day? Do I pay attention at Mass, especially at the Consecration, thinking of what's happening?

2. Have I saddened my parents, teachers, or others by my behavior? Am I disobedient to them?

3. Do I know and accept the fact that my "job" right now consists of schoolwork and my tasks at home? Do I look for ways to get out of these jobs, or do I do them poorly?

4. Do I give bad example to my brothers, sisters, or friends in my attitude or actions?

5. Do I get carried away by bad moods and get angry often without real reason?

6. Do I have the bad habit of always thinking of myself first? For example, am I unhappy unless I win a game, am first in line, get all the food I like, get to go where I want to go, etc.?

7. Am I selfish about my things? Does it bother me to have to share them with my brothers and sisters?

8. When I am sick or hurt, do I try not to complain? Do I try to offer up times when I hurt as a private sacrifice to God?

9. Do I try to help my friends and family when they need it? Do I wait to be asked to help, or do I look for ways to do so on my own?

10. Do I realize how important it is to tell the truth and to be sincere at home, at school, and in talking to God in prayer?

For Ages Eleven to Sixteen

1. Do I say my morning and night prayers with real purpose, and do I try to think of God at different times of the day?

2. Have I missed Mass on Sundays or Holy Days by making no real effort of my own to get there? Was I voluntarily distracted at Mass?

3. Have I spoken irreverently about holy things, the sacraments, the Church, or its ministers? Have I uttered the name of God in disrespectful ways?

4. Do I have an excessive desire for independence which causes me to receive badly the commands of my parents and teachers? Do I realize that this reaction stems from pride?

5. Have I quarreled too much with my brothers and sisters?

6. Do I try to control my appetite for material things (food, possessions, entertainment)? Do I get angry if things don't work out as I plan or want? Do I respect authority and try to tolerate disappointments rather than letting them get the best of me?

7. Do I study hard and with order, realizing that by doing so I make best use of the talents God has given me, and show appreciation for the effort my parents make to educate me?

8. Do I treat my peers with respect and am I aware of the needs of others around me?

9. Have I given in to dishonesty, especially by lying and cheating, either to avoid getting into trouble or for my personal benefit?

10. Have I really worked on my personal relationships with God, asking for special graces in times or temptation or important discussions?

11. Do I observe the details of modesty which safeguard purity? Have I seen bad movies or TV shows, or have I read immoral magazines or other material? Have I allowed my companions to convince me to succumb to any of these? Have I allowed myself to be carried away by desires opposed to the virtues of purity?

Act of Contrition

O my God, I am heartily sorry for having offended you, and I detest all my sins, because I dread the loss of heaven and the pains of hell; but most of all because they offend you, my God, who are all good and deserving of all my love. I firmly resolve, with the help of your grace, to confess my sins, to do penance, and to amend my life. Amen.

The Rosary

Although the Rosary has been said since apostolic times, it was put into its current form by St. Dominic in 1214 when Our Lady appeared to him. The Rosary consists of fifteen "mysteries." Each mystery is meditated upon during ten Hail Mary's (a decade). Each decade begins with an Our Father and ends with a Glory Be. There are five Joyful Mysteries, five Sorrowful, and five Glorious. The prayers should be said slowly, in order to be said devoutly, while meditating on the mysteries. A good way to set your mind and heart on the mystery is to pause before each one and ponder its meaning. If you have not said the Rosary much in the past, a good way to start is by saying one decade at a time, gradually increasing to one set of five mysteries and then all fifteen.

To begin a set of five mysteries, say the Apostles Creed while holding the crucifix of your Rosary. Then on the next bead say an Our Father, followed by three Hail Mary's. These are said for the intention of an increase in the virtues of faith, hope, and charity. Follow with a Glory Be, then set your mind on the first mystery. The large bead following the three Hail Mary's is for the Our Father of the first mystery.

The mysteries are:

The Glorious Mysteries (usually said on Saturday, Sunday, Wednesday)
The Resurrection
The Ascension
The Descent of the Holy Spirit
The Assumption of Mary
The Coronation of Mary

The Joyful Mysteries (usually said on Monday, Thursday)

The Annunciation
The Visitation
The Birth of Our Lord
The Presentation in the Temple
The Finding in the Temple

The Sorrowful Mysteries (usually said on Tuesday, Friday)

The Agony in the Garden
The Scourging at the Pillar
The Crowning with Thorns
The Carrying of the Cross
The Crucifixion

When all five are done, the final Glory Be is followed by the Hail Holy Queen:

Hail, holy Queen, mother of mercy,
our life, our sweetness, and our hope.
To you do we cry,
poor, banished children of Eve.
To you do we send up our sighs,
mourning and weeping in this valley of tears.
Turn then, most gracious advocate,
your eyes of mercy toward us,
and after this exile
show unto us the blessed fruit of your womb, Jesus.
O clement, O loving, O sweet Virgin Mary.

Prayer for the Home

Visit, we beseech Thee, O Lord, this home, and drive far from it all snares of the enemy; let Thy holy Angels dwell herein to preserve us in peace and let Thy blessing always be upon us. Amen.

Anima Christi

This beautiful prayer was written during the fourteenth century. The author is unknown, but we do know that it is traditionally said silently after receiving Holy Communion.

Soul of Christ, sanctify me.
Body of Christ, heal me.
Blood of Christ, drench me.
Water from the side of Christ, wash me.
Passion of Christ, strengthen me.
Good Jesus, hear me.
In your wounds shelter me.
From turning away keep me.

From the evil one protect me.
At the hour of my death call me.
Into your presence lead me,
to praise you with all your saints
for ever and ever. Amen.

Prayer for Families

O dear Jesus, I humbly implore you to grant your special graces to our Family. May our home be the shrine of peace, purity, love, labor, and faith. I beg you, dear Jesus, to protect and bless all of us, absent and present, living and dead. Amen.

Consecrations

Consecration to the Sacred Heart

This is the formal dedication of oneself, of one's family, community, society, or even of the whole human race to the Sacred Heart of Jesus. Consecration implies a total surrender to the Savior in gratitude for His blessings in the past and as a pledge of fidelity in the future. This devotion has been said to "impose itself in a special way" (Pope Paul VI) and to be obligatory to all Catholics (see *Heart of the Redeemer,* by Timothy T. O'Donell).

One of the oldest known acts of consecration and reparation to the Sacred Heart dates from the fifteenth century and was popularized by the Benedictine monks at the Abbey of St. Matthias at Trier in the German Rhineland. After St. Margaret Mary, the practice of the consecration to the Heart of Jesus became widespread in the Catholic world. Personal consecration of the individual can be made often and informally and, in fact, the Morning Offering of the Apostleship of Prayer is a daily act of consecration.

Family consecration has been strongly recommended by the modern popes, including Pope Pius XII, who declared:

"It is our heartfelt desire that the love of Jesus Christ of which His Heart is the fountain, should again take possession of private and public life. May our divine Savior reign over society an home life through His law of love. That is why we make a special appeal to Christian families to consecrate themselves to the Sacred Heart."

Group consecrations go back to at least 1720, when the city of Marseilles, through its bishop and civil officials, made the dedication. Pope Leo XIII consecrated the world to the Sacred Heart in 1899 in anticipation of the Holy Year at the turn of the century. In 1925, Pope Pius XI ordered a formal Act of Consecration of the Human Race to the Sacred Heart of Jesus, to be publicly recited annually on the feast of Jesus Christ the King. (Taken from *Pocket Catholic Dictionary,* by John A. Hardon, S.J.)

The following organizations can be contacted for literature and devotional materials:

Apostleship of Prayer
Auriesville, NY 12012

National Enthronement Center
3 Adams St.
Fairhaven, MA 02719

International Institute of the Heart of Jesus
770 W. Blue Mound Road
Milwaukee, WI 53213
or
14 Borgo Angelico
00193 Rome Italy

Sacred Heart League
Walls, MS 38686

Families for Christ or Men of the Sacred Heart
6020 W. Harwood Ave.
Orlando, FL 32811

Consecration to Mary

The Consecration to Mary is an act of devotion, promoted by St. Louis de Montfort (1673-1716), that consists of the entire gift of self to Jesus through Mary. It is, moreover, a habitual attitude of complete dependence on Mary in one's whole life and activity. In making the act of consecration, a person gives himself to Mary and through her to Jesus as her slave. This means that a person performs good works as one who labors without wages, trustfully hoping to receive food for shelter and have other needs satisfied by the master, to whom one gives all one is and does, and on whom one depends entirely in a spirit of love. The act of consecration reads:

"I, (name), faithless sinner, renew and ratify today in your hands the vows of my baptism; I renounce forever Satan, his pomps and works; and I give myself entirely to Jesus Christ, the Incarnate Wisdom, to carry my cross after Him all the days of my life, and to be more faithful to Him than I have ever been before. In the presence of all the heavenly court I choose you this day for my mother and queen. I deliver and consecrate to you, as your slave, my body and soul, my good actions, past, present, and future; leaving to you the entire and full right of disposing of me, and all that belongs to me, without exception, according to your good pleasure, for the greater glory of God, in time and in eternity. Amen." (Taken from *Pocket Catholic Dictionary*, by, John A. Hardon S.J.)

Consecration of the Family to the Holy Family

The following prayer is a consecration to the Holy Family:

O Jesus, our most loving Redeemer, Who having come to enlighten the world, with Your teaching and example, willed to pass the greater part of Your life in humility and subjection to Mary and Joseph in the poor home of Nazareth, thus sanctifying the Family that was to be an example for all Christian families, graciously receive our family as it dedicates and consecrates itself to You this day. Defend us, guard us and establish among us Your holy fear, true peace and concord in Christian love: in order that by conforming ourselves to the divine pattern of Your family we may be able, all of us without exception, to attain to eternal happiness.

Mary, dear Mother of Jesus and Mother of us, by your kind intercession make this our humble offering acceptable in the sight of Jesus, and obtain for us His grace and blessings.

St. Joseph, most holy Guardian of Jesus and Mary, assist us by your prayers in all our spiritual and temporal necessities; that we may be able to praise our divine Savior Jesus, together with Mary and you, for all eternity.

Our Father, Hail Mary, and Glory Be three times.

The Chaplet of Divine Mercy

This beautiful and powerful intercessory prayer extends the offering of the Eucharist. Each part of the Chaplet reflects the combination of Sacred Scripture, Tradition, and a powerful pleading for mercy. In private revelation, our Lord taught this prayer to Sister Faustina Kowalska of Poland (now Blessed Faustina). For more information about this devotion, call Marian Helpers, Stockbridge, MA, 01263, 800-462-7426, 800-344-2836 (in Canada).

Using ordinary Rosary beads of five decades, begin with the Our Father, Hail Mary, and the Apostles Creed. (See the Holy Week activities for the intentions of each decade.)

Then, on the large beads pray:

Eternal Father,
I offer you
the Body and Blood,
Soul and Divinity
of Your dearly beloved Son,
Our Lord Jesus Christ,
in atonement for our sins
and those of the whole world.

On the small beads pray:

For the sake of His sorrowful Passion,
have mercy on us
and on the whole world.

At the end pray three times:

Holy God,
Holy Mighty One,
Holy Immortal One,
have mercy on us
and on the whole world.

Enthronements

To find out about arranging your own Eucharistic home shrine, write to: Mrs. Marion Barnwell, 1207 East Maple Avenue, El Segundo, CA 90245.

For specific information on the Enthronement of the Sacred Heart, contact: Sacred Heart Apostolate, Syracuse, NY, telephone 315-492-6308.

Blessings

Blessings are a means of asking for extra grace for a person or setting aside a particular place, thing, or circumstance, and a way of giving praise to God while giving thanks. They invoke God's care and protection to sanctify and make us holy.

The Catholic Church has approved over two hundred blessings for liturgical use and hundreds more for use by lay Catholics. Some blessings involve sacraments and are only conducted by a priest or member of the clergy, but many may be said by laymen during the ordinary circumstances of daily life. Sacred actions such as making a sign of the cross, the sprinkling of holy water, or anointing with holy chrism, accompany some blessings.

The United States Catholic Conference's *Catholic Household Blessings and Prayers* states:

"[Blessings] are not luxuries, pieties for the few, but are the fibers that bind a baptized person to Church, to Christ, and to each other. Without them, we drift. Without them, the notion of being a Church is lost to us. In the time and culture where we live, that is a very real danger."

Daily Blessings for Children

Blessings can be given upon getting up in the morning, leaving for school, and going to bed at night, and also at anytime throughout the day that a child seems to need your approval and the grace of God. A father we know blesses his daughter every morning before she leaves for school in this way:

"The LORD bless you and keep you!
"The LORD let his face shine upon you, and be gracious to you!
"The LORD look upon you kindly and give you peace!" (Numbers 6:24-26, NAB).

You could say one or more of the following:
"May God bless you."
"May God keep you safe."
"God be with you."
"God be in your heart."
"May God bless and protect you."

Evening Blessing

Lord, bless this household and each one. Place the cross of Christ on us with the power of your love until we see the land of joy. Amen.

Blessing for Christmas Tree

Reprinted with permission from *Advent and Christmas in a Catholic Home* by Helen McLaughlin (St. Raphael Press).

Father: This is that most worthy Tree in the midst of Paradise.
All: On which Jesus by His death overcame death for all.
Father: Let the heavens be glad and the earth rejoice;
All: Let the sea and what fills it resound;

let the plains be joyful and all that is in them!

All the trees of the forest shall exult before the Lord, for He comes;

for He comes to rule the earth.

He shall rule the world with justice and the people with His constancy.

Glory be to the Father, and to the Son, and to the Holy Ghost.

As it was in the beginning, is now and ever shall be, world without end. Amen.

All: This is the most worthy tree in the midst of Paradise on which Jesus by His death overcame death for all.

Mother: God said: Let the earth bring forth the vegetation: seed-bearing plants and all kinds of fruit from trees that bear fruit containing their seed. And so it was. The earth brought forth vegetation, every kind of seed-bearing plant and all kinds of trees that bear fruit containing their seed. The Lord God made to grow out of the ground all kinds of trees pleasant to the sight and good for food, the tree of life also in the midst of the garden, and the tree of the knowledge of good and evil. And God saw that it was good.

All: Thanks be to God.

Father: O Lord, hear my prayer.

All: And let my cry come to You.

Father: Let us pray. O Lord Jesus Christ, who by dying on the tree of the Cross did overcome the death of sin caused by our first parents' eating of the forbidden tree of paradise, grant, we beseech You, the abundant graces of Your Nativity, that we may so live as to be worthy living branches of Yourself, the good and ever green Olive Tree, and in Your strength bear the fruit of good works for eternal life. Who lives and reigns for ever and ever.

All: Amen.

Novenas

A "novena," meaning "nine," is a prayer or devotion that takes place over nine consecutive days, weeks, or months, with one day set aside for the special prayer. This can be either public or private prayer, usually with a special request or thanksgiving. The nine days of prayer is in imitation of Mary and the disciples spending nine days in continuous prayer between the Ascension of the Lord and the coming of the Holy Spirit at Pentecost.

There are many novenas available in booklet form (see the Bibliography). Some novenas are begun nine days before a feast day.

Making a novena means to persevere in prayer, asking for some favor with a sincere heart. As you talk with God in your own words during your novena, you will find that the Holy Spirit is enlightening your mind and strengthening you to do God's will.

There are many novenas to pray throughout the liturgical year for the various seasons and feast days. The following novenas were taken from *Treasury of Novenas* by Rev. Lawrence Lovasik, S.V.D.. Each prayer should be said once a day for nine consecutive days or once a week for nine consecutive weeks.

Advent Novena

Father, all-powerful and ever-living God, I give You thanks through Jesus Christ our Lord. When He humbled Himself to come among us as a man, He fulfilled the plan You formed long ago and opened for us the way to salvation.

Now I watch for the day, hoping that the salvation promised us will be ours, when Christ our Lord will come again in His glory. His future was proclaimed by all the prophets. The Virgin Mother bore Him in her womb with love beyond all telling. John the Baptist was His herald and made Him known when at last He came. In His love He has filled us with joy as we prepare to celebrate His birth. When He comes, may He find me watching in prayer, my heart filled with wonder and praise.

In memory of the coming of our Lord and Savior, I beg you, Father, to grant me all the graces I need to be prepared for His coming to my soul on Christmas. I ask in particular this favor: (mention your request). For the love of Jesus, Your Son, has shown us in becoming man to save us, I beg You to grant my prayer, if it be Your holy Will.

Lenten Novena

Father, all-powerful and ever-living God, during the holy season of Lent You call us to a closer union with Yourself. Help me to prepare to celebrate the Paschal mystery with mind and heart renewed. Give me a spirit of loving reverence for You, our Father, and of willing service to my neighbor. As I recall the great events that gave us new life in Christ, bring the image of Your Son to perfection within my soul.

This great season of grace is Your gift to Your family to renew us in Spirit. Purify my heart and give me strength to control my desires and so to live in this passing world with my heart set on the world that will never end. I ask for grace to master my sinfulness and conquer my pride. I want to show to those in need Your goodness to me by being kind to all. Through my observance of Lent, help me to correct my faults and raise my mind to You, and thus grow in holiness that I may deserve the reward of everlasting life. In Your mercy grant me this special favor: (mention your request).

The day of the life-giving death and glorious resurrection of Jesus Christ, Your Son, are approaching. This is the hour when He triumphed over Satan's pride, the time when we celebrate the great event of our Redemption. The suffering and death of Your Son brought life to the world, moving our hearts to praise Your glory. The power of the cross reveals Your judgment on this world and the Kingship of Christ crucified. Father, through His love for us and through His sufferings, death and resurrection, may I gain eternal life with You in heaven.

Novena to the Immaculate Heart of Mary

Immaculate Heart of Mary, full of love for God and mankind, and of compassion for sinners, I consecrate myself entirely to you. I entrust to you the salvation of my soul. May my heart be ever united with yours, so that I may hate sin and reach eternal life together with those whom I love.

Mediatrix of all graces and Mother of Mercy, remember the infinite treasure which your Divine Son has merited by His sufferings and which he has confided to you for us your children. Filled with confidence in your motherly heart, which I venerate and love, I come to you with my pressing needs. Through the merits of your loving heart, and for the sake of the Sacred Heart of Jesus, obtain for me the favor I ask: (mention your request).

Dearest mother, if what I ask for should not be according to God's will, pray that I may receive that which will be of greater benefit to my soul. May I experience the kindness of your motherly heart and the power of your intercession with Jesus during life and at the hour of my death. Amen.

Novena to St. Joseph

St. Joseph, you are the faithful protector and intercessor of all who love and venerate you. I have special confidence in you. You are powerful with God and will never abandon your faithful servants. I humbly invoke you and commend myself, with all who are dear to me, to your intercession. By the love you have for Jesus and Mary, do not abandon me during life, and assist me at the hour of my death.

Glorious St. Joseph, spouse of the immaculate virgin, foster-father of Jesus, obtain for me a pure, humble and charitable mind, and perfect resignation to the Divine Will. Be my guide, my father, and my model through life that I may merit to die as you did in the arms of Jesus and Mary.

Loving St. Joseph, faithful follower of Christ, I raise my heart to you to implore your powerful intercession in obtaining from the Heart of Jesus all the graces necessary for my spiritual and temporal welfare, particularly the grace of a happy death, and the special grace I now implore: (mention your request).

Guardian of the Word Incarnate, I am confident that your prayers in my behalf will be graciously heard before the throne of God.

Petition to the Holy Family for Your Family:

Dear Jesus, Mary, and Joseph, to you we consecrate our family and all that we have. We want our home to belong entirely to you. You made family life holy by your family life at Nazareth. Your home was a home of prayer, love, patient endurance and toil.

It is our earnest wish to model our home upon yours at Nazareth. Remain with us, so that with your help the purity of our morals may be preserved , that we may obey the Commandments of God and teachings of the Church and receive the sacraments frequently.

Willingly, we surrender our entire freedom to you, our Queen and our Mother. We place under your care our body and its senses, our soul and its faculties, our thoughts and desires, our words and deeds, our joys and sorrows, our life and our death.

Give your aid to our family, our relatives and (our friends). Under your guidance may we always follow the Holy Spirit and never hinder His grace in us through sin.

Help us to tread our way successfully through the dangers of this life so to win passage to our home in heaven. As Saints there with you, may we sing the praises of each Person of the Blessed Trinity for all eternity.

Keep love and peace in our midst. Console us in our troubles. Help us to preserve the innocence of our children. Enlighten and strengthen our growing sons and daughters. Assist us all at the hour of death, so that we may be united with each other and with you in heaven.

Litanies

The word "litany" comes from the Latin "*litania,*" which stands for a form of responsory prayer that involves a number of petitions (sometimes called invocations) centered around one main subject or sacred theme. Litanies have been said in the Church for a long time, but only a few are authorized by the Church for use in public devotions and at public services.

Some may be said in private recitation by an individual or a group. The *Litany of the Saints* is the oldest litany in the Church and the model for all other litanies. The key element in a litany's form of prayer is its series of invocations, followed by the same repetitive response. One person leads the invocations, and others answer with the response. *A Prayerbook of Favorite Litanies*, by Father Albert J. Hebert, S.M., published by TAN, is full of great information and great litanies.

Many Catholics recite litanies in honor of Jesus, the Holy Spirit, Mary, and the saints. You can recite them alone or with others. A member of the family may lead the litany with the rest of the family chiming in with the response. Praying litanies lifts our hearts and voices in praise to God. The repetition and beauty of the litanies bring us to a peaceful, meditative state. Most Catholic bookstores have small, inexpensive litany leaflets for purchase. For litanies to Mary, Joseph, and the saints, you may refer to a book called *Traditional Catholic Prayers*, compiled and edited by Monsignor Charles J. Dollen, and published by Our Sunday Visitor.

Litany of All Saints

Lord, have mercy.	**Lord, have mercy.**
Christ, have mercy.	**Christ, have mercy.**
Lord, have mercy.	**Lord, have mercy.**
Christ, hear us.	**Christ, hear us.**
Christ, graciously hear us.	**Christ, graciously hear us.**

God, our heavenly Father,   **have mercy on us.**
God the Son,
Redeemer of the world,
God the Holy Spirit,
Holy Trinity, one Gaod,

Holy Mary,   **pray for us.**
Holy Mother of God,
Holy Virgin of virgins,
St. Michael,
St. Grabriel,
St. Raphael,
All you holy Angels and Archangels,
All you holy orders of blessed Spirits,

St. John the Baptist,   **pray for us.**
St. Joseph,
All you holy Patriarchs and Prophets,

St. Peter,   **pray for us.**
St. Paul,
St. Andrew,

St. James,
St. John,

St. Thomas,   **pray for us**.
St. James,
St. Philip,
St. Bartholomew,
St. Matthew,
St. Simon,
St. Thaddeus,
St. Matthias,
St. Barnabas,
St. Luke,
St. Mark,
All you holy Apostles and Evangelists,
All you holy Disciples of the Lord,
All you holy Innocents,

St. Stephen,   **pray for us.**
St. Laurence,
St. Vincent,
St. Fabian and St. Sebastian,
St. John and St. Paul,
St. Cosmas and St. Damian,
St. Gervase and St. Protase,
All you holy Martyrs,

St. Silvester,   **pray for us.**
St. Gregory,
St. Ambrose,
St. Augustine,
St. Jerome,
St. Martin,
St. Nicholas,
All you holy Bishops and Confessors,
All you holy Doctors,

St. Anthony,   **pray for us.**
St. Benedict,
St. Bernard,
St. Dominic,
St. Francis,
All you holy Priests and Clergy,
All you holy Monks and Hermits,

St. Mary Magdalene,　　　　　**pray for us.**
St. Agatha,
St. Lucy,
St. Agnes,
St. Cecilia,
St. Catherine,
St. Anastasia,
All you holy Virgins and Widows,
All you St.s of God,

Be merciful,　　　　　**Lord, save your people.**
From every evil,
From every sin,
From your anger,
From sudden and unforeseen death,
From the snares of the devil,
From anger, hatred, and all ill-will,
From the spirit of uncleanness,
From lightening and tempest,
From the scourge of earthquake,
From plague, famine, and war,
From everlasting death,
By the mystery of your holy Incarnation,
by your coming,

By your birth,　　　　　**Lord, save your people.**
By your baptism and holy fasting,
By your Cross and suffering,
By your death and burial,
By your holy resurrection,
By your wonderful ascension,
By the coming of the Holy Spirit, the Paraclete,
On the day of Judgement,
Be merciful to us sinners,
That you will spare us,
That you will pardon us,
That it may please you to bring us to true repentance,
To govern and preserve your holy Church,
To preserve in holy religion the Pope,
and all those in holy Orders,
To humble the enemies of holy Church,
To give peace and unity to the whole Christian people,
To recall to the unity of the Church all those who are straying, to bring all unbelievers to
　　the light of the Gospel,

To strengthen and preserve us in your holy service,
To raise our minds to desire the things of heaven,
To reward all our benefactors with eternal blessings,
To deliver our souls form eternal damnation,
and the souls of our brethren, kinsmen, and benefactors,
To give and preserve the fruits of the earth,
To grant eternal rest to all the faithful departed,
That it may please you to hear and heed us, Jesus,
Son of the living God, **Lord, hear our prayer.**

Lamb of God, who takes away the sins of the world, **spare us, Lord.**
Lamb of God, who takes away the sins of the world, **graciously hear us.**
Lamb of God, who takes away the sins of the world, **have mercy on us.**

Christ, hear us.	**Christ, hear us.**
Lord Jesus,	**Lord Jesus,**
hear our prayer.	**hear our prayer.**
Lord, have mercy.	**Lord, have mercy.**
Christ, have mercy.	**Christ, have mercy.**
Lord, have mercy.	**Lord, have mercy.**

Other beautiful litanies for the family:
Litany of the Blessed Virgin Mary
Litany of St. Joseph
Other litanies of the saints

Sacramentals and Popular Piety

"Sacramentals are sacred signs instituted by the Church. They prepare men to receive the fruit of the sacraments and sanctify different circumstances of life" (CCC 1677).

Sacramentals are objects or actions that are used by the Church in order to achieve through the merits of the faithful certain effects, mainly of a spiritual nature. They are not the same as sacraments, since their efficacy does not depend on the rite, but on the influence of prayerful petition. There are many sacramentals and they have varied through the years. A few examples might be the Rosary, the brown scapular, images of our Lord, the blessing of oneself with holy water, as well as the water itself.

The scapular of Our Lady of Mount Carmel is a common sacramental. "Just as Our Lady clothed the Baby Jesus in swaddling clothes, she clothes us in her brown cloth of Carmel" (from *You Can Become A Saint*, Mary Ann Budnik).

"Whosoever dies clothed in this (scapular) shall not suffer eternal fire." This is Mary's promise made on July 16, 1251, to St. Simon Stock. The scapular is worn not only as a public profession of devotion to Our Lady, but also a sign of consecration to her. It is worn next to the skin with one brown patch in front and the other in back. To receive information on the scapular, you can go to a local Catholic store or write: Christ in the Home Apostolate, P.O. Box 9608, Pittsburgh, PA 15226.

"Among the sacramentals blessings occupy an important place. They include both praise of God for his works and gifts, and the Church's intercession for men that they may be able to use God's gifts according to the spirit of the Gospel" (CCC 1678).

As the head of the household, it is appropriate for the father to say any relevant blessings for his family. In some families, the father will give each child a blessing before he or she goes to bed at night. This may be done by making the sign of the cross with the thumb on the child's forehead and saying, "May the Lord bless you and keep you safe," or something similar.

The father may also want to bless the house. This is traditionally done on Epiphany, and a version of that blessing is included in the Christmas section of this book.

Sacrament Days

The sacraments are the actions of Christ Himself in the world. Through the sacraments, Christ reaches through time and space and fills us with His life. This "Spirit of adoption makes the faithful partakers in the divine nature [Cf. *2 Peter* 1:4] by uniting them in a living union with the only Son, the Savior" (CCC 1129).

The sacraments, then, are momentous occasions in our lives and in the lives of our loved ones. In many ways, these are more momentous than birth itself, because on a birthday we celebrate our physical life, which will someday end. However, in the sacraments we receive the grace necessary for eternal life in Christ, which of course will never end.

It is important in family life to mark these special days and their anniversaries with celebrations. The anniversaries of days such as baptisms, confirmations, marriages, and first communions can be marked with special activities and privileges. When a family member receives a sacrament for the first (or only) time, it is important that he or she is mentally prepared for the sacred occasion. One way to help the person keep that sense of the sacredness of the moment throughout the day is to make the celebrations (and their subsequent anniversaries) sacred, solemn, and holy. Avoid amusements and gifts that have no relation or meaning to the day itself. (For example, a trip to an amusement park would not be an appropriate way to celebrate any sacrament.)

There are many ways one *can* celebrate a sacrament and each family should develop their own traditions to pass on through the generations. Following are just a few ideas.

Sacrament Bulletin Board

Set up a bulletin board in a prominent place which can be decorated for whichever anniversary needs to be acknowledged. Pictures, certificates, newspaper clippings, and other relevant decorations can be used (laminate them if possible so that they can be used every year).

The family member who is celebrating the anniversary can do this themselves, or this can be done for them by the rest of the family.

Dinner Celebration

The menu can be chosen by the honoree and a special dessert prepared. It is important to spend some time remembering the significance of the event in the family member's life and special prayers should be said. The father can do a special blessing and family members can toast the person, giving their impressions of the importance of the sacrament in the life of the family member. For example: On a baptismal day, the family can help the family member renew his or her baptismal vows by responding, if the child is too young, or by making the statements to which the person can respond. Also, each family member can share how they encounter Christ's saving grace, received at baptism, in that person.

Guests to Help Celebrate

It is often difficult to keep in touch with important people in our lives, such as our godparents, our confirmation sponsor, the priest who gave us our First Holy Communion, the teacher who prepared us for a sacrament, the best man and maid of honor at our wedding, or the priest who witnessed it. These celebrations are the perfect time to touch base with these people and let them know how important their contribution to these days are to us. If any of these people cannot attend, they might be asked to write a letter to the person, thus keeping the spiritual relationship alive.

The Sacraments Themselves

Baptism: This can be celebrated as a birthday is celebrated. Some families replace their usual birthday celebrations with a small-scale acknowledgment and really celebrate the baptismal days.

First Reconciliation: This is a good one to celebrate quietly, alone with God. However, children will need your help and encouragement to do this. Provide them with the opportunity to go alone (mom may want to sit as inconspicuously as possible in the back) to a church and pray or receive the sacrament again.

First Holy Communion: It is important that this and all sacrament days are celebrated as a sacred day, and not a day to parade the finest dresses and be showered with gifts and distracted with amusements. The anniversaries should also have a sacred character. Attending Mass as a family would be appropriate, and/or a reenactment of the Last Supper, at which Christ instituted this sacrament, would also give the celebration a sacred character.

Confirmation: This sacrament is given at different ages, depending on your local bishop. Even so, it is an important marker in a child's life. Generally, in the United States, confirmation is received just prior to or during adolescence, and is sometimes seen as a rite of passage. Celebration of this sacrament and its anniversary can be done in a more grown-up way as a result. Perhaps a private dinner with Mom and Dad would be appropriate. This could also be a good way to introduce the habit of yearly retreats by finding an appropriate retreat (or making one up) to attend on or around the anniversary.

Marriage: This anniversary is already celebrated by most. However, the sacred celebration of the sacrament is not always emphasized. As the children grow older, they should be included in this celebration, since it is a perfect opportunity to implant in their young minds a deep respect for the importance of this great sacrament. A discussion of the character of marriage and its indissolubility, as well as a reading of the nuptial blessings and restatement of the vows are all ways to do this.

Glossary

Abbot: Superior of a monastery of monks having a settled location.

Abstinence: Refraining from certain foods or drink. Can be done spontaneously by an individual or may be prescribed be ecclesiastical law.

Commemoration: A memorial in Lent. A memorial does not override the fast and abstinence of the Lenten season.

Conscience: The judgment of the practical intellect deciding, from general principles of faith and reason, the goodness or badness of a way of acting that a person now faces.

Contrition: The act or virtue of sorrow for one's sins.

Cult: A definite form of worship or of religious observance. Also, a particular religious group centered around some unusual belief, generally transient in duration and featuring some exotic or imported ritual and other practices.

Doctor of the Church: A title given since the Middle Ages to certain saints whose writing or preaching is outstanding for guiding the faithful in all periods of the Church's history.

Ecumenism: The modern movement toward Christian unity whose Catholic principles were formulated by the Second Vatican Council in 1964: 1) Christ established his Church on the Apostles and their episcopal successors, whose visible head and principle of unity became Peter and his successor, the Bishop of Rome; 2) Since the first century there have been divisions in Christianity, but many persons now separated from visible unity with the successors of the apostles under Peter are nevertheless Christians who possess more or less of the fullness of grace available in the Roman Catholic Church; 3) Catholics are to do everything possible to foster the ecumenical movement, which comprehends all "the initiatives and activities, planned and undertaken to promote Christian unity, according to the Church's various needs and as opportunities offer" (*Decree on Ecumenism* I, 4).

Encyclical: A papal document treating of matters related to the general welfare of the Church, sent by the pope to the bishops. Used especially in modern times to express the mind of the pope to the people.

Fasting: A form of penance that imposes limits on the kinds or quantities of food eaten. Usually requires only one full meal a day with two small snack-size meals. Required fast days include Ash Wednesday and Good Friday, although it is recommended on all Fridays, especially those in Lent.

Feast: Days set apart by the Church for giving special honor to God, the Savior, angels, saints, and sacred mysteries and events. Some are fixed festivals, such as Christmas and the

Immaculate Conception; others are movable, occurring earlier or later in different years. Festivals are now divided, since the Second Vatican Council, into solemnity, feast, and memorial, in descending order of dignity. Memorials are further classified as prescribed or optional. Below these are ferial (or week) days with no special ritual rank. And in a class by themselves are the Sundays of the year, and the various liturgical seasons, such as Advent and Lent. All of these represent what is called "sacred times," whose religious purpose is to keep the faithful mindful throughout the year of the cardinal mysteries and persons of Christianity.

Heresy: Commonly refers to a doctrinal belief held in opposition to the recognized standards of an established system of thought. Theologically it means an opinion at variance with the authorized teachings of any church, notably the Christian, and especially when this promotes separation form the main body of faithful believers.

Icon: A flat painting, a sacred picture of the Eastern Church. It is generally painted on wood and covered, except the face and hands, with relief of seed pearls and gold or silver.

Iconoclasm: A heresy that rejected as superstitious the use of religious images and advocated their destruction.

Infallibility (of pope): Freedom from error in teaching the Universal Church in matters of faith or morals. The condition of the infallibility is that the pope speaks *ex cathedra*. For this is required that: 1) He have the intention of declaring something unchangeably true; and 2) He speak as shepherd and teacher of all the faithful with the full weight of his apostolic authority, and not merely as a private theologian or even merely for the people of Rome or some particular segment of the Church of God. The supernatural assistance of the Holy Spirit is the source of this authority and infallible statements cannot be changed.

Liturgical Year: The liturgical cycle of the mysteries of Christ, the Blessed Virgin, angels, and saints, which the Church commemorates in the Mass, the Divine Office, and other forms of public worship. The liturgical year begins with the first Sunday of Advent and closes with the thirty-fourth week "through the year."

Magisterium: The Church's teaching authority, vested in the bishops, as successors of the apostles, under the Roman Pontiff, as successor of St. Peter. Also vested is the pope, as Vicar of Christ and visible head of the Catholic Church.

Martyr: A person who chooses to suffer, even to die, rather than renounce his or her faith or Christian principles. After the example of Christ, one does not resist one's persecutors when they use violence out of hatred or malice against Christ, His Church, or some revealed truth of the Catholic religion.

Memorial: One of three levels of festivals — solemnity, feast, and memorial. Memorials can be prescribed or optional.

Monk: Originally the term "monk" referred to a hermit, but soon in the early Church the word applied to men living a community life in a monastery, under vows of poverty, chastity, and obedience.

Orthodoxy: Right belief as compared with heterodoxy or heresy. The term is used in the East to identify those churches now united with Rome, which call themselves the "holy, orthodox, catholic, Eastern Church."

Pagan: In general one who practices idolatry. Formerly used to describe anyone who did not profess monotheism, belief in one God.

Glossary

Patron Saint: A saint or blessed who, since early Christian times, has been chosen as a special intercessor with God for a particular person, place, community, or organization. The custom arose from the biblical fact that a change of personal name indicated a change in the person, such as, Abram to Abraham, Simon to Peter, Saul to Paul, and for the practice of having churches built over the tombs of martyrs.

Penance: The virtue or disposition of the heart by which one repents of their sins and converts to God. Also, the punishment endured in reparation for sins committed by oneself or others (one can offer up hardship and difficulty for the sins of others).

Religious: Those who have professed public vows of poverty, chastity, and obedience.

Reparation: The act or fact of making amends. It implies an attempt to restore things to their normal or sound conditions, as they were before something wrong was done. With respect to God, it means making up with greater love for the failure in love through sin.

Schism: A willful separation from the unity of the Christian Church. It is fundamentally volitional, as opposed to heresy, which by its nature refers to the mind.

See (of Peter): Refers to "seat" of the Church's authority.

Solemnity: The highest liturgical rank of a feast in the ecclesiastical calendar.

Veneration of the Saints: Honor paid to the saints who, by their intercession and example and in their possession of God, minister to human sanctification, helping the faithful grow in Christian virtue. Venerating the saints does not detract form the glory given to God, since whatever good they posses is a gift from his bounty.

Virgin: A title given to an unmarried or Religious woman who, with the help of God, has preserved her innocence and lived fully the virtue of chastity.

Vocation: A call from God to a distinctive state in life in which the person can reach holiness. Vatican II made it clear that there is a *universal* call to holiness.

(Excerpts from* A Pocket Catholic Dictionary, *John A. Hardon, S.J.)

Bibliography

Mary Achterhoff, *Grace in Every Season: Through the Year with Catherine Doherty* (Ontario, Canada: Madonna House Publications, 1992).

Ann Ball, *Catholic Traditions in Cooking* (Huntington, Indiana: Our Sunday Visitor, 1993).

_____, *Catholic Traditions in Crafts* (Huntington, Indiana: Our Sunday Visitor, 1997).

_____, *Catholic Traditions in the Garden* (Huntington, Indiana: Our Sunday Visitor, 1998).

_____, *A Handbook of Catholic Sacramentals* (Huntington, Indiana: Our Sunday Visitor, 1991).

William Bennet, *The Book of Virtues* (New York: Simon & Shuster, 1993).

Florence S. Berger, *Cooking for Christ, The Liturgical Year in the Kitchen* (San Diego: National Catholic Rural Life Conference, 1944. Also reprinted by Firefly Press).

Richard Beron, O.S.B., *With the Bible Through the Church Year* (New York: Pantheon Books, 1953).

Mary Ann Budnik, *You Can Become A Saint* (Houston: Lumen Christi Press, 1990).

Margaret, Matthew, and Stephen Bunson, *Our Sunday Visitor's Encyclopedia of Saints* (Huntington, Indiana: Our Sunday Visitor, 1998).

Rhonda De Sola Chervin, *Quotable Saints* (Ann Arbor, Michigan: Servant Publications, 1992).

Rhonda De Sola Chervin and Carla Conley, *The Book of Catholic Customs and Traditions: Enhancing Holidays, Special Occasions, and Family Celebrations* (Ann Arbor, Michigan: Servant Publications, 1994).

G.K. Chesterton, *Brave New Family* (San Francisco: Ignatius Press, 1990).

Shirley Dobson and Gail Gaither, *Let's Make a Memory* (Waco, Texas: Word Books, 1983).

Monsignor Charles J. Dollen, *Traditional Catholic Prayers* (Huntington, Indiana: Our Sunday Visitor, 1990).

Donna Erickson, *Primetime Together with Kids* (Discovery Toys Publishing, 1989).

Josemaría Escrivá, *The Way of the Cross* (London: Scepter, 1982).

_____, *The Way* [originally *Consideraciones Espirituales*] (London: Scepter, 1934).

_____, *The Furrow* (London: Scepter, 1986).

_____, *The Forge* (London: Scepter, 1987).

_____, *Christ is Passing By* (London: Scepter, 1974).

Faith and Life Series (Grades 1-8), Catholics United for the Faith (San Francisco: Ignatius Press).

Francis Fernandez, *In Conversation with God, Daily Meditations*, Volumes 1-5 (London: Scepter, 1991).

Monsignor John Hagen, *The Absolute Essentials of Bringing up Children* (Australia, Kansas City, and Michigan: Instauratio Press, distributed by Angelus Press, 1994).

John A. Hardon, S.J., *Pocket Catholic Dictionary* (New York: Image Books, Doubleday, 1985).

Reverend Albert J. Hebert, S.M., *A Prayerbook of Favorite Litanies, 116 Favorite Catholic Litanies and Responsory Prayers* (Rockford, Illinois: TAN Books and Publishers, Inc., 1985).

Thomas Howard, *Hallowed Be This House* (San Francisco: Ignatius Press, 1979).

_____, *If Your Mind Wanders at Mass* (Steubenville, Ohio: Franciscan University Press, 1995).

David Isaacs, *Character Building, A Guide for Parents and Teachers* (Four Courts Press, 1984).

Kay Lynn Isca, *Catholic Etiquette* (Huntington, Indiana: Our Sunday Visitor, 1997).

Mollie Katzen, *Moosewood Cookbook* (Berkeley: Ten Speed Press, 1977).

Reverend George A. Kelly, *The Catholic Family Handbook* (New York: Random House, 1959).

Wendy Leifeld, *Mothers of the Saints* (Ann Arbor, Michigan: Servant Publications, 1994).

Reverend Lawrence Lovasik, S.V.D., *Treasury of Novenas* (New York: Catholic Book Publishing Co., 1986).

Alfred McBride, O.Praem., *Father McBride's Family Catechism* (Huntington, Indiana: Our Sunday Visitor, 1998).

Helen McLaughlin, *Advent and Christmas in a Catholic Home* (Lancaster, California: St. Raphael Press, 1994).

_____, *Family Advent Customs* (Collegeville, Minnesota: Liturgical Press, 1979).

_____, *My Name-day Come For Dessert* (Collegeville Minnesota: Liturgical Press, 1962).

Albert J. Nevins, M.M., *A Saint for Your Name — Boys/Girls* (Huntington, Indiana: Our Sunday Visitor, 1980).

Mary Reed Newland, *We and Our Children, Molding the Child in Christian Living* (New York: P.J. Kennedy and Sons, 1954).

_____, *The Year and Our Children, Planning the Family Activities for Christian Feasts and Seasons* (San Diego: Firefly Press, 1994).

_____, *The Saints and Our Children* (Rockford, Illinois: TAN, 1995).

_____, *Our Children Grow Up* (New York: J.P. Kennedy and Sons, 1965).

Terry and Mimi Reilly, *Family Nights Throughout the Year* (St. Meinrad, Indiana: Abbey Press, 1978).

Routley, Erik, *The English Carol* (Greenwood Publishing Group, Inc., 1973).

Saints and Feast Days, adapted from the "Christ Our Life Series" (Chicago: Loyola University Press).

Edith Schaeffer, *The Hidden Art of Homemaking, Living Studies* (Wheaton, Illinois: Tyndale House Publishers, Inc., 1986).

Mike and Sandy Scherschligt, *From the Kitchen of the Scherschligt Palace: A Guide to Feasting* (Christmas, 1993).

Sara Wenger Shenk, *Why Not Celebrate* (Intercourse, Pennsylvania: Good Books, 1987).

Gary Smalley and John Trent, Ph.D., *The Hidden Value of a Man* (Focus on the Family Publishing, 1994).

Demetria Taylor, *The Cook's Blessings* (New York: Random House, 1965).

Mary Dixon Thayer, *The Child on His Knees* (Harrison, New York: CMA Press, 1994).

Maria Augusta von Trapp, *Around the Year with the Trapp Family, Keeping the Feasts and Seasons of the Christian Year* (New York: Pantheon Books, 1955).

_____, *Yesterday, Today, and Forever* (New York: J.B. Lippincott Company, 1952).

Jesus Urtega, *God and Children* (Manila, Philippines: Sinag-Tala Publishing, Inc., 1984).

Evelyn Birge Vitz, *A Continual Feast* (San Francisco: Ignatius Press, 1985).

Father Paul Wickens, *Handbook For Parents, Common Sense Rules for Catholic Mothers and Fathers* (Long Prairie, Minnesota: Neumann Press, 1985).

_____, *Husband and Wife, Joys and Sorrows and Glories of Married Life* (Long Prairie, Minnesota: Neumann Press, 1992).

Catalogs

Ignatius Press, 33 Oakland Ave., Harrison, NY 10528; 1-800-651-1531.

Leaflet Missal Company, 976 W. Minnehaha Ave., St. Paul, MN 55104-1556; 1-800-328-9582, Fax 612-487-0286.

Lifetime Books and Gifts: Always Incomplete Catalog, 3900 Chalet Suzanne Dr., Lake Wales, FL 33853-7763; 813-676-6311; Fax 813-676-2732.

The Mother of Our Savior Co., Inc., 153 B. Mann Rd., P.O. Box 100, Pekin, IN 47165; 1-800-451-3993.

Our Sunday Visitor, 200 Noll Plaza, Huntington, IN 46750; 1-800-348-2440.

The Printery House, Conception Abbey, Conception, MI 64433; 816-944-2331; Fax 816-944-2582.

TAN Books and Publishers, Inc., P.O. Box 424, Rockford, IL 61105; 1-800-437-5876.

Periodicals

The Catholic Answer, 200 Noll Plaza, Huntington, IN 46750, 1-800-348-2440.

The Catholic Hearth, Route 2, Box 29A, Long Prairie, MN 56347; 1-800-746-2521.

Catholic Heritage, 200 Noll Plaza, Huntington, IN 46750, 1-800-348-2440.

The Catholic Family's Magnificat, P.O. Box 43-1015, Pontiac, MI 48343-1015; 810-412-1959.

The Catholic Home Educator, P.O. Box 420225, San Diego, CA 92142.

Catholic Parent, 200 Noll Plaza, Huntington, IN 46750; 1-800-348-2440.

Catholic World Report, Ignatius Press, 1-800-651-1531.

Inside the Vatican, Subscription Dept., New Hope, KY 40052; 1-800-789-9494.

Laywitness, 827 N. 4th St., Steubenville, OH 43952; 1-800-693-2484.

Life After Sunday Newsletter, WPR Co., Inc., 2102 Dayton St., Silver Springs, MD 20902-4222; 1-800-473-7980; Fax 301-649-6593.

New Covenant, 200 Noll Plaza, Huntington, IN 46750; 1-800-348-2440.

Our Sunday Visitor, 200 Noll Plaza, Huntington, IN 46750; 1-800-348-2440.

Appendix

Jesse Tree symbols

Jesse Tree symbols

Index

A
Abbot Chautard, 48
abbot, 97, 117, 130, 150, 177
abstinence, 47, 80, 177
act of charity, 32, 77, 88
act of contrition, 79, 162
act of faith, 72-73, 77
act of hope, 75
act of love, 77-78
Adam, 12, 13, 15, 31, 90, 158
Adam and Eve, 13, 15, 90, 158
Adopt-a-Grandparent, 44
Advent House, 18, 20, 156-158
Advent Novena, 168
Advent Wreath, 20-21, 22, 49
All Saints Day Eve, 145
almsgiving, 31, 34
Angel Food Cake, 51-52
Angel on My Shoulder, 71
Anima Christi, 163
Annunciation of Our Lord, 106, 163
Anointing of the Sick, 60-61, 62
Apostles Book, 73, 81
Apple Fritter and Caramel Sundaes, 122
Archangel Gabriel, 106, 138
Archangel Michael, 70, 72, 138, 171
Archangel Raphael, 71, 138, 171
Ascension Thursday, 51, 57
Ash Wednesday, 25, 30, 31, 46, 177
B
Banbury Tarts, 143-144
Baptism, 23, 31, 51, 60-61, 83, 89, 118, 129, 165, 173, 176
Bedtime Chats, 79
Beer Bread, 105
Beheading of St. John the Baptist, 133
Bernadette, 86
Birth of the Blessed Virgin Mary, 134
Bless Your Seedlings, 56
Blessed Josemaría Escrivá de Balaguer, 118
Blessed Juan Diego, 155
Blessed Kateri Tekakwitha, 122
Blessed Katherine Drexel, 104
Blessed Laura Vicuña, 98
Blessed Pier Giorgio, 121
Blessed Teresa Benedicta, 128
Blessing for Christmas Tree, 12, 167
Blessing of Chalk, 96
Blessing of Homes, 96
Blessing of Throats, 101
Broiled Fish, 26, 51
Bubble Party, 68
Butterfly Mobile, 55

Butterfly Project, 55
C
C&H Box, 71
Calzones, 42
Candelabrum, 45
Carnival, 23, 25-30
Catechism of the Catholic Church (CCC), 10, 36, 56, 59, 60, 61, 62, 145, 155
Caterpillar Hunt, 56
Chair of St. Peter the Apostle, 103
Chaplet of Divine Mercy, 47, 166
chastity, 59, 60, 76, 96, 101, 103-104, 121, 178, 179
Chick Pea Curry, 132
Christ Candle, 12, 22, 101
Christ the King, 65, 115, 151, 164
Christkindl, 13, 20, 21
Christkindl Brief, 14
Christmas Eve, 8, 12, 20
Christmas Lady Cookies, 16
Christmas Punch for Children, 17
Christmas Tree, 12, 13, 48, 167
Christmastide, 23, 25
Christ's Ancestors, 13
Christstollen, 15
cinquain, 53, 88
Clam Sauce, 43
Collect Toys for the Needy, 33
Color Eggs, 47
commemoration, 101, 102, 149, 157, 158, 160, 177
confession, 31, 52, 61, 83-84, 115, 126, 139
Confirmation, 10, 60, 61, 85, 89, 176
conscience, 59, 61, 62, 74, 76, 126, 161, 177
Consecration of the Family to the Holy Family, 165
Consecration to Mary, 126, 165
Consecration to the Sacred Heart, 65, 164-165
contrition, 79, 83, 162, 177
Corn Tortillas, 154-155
corporal works of mercy, 37-38, 43
Corpus Christi, 64
Cranberry Bread, 69
Cranberry Muffins, 16
Cream Puffs, 41, 106
cross, 32, 35, 38, 45, 46, 61, 80, 81, 110, 134, 135, 163, 165, 167, 168, 169, 173
Crown Cake, 11, 65
Cucumbers with Cumin and Yogurt, 26
cult, 155, 177
D
Dad's Day, 75
Daily Blessings for Children, 167
Dark Rye Bread, 40
David, 13, 15, 18-19, 57, 65, 157, 159

Dedication of St. John Lateran Basilica, 147
Dedication of the Basilica of Saints Peter and Paul, 149
Dedication of the Basilica of St. Mary Major, 126-127
Divine Infancy, 151
Divine Mercy Novena and Chaplet, 47-48
Divine Office, 7, 178
doctor of the church (definition of), 177

E

Easter, 8, 31, 34, 35, 38, 46, 48, 49-57, 67, 80, 103, 120, 159
Easter Garden, 46-47
Easter Vigil, 35, 47
ecumenism, 177
Edelweiss Coffeecake, 85
Stein, Edith (St. Thersia Benedicta) 128
Egg Nog, 17
Emmaus Walk, 51
encyclical, 177
English Toffee, 159
Enthronements, 166
Epiphany, 22-23, 95-96, 175
epistle, 32, 74, 78, 112, 150
Eternity Cake, 50-51
Eucharist, 12, 36, 46, 49, 52, 53, 60, 61, 64, 67, 77, 78, 79, 80, 104, 107, 120, 146, 166
Eve, 13, 15, 90, 158, 163
Evening Blessing, 55, 167
Examination of Conscience, 62, 126, 160-161
Exploring Scripture, 89

F

Fajitas, 154-155
Family Activity Box, 67, 69
Family Altar, 14, 31, 33, 64
Family Christmas Letter, 14
Family Service Chart, 82
Family Time, 12, 48, 53, 56, 60, 89
Family Tree Centerpiece, 76-77
fasting, 25, 31, 34, 105, 132, 173, 177
feast (definition of), 10, 177
Feast of All Souls, 145
Feast of Christ's Birth, 22
Feast of St. Mark, 50
Feast of the Baptism of Our Lord, 23
Feast of the Epiphany, 22-23, 95
Feast of the Guardian Angels, 118, 139-140
Feast of the Holy Family, 22
Feast of the Immaculate Conception, 151
Feast of the Transfiguration, 127
Feast of the Visitation, 115
First Communion, 61, 65, 112, 176
First Martyrs of the Church of Rome, 120
Flower Walk, 67
foreign missions, 13, 142, 152
fortitude, 58, 76, 81
French-Canadian crêpes, 96-97
Fruitcakes, 26, 28

fruits of the Holy Spirit, 49, 57-59

G

German Pound Cake, 107
gift of counsel, 58
gift of fortitude, 58
gift of knowledge, 57
gift of piety, 58
gift of the fear of the Lord, 58
gift of understanding, 58
gift of wisdom, 58-59
Glorious Mysteries, 87, 162
Good Friday, 31-32, 34, 46-47, 177
Good-Deed Counter Jar, 32
goodness, 59, 96, 123, 169
guardian angel, 37, 70-71, 72, 140

H

haiku, 53
Hail Mary, 79, 86, 88, 139, 162, 166
Halloween, 145
Hearty Vegetable Soup, 113
Herbed Lentils and Rice, 42-43
Herbergsucher, 20
heresy, 94, 97, 109, 111, 113, 117, 119, 126, 127, 131, 144, 178, 179
Holy Angels, 36, 52, 67, 70, 138, 163, 171
Holy Bible, 48
Holy Day of Obligation, 57, 129, 145, 153, 159
Holy Innocents, 18, 160, 172
Holy Orders, 60, 61-62, 171, 173
Holy Thursday, 36, 46-47, 57, 64, 67, 77
Holy Saturday, 47-48
Holy Week, 34, 45, 64, 122, 166
Honor St. Joseph, 36, 55, 67, 75, 76, 103, 111
Honor the Apostles, 54, 67, 149
Honor the Blessed Virgin Mary, 54
Horseshoe Cookies, 146
Hot Cross Buns, 40

I

icon, 178
iconoclasm, 178
Immaculate Conception of the Blessed Virgin Mary, 153, 155
Immaculate Heart of Mary, 125, 169
infallibility, 76, 178

J

Jambalaya, 150-151
Jesse Tree, 12, 13, 14, 185-186
Jesse, 13, 14, 15, 19, 157
Jesus' Ancestors, 13, 15
Jonah Project, 34
Jonah Story, 33
joy, 59, 69, 140, 146, 156, 167, 169
Joyful Mysteries, 87, 115, 162-163
justice, 19, 38, 66, 76, 86, 157, 168

K-L

kindness, 22, 59, 104, 169
Laetare (Rejoice) Sunday, 32
Lamb-and-Flag Drawing, 55

Last Supper Meal, 44
Lenten Novena, 169
Lenten Reading Program, 37, 48
Lenten Yule-Log, 49
Lentils with Cumin and Coriander, 26-27
Life Cakes, 156
Litany of All Saints, 51, 171-174
liturgical year, 5, 7, 25, 93, 168, 178, 181
Liturgy of the Hours, 7, 10, 18, 29, 30
long-suffering, 60
Louisiana Red Beans and Rice, 40
love (as a fruit of the Holy spirit), 59

M
magisterium, 76, 178
Manger, 13-14, 17, 95
Mardi Gras, 25, 28, 30
Marian Pancakes, 84
Marian Shrine, 84-85
martyr, 178
Mary Poem, 88
Matrimony, 60, 62
Memorare, 86, 88
memorial, 178
Mercy Sunday, 47, 50, 171
Messianic Prophecies, 14, 18
Methodius, 102
Middle Cross Day, 32
mildness, 60, 96
modesty, 59-60, 162
monk, 102, 116, 147, 152, 178
mortal sin, 31, 66, 121
mortification, 31
music, 25, 29, 54, 62, 67, 68, 69, 91
My Best Friends, 71
Mystical Rose, 87

N
name-days, 10
Nativity, 15, 17, 22, 75, 87, 95, 168
New Years Eve, 160
Novena to St. Joseph, 103, 170
Novena to the Immaculate Heart of Mary, 169
novena, 20, 47-48, 59, 76, 84, 103, 168-170

O
O Antiphons, 18-19, 20, 156-158
Octave of Christmas, 20, 159
orthodoxy, 111, 178
Our Lady of Guadalupe, 155
Our Lady of Knock, 130
Our Lady of Lourdes, 84, 102
Our Lady of Mt. Carmel, 123
Our Lady of Ransom, 137
Our Lady of Sorrows, 38, 134-135
Our Lady of the Rosary, 141

P
pagan, 96, 115, 116, 120, 135, 143, 147, 155, 178
Palm Sunday, 45-46
Party Ideas, 25
Paschal candle, 35, 49, 54, 56, 59, 62

Passion Sunday, 31, 33, 37, 67
patience, 34, 59, 104, 109, 126
patron saint:, 9-10, 21, 52, 94, 112, 141, 179
Paul, Apostle, 98-99, 143
peace, 59, 64, 66, 74, 93, 110, 116, 130, 133, 139,
    140, 148, 150, 160, 163, 164, 165, 167, 170, 173
penance, 20, 31, 32, 34, 38, 39, 50, 51, 52, 60-61,
    66, 96, 110, 124, 132, 140, 162, 177, 179
Pentecost Sunday, 49, 59, 63-64
Perpetual Adoration, 78
Petition to the Holy Family for Your Family, 170
Pfeffernuesse, 16
Picnic Breakfast, 51
Polenta, 63
Pope Pius IX, 102, 151
Pope St. John I, 113
Potato Salad, 69
Potatoes a la *Huancaina*, 131-132
Prayer for Families, 164
Prayer for Peace of St. Francis of Assisi, 140
Prayer for the Home, 9, 163
Prayer to the Guardian Angels, 37, 52, 72
Presentation of Our Lord, 100, 163
pretzels, 39, 41, 83
prudence, 74, 76, 123, 156
Purgatory, 31, 47, 145-146

Q-R
Queenship of Mary, 131
Reader's Theater, 82
reconciliation, 61, 176
Religious Art Fair, 80
religious, 179
reparation, 61, 84, 164, 179
Roasted Lamb, 44
Rosary Shrine, 87
Rosary, 31, 47, 52, 83-84, 87, 88, 100, 115, 129,
    131, 134, 139, 141, 162, 166, 174
Rum Balls, 16

S
Sacrament Bulletin Board, 175
sacramentals, 56, 58, 174-175, 181
sacraments, 7, 24, 48, 54, 56, 60-62, 65, 68, 89, 161,
    167, 170, 174, 175-176
Sacred Heart, 64-65, 115, 125, 142-143, 148, 164-
    165, 166, 169
Saints Ann and Joachim, 125
Saints Marcellinus and Peter, 115
Saints Nereus and Achilleus, 112
Saints Perpetua and Felicity, 104
Saints Philip and James, 111-112
Saints Timothy and Titus, 99
schism, 142, 179
Scones, 148
Scripture Cake, 70
Scrumptious Sundaes, 87
Sea Scallop Supper, 124-125
Secret Buddies Game, 74
Secret Pancake Recipe, 82

see (of Peter), 147, 179
self-control, 59, 60
seven gifts of the Holy Spirit, 49, 57, 59
Seven Holy Founders of the Servite Order, 102
seven sorrows of Mary, 38, 46, 134, 135
Seven-Herb Soup, 43-44
Sfinge, 36, 41, 106
Shrouding, 33, 37
sign of the cross, 10, 63, 175
Simmel Cake, 32
solemnity, 93, 94, 106, 118, 119, 129, 145, 151, 153, 159, 178, 179
Solemnity of All Saints, 58, 63, 145
Solemnity of Christ the King, 151
Solemnity of Mary the Mother of God, 93-94
Solemnity of Our Lady's Assumption, 129
Solemnity of Saints Peter and Paul, 119
Solemnity of the Birth of John the Baptist, 118
Song of Bernadette, 86, 102
Sorrowful Mysteries, 47, 80, 87, 162, 163
Soup of Health, 42
spiritual communion, 37, 54, 77, 78, 79
spiritual works of mercy, 37
Sprouts in an Eggshell, 68
St. Agatha, 101
St. Agnes, 98
St. Albert the Great, 100, 148
St. Ambrose, 98, 133, 153
St. Andre Kim Taegon, 136
St. Andrew, 151, 160
St. Angela Merici, 99
St. Anne, 13, 153
St. Anselm, 109
St. Ansgar, 101
St. Anthony Mary Claret, 144
St. Anthony of Padua, 117
St. Anthony the Abbot, 97
St. Anthony Zaccaria, 121
St. Athanasius, 111
St. Augustine of Canterbury, 115
St. Augustine, 23, 48, 60, 76, 133
St. Barnabas, 110, 117, 172
St. Bartholomew, 132
St. Basil, 34, 72, 94
St. Basil's Cupcakes, 94
St. Benedict, 102, 104, 114, 121
St. Bernadette Soubirous, 102
St. Bernardine of Siena, 113
St. Bernard of Clairvaux, 88, 130
St. Bonaventure, 123
St. Boniface, 116
St. Bridget, 124
St. Bruno, 141
St. Cajetan, 127
St. Callistus, 127, 135, 142
St. Casimir, 104
St. Catherine Labouré, 151
St. Catherine of Alexandria, 150-151

St. Cecilia, 150
St. Charles Borromeo, 146
St. Charles Lwanga and Companions, 116
St. Clare of Assisi, 128
St. Clement I, 150
St. Columban, 150
St. Cornelius, 135
St. Cyprian, 135
St. Cyril (monk), 102
St. Cyril of Alexandria, 119
St. Cyril of Jerusalem, 105
St. Damasus I, 155
St. Denis, 141
St. Dominic, 84, 110, 127-128, 139, 162
St. Elizabeth Ann Seton, 81, 95
St. Elizabeth of Hungary, 149
St. Elizabeth of Portugal, 120-121
St. Ephrem of Syria, 116
St. Eusebius of Vercelli, 126
St. Fabian, 97
St. Fidelis of Sigmaringen, 110
St. Frances of Rome, 104
St. Frances Xavier Cabrini, 148
St. Francis de Sales, 48, 98, 129-130
St. Francis of Assisi, 78, 128, 140
St. Francis of Paola, 108
St. Francis Xavier, 152
St. George, 109
St. Gertrude the Great, 149
St. Gregory Nazianzen, 94
St. Gregory the Great, 115, 134
St. Gregory VII, 114
St. Hedwig, 143
St. Henry II, 122, 129
St. Hilary of Poitiers, 96
St. Ignatius of Antioch, 103, 143, 147
St. Ignatius of Loyola, 125
St. Irenaeus, 119
St. Isaac Jogues, 144
St. Isidore of Seville, 108
St. Isidore the Farmer, 112
St. James, 112, 124-125
St. Januarius, 136
St. Jean Baptist de la Salle, 108
St. Jean Marie Vianney, 126
St. Jeanne Frances de Chantal, 129
St. Jerome, 102, 138-139
St. Jerome Emiliani, 102
St. Joachim, 13, 125
St. John, 159
St. John Bosco, 100
St. John Chrysostom, 9, 135
St. John Damascene, 152-153
St. John de Brébauf, 144
St. John Eudes, 130
St. John Fisher, 118
St. John Kanty, 158
St. John Leonardi, 142

St. John Neumann, 95
St. John of Capistrano, 144
St. John of God, 104, 126
St. John of the Cross, 48, 156
St. John's Wine, 158, 160
St. Josaphat, 147
St. Joseph Calasanz, 133
St. Joseph Table, 36
St. Joseph the Worker, 111
St. Joseph, husband of Mary, 103, 111
St. Jude, 145
St. Junípero Serra, 120
St. Justin, 113, 115
St. Lawrence, 128
St. Lawrence of Brindisi, 123
St. Leo the Great, 147
St. Louis, 122, 133, 165
St. Lucy, 156
St. Luke, 143-144
St. Margaret Mary Alacoque, 64, 142
St. Margaret of Scotland, 148-149
St. Marguerite Bourgeoys, 96
St. Maria Goretti, 121
St. Mark, 110, 123, 127
St. Martha, 125
St. Martin de Porres, 146
St. Martin I, 109
St. Martin of Tours, 147
St. Mary de Pazzi, 114
St. Matthew, 136
St. Matthias, 112, 164
St. Maximilian Mary Kolbe, 128
St. Monica, 81, 133
St. Nicholas Cookies, 152-153
St. Nicholas Story, 21, 153
St. Nicholas, 21, 152-153
St. Norbert, 116
St. Patrick of Ireland, 105, 147
St. Paul Chong Hasang and Companions, 136
St. Paul Miki and Companions, 101
St. Paul of the Cross, 144
St. Peter Canisius, 157
St. Peter Chanel, 110
St. Peter Claver, 134
St. Peter Damian, 103
St. Peter Fournier, 155
St. Philip Neri, 114-115
St. Pius V, 111, 141
St. Pius X, 131
St. Polycarp, 103
St. Raymond, 96
St. Robert Bellarmine, 136
St. Romuald, 117

St. Rose of Lima, 132
St. Scholastica, 102
St. Sebastian, 97
St. Simon, 145, 174
St. Sixtus II, 127, 128
St. Stanislaus, 109
St. Stephen, 129, 159
St. Sylvester, 160
St. Thérèse of Lisieux, 48, 79, 139
St. Teresa of Ávila, 48, 142, 156
St. Teresa Benedicta (Edith Stein), 128
St. Thomas Aquinas, 74, 100
St. Thomas Becket, 160
St. Thomas More, 117
St. Thomas, 74, 100, 120
St. Turibius of Mogrovejo, 106
St. Vincent de Paul, 137, 151
St. Vincent Ferrer, 108
St. Vincent the Deacon, 98
St. Wenceslaus, 138
Start a Novena, 84
Stations of the Cross Booklets, 36
Stations of the Cross Trail, 81
Stations of the Cross, 31, 35-36, 45, 47, 52, 81-82, 100
Strawberry Cake, 50
Summer Truffle, 129
T
temperance, 75-76
The Day the Sun Danced, 86, 139
Three Days Before Ascension, 50
Tomato-Lentil Soup, 42
Tree Decorations, 13-14
Trinity Sunday, 49, 63-64
Triumph of the Holy Cross, 135
Twelve Days of Christmas, 23, 159
12 Fruits Salad, 49
U-V
Unleavened Bread, 44, 79
Vegetable Soup, 43, 113
Venerable Bede, 114
veneration of the Saints, 179
venial sin, 31
Vigil of Passion Sunday, 37
virgin, 179
vocation, 72, 179
W
Weekend Retreat, 87
Wheat and Barley Loaves, 26, 27
Wheatless Fruit Bread, 98-99
Whole Wheat Bread, 39
wine, 26, 36, 42, 43, 44, 69, 78, 107, 154, 158, 160
Work as an Offering, 53
Works of Mercy Mobile, 38

Our Sunday Visitor...
Your Source for Discovering the Riches of the Catholic Faith

Our Sunday Visitor has an extensive line of materials for young children, teens, and adults. Our books, Bibles, booklets, CD-ROMs, audios, and videos are available in bookstores worldwide.

To receive a FREE full-line catalog or for more information, call **Our Sunday Visitor** at **1-800-348-2440**. Or write, **Our Sunday Visitor** / 200 Noll Plaza / Huntington, IN 46750.

Please send me:__ A catalog
Please send me materials on:
  __ Apologetics and catechetics   __ Reference works
  __ Prayer books   __ Heritage and the saints
  __ The family   __ The parish

Name_____

Address_____Apt._____

City_____State ____Zip_____

Telephone (   ) _____

A93BBABP

Please send a friend:__ A catalog
Please send a friend materials on:
  __ Apologetics and catechetics   __ Reference works
  __ Prayer books   __ Heritage and the saints
  __ The family   __ The parish

Name_____

Address_____Apt._____

City_____State ____Zip_____

Telephone (   ) _____

A93BBABP

 **Our Sunday Visitor**
200 Noll Plaza
Huntington, IN 46750
1-800-348-2440
osvbooks@osv.com

OurSundayVisitor

Periodicals • Books • Tapes • Curricula • Software • Offering Envelopes. For a free catalog call 1-800-348-2440.